GW00382208

The Economics of Law

Antony W. Dnes

Professor of Economics
Nottingham Trent University

INTERNATIONAL THOMSON BUSINESS PRESS
I ⓣ P An International Thomson Publishing Company

London • Bonn • Boston • Johannesburg • Madrid • Melbourne • Mexico City • New York • Paris
Singapore • Tokyo • Toronto • Albany, NY • Belmont, CA • Cincinnati, OH • Detroit, MI

The Economics of Law

Copyright © 1996 Antony Dnes

First published 1996 by International Thomson Business Press

 I(T)P A division of International Thomson Publishing Inc.
The ITP logo is a trademark under licence

British Library Cataloguing-in-Publication Data
A catalogue record for this book is available from the British Library

First edition 1996

Typeset in 10/12pt Times by Photoprint, Torquay, Devon
Printed in the UK by The Alden Press, Oxford

ISBN 0-412-62800-7

International Thomson Business Press
Berkshire House
168–173 High Holborn
London WC1V 7AA
UK

International Thomson Business Press
20 Park Plaza
14th Floor
Boston MA 02116
USA

http://www.thomson.com/itbp.html

Contents

Preface

In this book I provide an accessible survey of law and economics that is aimed at practitioners and advanced students of both economics and law, particularly those located in England or in other Commonwealth countries. The material is drawn from English, Commonwealth and US case law. Consequently, there is a comparative element to the book that should make it interesting in several countries.

The focus is mainly on the economics of core areas of the common law (mainly property, contract and tort, with some attention given to criminal law) in the chapters that follow. I have resisted the temptation to include regulatory topics, except where regulation bears on the core areas, because there are good existing treatments of topics such as competition law or natural monopoly. Crime is covered in the book because experience shows that students particularly enjoy this application of economics to legal issues. The chapter on procedural issues reflects some particularly interesting contemporary questions.

The economic analysis and the legal principles are treated in a self-contained manner as the book progresses. This approach should mean that lawyers and economists can use the book without any prior knowledge of the other 'parent' subject. I have substituted common language for specialist jargon in places (usually to define the jargon *in situ*) and have used economic analysis just up to the point necessary to show particular results.

Acknowledgements

I would like to thank the many people who have commented on earlier drafts of this book. In particular, I wish to thank Bruce Chapman (Toronto), Eirik Furubotn (Texas), Nick Tilley (Nottingham Trent) and Steve Smith (St Anne's, Oxford) who made many helpful suggestions. The usual disclaimers apply.

The economic analysis of law: an introduction

1

There has been a considerable growth of interest in the combined study known as law and economics (for which the 'economic analysis of law' is really a better description). The new work represents a trend in economic thinking that governments and business should find useful. The application of economic principles to legal instruments, questions and procedures, which is one way to define the economic analysis of law, is not really new: in the eighteenth and nineteenth centuries it was common for political economists to have had exposure to legal training and to work on institutionally focused questions.

In the *Wealth of Nations*, Adam Smith (1776) saw institutional factors like primogeniture and the English Poor Laws as inhibiting the economic development of society from mercantilism towards industrialism. Primogeniture caused land to be transferred in large parcels which in practice meant some of it often remained unused. The Poor Laws, much like public housing in our own time, made labour mobility difficult as the labourer was restricted from moving to another parish – an unintended consequence of a policy intended to stop the poor of one parish becoming a burden on landowners in another.

From the 1950s onwards, many economists analyzed regulatory issues in considerable depth. Their work was an early kind of law and economics mainly concerned with antitrust and the regulation of natural monopoly (Stigler, 1971; Peacock and Rowley, 1972; Priest, 1993). Regulatory economics certainly paved the way for the extension of economics to the analysis of further areas of the law.

Following the publication by the 1991 Nobel prize winner Ronald Coase (1960) of his article 'The Problem of Social Cost' modern law and economics has particularly focused on issues arising in the common law of countries like England, other Commonwealth nations and the USA.[1] The common-law countries may be contrasted with the civil law tradition characterizing continental Europe (and Scotland). The civilian tradition is to limit judges to the interpretation of statutory codes.[2] The key distinction is whether judges can independently make law, creating 'precedent' as they encounter cases not fully catered for by 'holdings' from earlier similar cases.

Common law coexists with the statute law that emanates from the legislature and it is quite possible to use economic analysis on both. It is fair to say, though, that earlier work, with its emphasis on regulatory questions, concentrated on statute whereas the economics of law now includes the analysis of property rights, contracts and 'tort' (e.g. nuisance or negligence issues) where much of the law is common law. In recent years, the criminal common law has been added to the list. A useful milestone in the development of law and economics was the publication in 1973 of Richard Posner's *Economic Analysis of Law* (Posner, 1992) which consolidated much of the old and the new.

1.1 SOME APPLICATIONS

Since modern economics studies rational behaviour, defined as the pursuit of consistent ends by efficient means (Cooter and Ulen, 1988), there is no difficulty in applying it to the law. Ends and means are clearly involved in setting and administering the law. A few simple examples of legal cases and issues will clarify what is meant by this application. We draw them from three classic areas of law to show that economic analysis can be fruitfully applied to some interesting legal questions.

1.1.1 Crime

We start with an example from criminal law as there is undoubtedly a great concern worldwide with the perceived breakdown of law and order. We examine economic issues of crime and punishment in depth in Chapter 7.

Some countries in the Far East impose death sentences on those convicted of smuggling hard drugs. Economic analysis shows why this might make sense. These countries are relatively poor and probably cannot afford to devote large amounts of money to detecting smugglers. If criminals are rational, they will respond to increases in the expected value of punishment by reducing their criminal activity. This response will follow even if criminals are often driven by irrational factors as long as they react rationally at the margin of their activities.

The expected value of punishment equals the probability of conviction multiplied by the sentence for the crime. If a country cannot afford to increase the conviction rate it can obtain the same effect in reducing smuggling by adopting severe sentences. The economist Gary Becker (1968) has conjectured that this trade-off explains the existence of severe punishments for non-capital crimes in earlier times in what are now more advanced societies.

A contemporary practical application of the reasoning involved in comparing deterrence through severity with that from probability of conviction is easy to make. Most modern societies are concerned about increasing levels of both violent and property crime. How should this be tackled? If the cost of increasing the severity of prison sentences is compared with that for increasing detection and conviction of criminals, it turns out to be much cheaper to obtain a target reduction in crime by increasing the length of sentences (Pyle, 1989). The economic analysis here is useful. It suggests that the common response of many governments around the world to rising crime – to increase expenditure on police – may not be the most cost-effective. Interestingly, it seems that developed economies have not moved that far from the predicament facing less developed ones.

1.1.2   Nuisance

Our second example comes from the legal treatment of nuisance which is a 'tort' – or private wrong – in common-law countries. Tort is covered extensively in Chapters 3 and 6. Our example is the famous case of *Sturges* v. *Bridgman* (1879) which concerned a confectioner who set up shop next to a physician whom he disturbed with the vibration and noise from equipment. The doctor (Sturges[3]) won the right (an injunction) to stop (enjoin) the nuisance. What are the economic implications of this?

Economists regard *Sturges* as a case of 'externality', i.e. there are spillover effects caused by conflicting property rights. Ronald Coase (1960) analyzed *Sturges* in 'The Problem of Social Cost', where he emphasized the inherently reciprocal nature of externalities: the confectioner affects the doctor but the latter has to be in the way for harm to arise. Both parties are exercising legitimate private property rights which conflict. Coase reached the surprising conclusion that it does not matter from the point of view of economic efficiency whether the person causing the nuisance (Bridgman) has the right to continue or whether the victim has the right to stop him as long as they can bargain at reasonably low cost. For illustration, assume that the confectioner's noise completely stops medical practice. If the medical business were more profitable but did not have the right to stop the noise the doctor could afford to bribe the confectioner to stop. Conversely, if the doctor did have the right the less profitable confectioner could not bribe the doctor to tolerate the noise. We examine the 'Coase theorem' in detail in Chapter 3 (section 3.1).

One observation on the operation of the law in nuisance cases like *Sturges* is that it tends to award an injunction rather than award compensatory damages wherever the number of parties is small. This would seem to be efficient since many small-numbers cases are likely to exhibit low bargaining costs. If such rules become well known to holders of property rights they may avoid taking their disputes to court, preferring to settle at an earlier stage and avoid the costs of litigation. Observations like this have led Posner (1992) to argue that the law evolves efficiently where efficiency is interpreted as wealth maximization (comparison of monetary gains and losses).

1.1.3   The economics of breach of contract

Our final introductory example is drawn from the study of contract. Economic efficiency is based on voluntary and informed trading which is supported by a law of contract that enforces terms of trade and may plug gaps in agreements that would otherwise be too costly to cover. Contract law enables resources to be transferred to their most valuable uses as people come to know what promises are enforceable and how enforcement may occur. Trebilcock (1993) gives a very full analysis of the detailed requirements for private agreements to be sufficiently voluntary and informed to promote social welfare.

Suppose a company does not wish to complete a service it has promised to undertake. Should it be forced to perform? Both economics and law suggest that it is unnecessary to require specific performance except in special cases. It is not the business of the law to force people to carry out tasks for which the economic justification may have disappeared but only to ensure they compensate for their non-performance. There can be such a thing as efficient breach of contract when the breacher is able to compensate the 'victim' for non-performance. Compensation is usually defined by the courts, although some economists have argued, following the Coase theorem, that enforcing specific performance of the original contract would ensure that the would-be breaching party were forced to pay accurate compensation to obtain the victim's consent to breach.

In a famous case, *Tsakiroglou* v. *Noblee Thorl* (1962), a company in the Sudan undertook to sell peanuts to a German firm on standard terms – in particular, at a price including insurance and freight. The Suez war erupted in 1956 and the company claimed delivery was impossible. The buyer claimed delivery was just more expensive (around the Cape) and won. The case is particularly useful as an illustration of the insurance function of contracts.

The courts concentrated upon the issue of whether performance was physically possible which is not how an economist would examine the case. The economist sees a contract as an attempt to increase efficiency by allocating future contingencies between the parties. By dealing with contingencies and allocating risks, contracts perform an insurance function. In *Tsakiroglou*, it seems the seller was in the best position – at the time the contract was written – to cover the contingency of blockage of the canal. It is also relevant that the price included insurance and freight suggesting these things were the responsibility of the seller. Efficient contracts would assign risks to those able to bear them at least cost. This is a useful principle for courts when they are asked to enforce a contract. If businesses discerned such a general tendency in the courts they could save themselves the costs of covering these details in contracts unless they wished explicitly to do something else. We cover further contract issues in Chapters 4 and 5.

1.2   ECONOMIC EFFICIENCY

Having used the notion of economic efficiency to appraise the role of injunctions against nuisance and to assess the effects of risk sharing in contracts, we should say something about the standard of efficiency used throughout this book. We follow Posner (1992) and adopt wealth maximization as a simple criterion of economic efficiency. Thus, a contract in which risk is borne by the person who can avoid the contingency at lowest cost is efficient, as this maximizes the joint surplus after costs of the parties. The thing to note is that wealth maximization ignores the distribution of benefits.

Very often we shall be asking normative questions using wealth maximization as a standard of comparison. An example was just given in the previous section: if we wish to encourage efficient contracting how should the courts allocate risks? It is also possible to make a positive (i.e. predictive) scientific argument that the common law evolves as though judges consciously sought to maximize wealth (Posner, 1992, p.534). The same conclusion can be reached by noting there is more to be gained from litigating an inefficient legal rule (Rubin, 1977). An alternative hypothesis is that special interest groups influence the development of the law for their own benefit (Rubin and Bailey, 1994), which Posner (1992, p.523) accepts in the case of statute law but not for the judge-made common law. Special interest groups operate as 'rent seekers' trying to shape legislation to give them monopolistic advantages, which does not necessarily maximize social wealth. Rent seeking is examined more closely in Chapter 2.

This book is mainly concerned with the normative economic analysis of law. It is not therefore strictly necessary to reach a conclusion on the debate over whether the law is efficient or not. However, the view of this author is that Posner is broadly correct.[4] Efficient rules can be found in, and may dominate, the common law, although instances of inefficiency (including rent seeking) can be found. Legislation on the other hand can often be seen to favour particular groups, although, this time, efficient exceptions can be found.

Returning to the normative economic analysis of law the main alternative to wealth maximization as a welfare criterion is utility maximization. Utility refers to the direct psychic benefits experienced by people as they consume money income. Although utility may often be measured well by individuals' willingness to pay for a benefit (or to avoid a cost) this is not always so. The principal difficulty arises when two individuals have very different levels of wealth. If the value placed on additional units of money falls in a similar manner for different people as wealth increases (based on the hypothesis of diminishing marginal utility of money income) then a unit of money is likely to be worth less to the rich man than to the poor one. It is often suggested that we should use utility measures of the costs and benefits in comparing, say, the costs of a nuisance to one individual with the benefits another enjoys from the same nuisance. However, there is simply no straightforward method to do this and the criterion of utility maximization is basically too complex for use. Using a test of utility maximization would require us to make assumptions about individuals' utility scales as we made interpersonal comparisons. The wealth-maximization approach avoids making difficult interpersonal comparisons of utility. Nonetheless, wealth maximization will influence the distribution of wealth, e.g. by conferring legal awards on some people rather than others.

If the legal system does tend towards wealth maximization a part of the reason may be that this is a simple criterion that courts can understand. Attempts to assess pay-offs in terms of utility would involve the courts in lengthy and costly assessment procedures (Posner, 1981, p.79). Many of the costs of court actions are not borne by the parties but are spread more widely by taxation. The possible gains to the parties from refining the measurement of their gains and losses (if feasible) could easily be outweighed by increased costs of measurement which would imply the loss of tax-funded projects to the wider community. Thus, it may be very sensible for the wider community to place limits on the measurement costs that can be incurred.

Posner (1981, p.88) has gone further and has argued that wealth maximization is morally superior to either utility maximization or other ethical standards for assessing welfare change. In particular, he holds that wealth maximization respects individual autonomy and encourages economic progress. Some philosophers of law are quite hostile to this view. Interestingly, Dworkin (1986, p.302) arrives at a similar approach to resolving the claims of different individuals but from a rights-based egalitarian perspective rather than one based on wealth maximization.

Much of the time, it will not matter much to the parties concerned whether their interests are measured by money or in terms of utility: money will do fine. This is because the law often requires compensation to be paid to an injured party. If A can breach his contract with B by paying £100 to cover B's losses it does not matter that the money is worth five 'utils' to A but 10 utils to B, assuming (unrealistically) that we have a black box able to measure utility. The expected benefits to B from the contract are preserved and A is free to pursue some alternative business deal giving him a net benefit greater than £100. If compensation is paid, we have an example of a Pareto improvement (named after the Italian economist Vilfredo Pareto) where at least one person is made better off without lowering the welfare of another.

Problems may arise when courts use market values to calculate compensation: e.g. governments are often required to compensate for the compulsory taking of land by paying market value. Awarding market value ignores any special benefits enjoyed by the owner although, as Fischel (1995b) has argued, trying to incorporate special factors may be too costly. In market-compensation cases there is a major issue concerning the effectiveness of compensation and we cannot be sure of a Pareto improvement

In general, wealth maximization does not necessarily result in a Pareto improvement but will always give a potential Pareto improvement. This is well illustrated by the courts' application of tort law which deals mainly with accidents. In standard cases of negligence, an injurer for whom the costs of preventing an accident are judged to have been too high relative to the victim's losses is held not to have been negligent. The non-negligent injurer is not required to pay damages to the victim. Encouraging only cost-effective precautions is a form of wealth maximization. The law effectively says that the net benefit from the injurer's activity (e.g. delivering parcels) is maximized if the accident victim (e.g. a pedestrian who may be run over) bears some of the risks. It reflects a potential Pareto improvement, i.e. a Kaldor-Hicks test of whether the injurer could in principle compensate the victim and remain better off from some change but with no requirement placed on the beneficiary to actually hand over compensation.

What about non-efficiency based criteria in relation to legal issues? An appealing approach to many is to seek fair solutions to conflict. Fairness criteria are notoriously difficult to define, as a browse through any text on the philosophy of ethics will show. It is a sad fact that many people see what is in reality only an expression of their own preferences for favouring the welfare of some individual or group relative to another as an expression of justice. The advantage of an economic approach is that it avoids interpersonal assessments and is more neutral in its efforts. Efficient changes, rules or policies have the capacity to make everyone better off (although such changes might be resisted by true egalitarians if they made the distribution of wealth more unequal).

Finally in this section, it is extraordinary how an efficiency criterion can illuminate legal issues. We may not be able to agree on an ideal distribution of benefits from economic activity, but we probably find it easy to accept that, whatever the distribution is, steps should be avoided that make everybody demonstrably worse off.

1.3 AVOIDING 'NIRVANA' COMPARISONS

It is worth elaborating a little further on the notion of economic efficiency. There may well have been a tendency among many writers on economic policy to ignore relevant constraints affecting a particular problem. These practitioners of 'nirvana' economics typically commit one or more of three fallacies. Demsetz (1969) argued that commentators often commit the 'fallacy of the free lunch' by ignoring the costs of corrective economic policy. According to Furubotn (1994) people see a dual-cost universe in which the cost of government intervention is ignored whereas the costs affecting business are recognized.

A second fallacy ('the people could be different') arises when commentators ignore the true tastes and preferences of the individuals who make up society. Some economists argue for increasing the taxes on oil products to slow down rates of depletion. They argue that oil companies heavily discount future benefits from conserving oil partly owing to their sensitivity to the risk of political appropriation of their assets. These risks are purely distributional and, so it is argued, society would prefer a slower rate of depletion. However, intervention to slow down depletion ignores people's preferences as they stand, for whatever reason and implies that the people could be different.

The fallacy of the 'grass is always greener' assumes that social situations are perfectible. This perfection may in reality be unattainable, e.g. there may be no set of policies that can improve on unregulated, open-access to high-seas fisheries. The major problem of over fishing attached to open access may in reality be no worse than problems, such as the encouragement of expensive lobbying by fishing groups, set up by attempts to control fishing.

Courts are not required to intervene in the economy in the interests of public policy although they do sometimes interpret policy. However, in judging cases they are frequently engaged in welfare comparisons albeit often on a modest scale. Consequently it is important for the courts to be realistic and to avoid the fallacies of 'nirvana' economics. In fact, the record may be good in this respect. The alternative to 'nirvana' economics is 'comparative institutionalism', in which feasible alternative institutional arrangements are realistically examined to see which is superior. The courts may be quite naturally led to comparative institutionalism owing to procedural rules that limit case costs and a traditional emphasis on the practical demonstration of injury.

1.4 PLAN OF THIS BOOK

We begin in Chapters 2 and 3 by examining the whole area of property rights which is a very well-established topic in law and economics. The idea is to see how a secure system of property rights is essential to support economic efficiency. Some less obvious property rights such as those for intellectual property are also considered. We move on in Chapters 4 and 5 to questions of contract which is a classic area of legal doctrine. The effect of contract can be seen as moving resources to their highest valuing users. In Chapter 6 we examine tort which is most simply seen as covering negligence issues. Chapter 7 covers criminal law which is our main area of public law. The final chapter covers procedural issues such as cost rules in court cases and contingency-fee litigation.

SUMMARY AND CONCLUSIONS

Economists have contributed much to recent legal analysis. An analysis motivated by an efficiency criterion can help to explain the function of many traditional legal instruments, questions and procedures. This has a positive-economics aspect to it where we are interested in explaining the world and making scientific predictions. It also has a normative aspect for we may wish to design new legal rules or procedures with economic efficiency in mind.

In North America, economics has had a terrific influence on law. There, academic lawyers have been heard to comment that one needs training in the economic analysis of law to understand the law literature, let alone the law and economics literature. This is not yet the situation on the other side of the Atlantic but there is a growing interest in law and economics in both of the parent disciplines.

ENDNOTES

1. Care should be taken not to overlook a recent growth in interest in the economics of law in countries with civil codes (rather than a reliance on common law) such as Germany.
2. Care is needed though, as some civilian countries have no code (e.g. Scotland) and some common-law countries have codes (e.g. the USA's Uniform Commercial Code).
3. The case is brought by the plaintiff, Sturges, whose name is recorded first on the case citation.
4. It seems better to state a view than duck the issue.

2 | Property

Property rights are central to the operation of any economy. There is a distinct literature in economics concerned with the significance of different property-rights regimes. Indeed, Demsetz's (1967) work in this area was partly responsible for the emergence of modern law and economics. A major economic issue in this chapter concerns the efficiency of alternative systems of property rights. As well as looking at resources like land and wildlife stocks we also examine intellectual property rights in inventions and works of art. Conflict over property rights and the effects of legal remedies to such conflict are dealt with in the next chapter.

2.1 SOME DEFINITIONS

Economists and lawyers regard property in terms of a bundle of rights specifying what a person can do with a resource. These rights are constrained by various statutes, by common law and by the details of contracts that may have been established. However, three things stand out as characterizing the bundle of rights attached to private property. In particular, private property rights are saleable. Secondly, the owner is free to exercise rights or neglect them. Finally, the interference of others is forbidden.

In addition to private property rights there are other categories that are of interest. In particular, private property contrasts with common property from which people may not be excluded. Examples of common property include open-access fisheries and common land. The legal rule applying to common-property wildlife stocks is that of first possession: the first person to capture the animal has possession of it, the ramifications of which are explored by Lueck (1989). Common property is generally judged to lead to overuse of a resource, which is inefficient. In addition to private and common property rights there are less obvious categories. For example, usufruct rights give the right to use privately and to exclude others but do not give the right to sell the resource. Primitive tribal societies often had usufruct rights (Posner, 1980). Another less obvious category is given by riparian rights which give certain ownership privileges over water to whoever owns the land it passes through.

Private property rights probably emerged as individuals protected favoured pieces of land by the use of force, or took land from others through force or negotiation, when the costs of doing so were outweighed by the expected benefits (Umbeck, 1981). Economies of scale in protection services suggest bargaining over the terms for creating some form of government to safeguard private property rights once they are established. Government then comes to have a natural monopoly of coercion and can be funded by the savings that individuals make from no longer needing private security measures. This is the familiar story of the move from anarchy to order associated with Hobbes (1651).

The most important factors in the creation of private property rights are the bargaining and enforcement costs involved. These transaction costs can be so high that it is not always worth creating private property rights. Hence, common property rights tend to persist for wildlife stocks such as fish and seals. If it were possible, e.g. electronically, to fence areas of the sea to contain stocks we would probably see attempts to create private rights.

2.2   ECONOMIC ANALYSIS OF PROPERTY RIGHTS

Economic analysis suggests that private property rights are more efficient than common rights. We can distinguish between a dynamic and a static view of the superiority of private rights.

Posner (1992) points out that the dynamic view is very old and can, e.g., be found in Blackstone (1766). It states that private property rights give an incentive for the long-term efficient use of a resource, e.g. you would not fertilize and prepare land if someone else could come along and use it to plant crops. Common property rights are often a feature of a nomadic lifestyle in which a local supply of a resource becomes exhausted before the tribe moves elsewhere. An indication of the low productivity of common rights is given by Anderson and McChesney (1994) who report that a settler needed about two acres of land to support a family in colonial America whereas a native Indian family needed 2000 acres.

Another dynamic view of the superiority of private rights emphasizes the role that transferability plays in encouraging efficient use of resources. Private property rights can be sold to higher valuing users, which is not possible with common rights. Therefore, private rights are necessary and transferable private rights are sufficient for efficiency. This search for long-run dynamic efficiency has also been applied as a theory of history (North, 1990).

The static view of the inefficiency of common rights is of comparatively recent origin and is associated with property-rights theorists like Gordon (1954), Demsetz (1967) and Furubotn and Pejovich (1972, 1974). The general argument here is that common property rights cause over-exploitation of a resource as new users ignore their impact on existing ones. We now examine this proposition analytically by looking at the economic theory of the open-access fishery.

2.3 THE ECONOMICS OF A COMMON-PROPERTY RESOURCE: THE FISHERY

High-seas fisheries furnish the most significant modern example of common property. The model in this section is a development of Gordon's (1954) seminal article. The economic theory of the open-access fishery is also applicable to any common-property resource, particularly other renewable resources like seal stocks or woodland.

Figure 2.1 shows a relationship between fishing effort (standard boats with crew) and total revenue which is based on an underlying effort–yield relationship. The yield (i.e. catch) can be measured in weight or as total revenue. To find total revenue, yield in weight is multiplied by the price of fish. We assume a given price, which would result from a competitive market for fish and which is normalized to a unit value. Therefore, the total revenue curve in Figure 2.1 is simply a relabelled yield curve.

The fish population will adjust to give the total revenue (yield) levels shown as fishing is varied on the horizontal axis. Increases in effort reduce the underlying population. The total-revenue curve shows the usual bell-shaped relationship that is used as a starting point in models of fisheries management (Clark, 1976).[1] At first, increasing fishing effort increases the yield as a smaller fish population puts less demand on its food sources and breeding and growth of the fish stock shows greater gains. However, past point M, the falling fish population implies that fish experience increasing difficulty in locating partners for

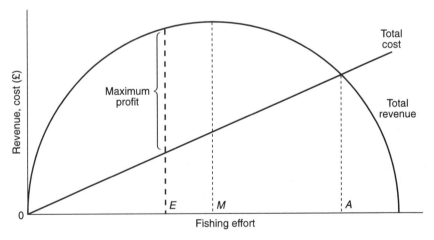

Figure 2.1 The fishery. E = point of maximum profit; M = point after which fish yield falls; A = level of effort given by open access.

breeding so that yield falls. Hence, the derived total-revenue curve has a bell shape, giving a maximum at point M.

Assuming a constant unit cost of fishing effort gives the linear total cost function. A private owner of the fishery would expand fishing effort to point E in Figure 2.1 where profit is maximized.[2] With common rights, people enter the fishery as long as there is any profit to be had in excess of the (normal) profit they could earn on their investments elsewhere in the economy. If we assume that the fishermen's costs include an element of required normal profit, open access gives a level of effort shown by point A. The entire surplus on the fishery is dissipated by open access. The lack of private property rights leads to overfishing. If we could reduce fishing effort from A to E, we could release inputs for use elsewhere in the economy and increase the catch in the fishery.

Unfortunately, the world's remaining examples of common property resources are almost certainly cases where it is just too costly to create the private rights. The costs are attached to enforcement and suppressing distributional conflict (Libecap, 1989; Furubotn, 1989 and 1987). The analysis of the fishery model leads to a 'first-best' optimum that ignores the very real costs of enforcing the ideal solution. Introducing the irremovable constraint of meeting costs of enforcement that would more than erode the maximum profit shown in Figure 2.1 would cause common property to be the 'second-best' optimum. Nonetheless, many economists make the general point that introducing common property where the cost of enforcing private rights is low would lead to over-exploitation of a resource.

One example of a fishery with some privately owned grounds is the US oyster fishery. Agnello and Donnelley (1975) test the prediction that private rights lead to a more efficient fishing industry using data on the oyster fisheries of 16 contiguous Atlantic and Gulf states from Massachusetts to Texas over the period 1950–69. They used averages of the 20 years' data for each state. The proportion of private property rights in oyster beds varies across states and years. Generally, natural oyster beds are treated as common property in the USA but other subaqueous areas may be leased and seeded for oyster farming, giving some private rights. Common-property oyster beds are likely to be less efficient since harvesting removes cultch,[3] which fishermen will not replace even though states often prohibit dredging and other very harmful techniques.

Agnello and Donnelley regressed the average product of labour on the property-rights variable and a number of other exogenous variables (such as the capital intensity of fishing and the presence of disease) using ordinary-least-squares analysis in six different specifications of a model. The property-rights variable was always statistically significant and of the expected positive sign, indicating that private rights increase labour productivity.

Before leaving this topic, it is interesting to note that fisheries regulation tends to favour approaches towards controlling overfishing that rely on simple enforcement mechanisms. There is a history of the regulations not working. Closed seasons are simple to enforce: if you see a boat, you arrest its skipper. However, fishermen will intensify their efforts during the open season. The regulation does not overcome the inherent problem of the intensive use of common property but just raises fishermen's costs. An even more striking case of irrational conservation occurred some years ago in the Pacific salmon fishery when powerboats were banned from the Bristol Bay (Crutchfield and Pontecorvo, 1969). What is ideally needed in these cases is a reduction of costs as effort is withdrawn, not an increase of costs.

2.4 RENT SEEKING

Another problem with common property rights is that they encourage rent seeking activity. Rent is defined in economics as any payment over and above the amount necessary to keep a factor of production in its current use. Rent seeking may be defined as the devotion of resources to gathering pure surpluses (Buchanan *et al.*, 1980), e.g. businessmen may try to influence the award of public contracts in favour of their companies. The idea can be applied to common property resources as participants seek rents, even if overuse means they get none.

Common rights imply an increased incentive to spend resources on conflict (Dnes, 1985). Taking the example of high-seas fishing once more, boats are equipped with technology designed to beat rivals to the stocks. Much of this expenditure on conflict could be saved if fishermen had more secure access to fish stocks. This is quite apart from the savings that would arise from avoiding the periodic episodes in which fishermen become aggressive with other boats and cut their nets, as in August 1994 when Spanish fishermen tried to deter French and British fishermen from fishing for tuna in the Bay of Biscay.[4] As already noted, in the case of fishing, it seems that the costs of establishing private rights are too high relative to the benefits. Nevertheless, fishing illustrates the kind of investment in conflict that can be avoided if private rights are feasible.

Ricketts (1987) argues that the usual notion of rent seeking implies a value judgement about what is an appropriate efficiency standard. He argues for the use of the *status quo ante* as a standard to define rent seeking: a person seeking to change status-quo property rights is rent seeking. Ricketts argues that otherwise there is a risk of defining all economic activity as rent seeking. Dnes (1989) argues that this may move the focus of rent-seeking analysis too far from some categories of behaviour that are clearly conflict orientated.

From a practical point of view, independently governed, well-defined and secure private property rights tend to make rent seeking unproductive. This encourages people to obtain income from productive, entrepreneurial activity where entrepreneurship refers to innovation in terms of products or production processes. Also, privately owned resources will only transfer by sale if there is a higher valued use. However, rent seeking might transfer resources to inefficient uses. A rule of first possession applies to wildlife stocks but the fastest fisherman or hunter is not necessarily the lowest-cost one.

Anderson and McChesney (1994) analyze the establishment of settlers' property rights as a result of conflict and negotiation with native Indian populations in America. One explanation of increased conflict between settlers and Indians after 1850 is that the move west brought settlers into contact with more nomadic Indians. This lack of established private rights over land made it much harder to negotiate. We discuss this study further below.

2.5   THE PROPERTY-RIGHTS PARADIGM

Starting in the 1960s, a number of economists sought to redefine economic theory in terms of the creation, enforcement and transfer of property rights. An extremely interesting paper in this regard is Demsetz (1967). Demsetz notes that a transaction implies that two bundles of property rights are exchanged. He argues that property rights emerge to control externalities, which are defined as unpriced spillover effects between the activities of different individuals. An externality is internalized when property rights cause its effects to be fully recognized. There is a tendency to see externalities as minor problems in a sea of otherwise well-functioning markets. The property-rights paradigm inverts this view: in the beginning there are externalities which individuals internalize by creating property rights whenever this is worth doing.

Demsetz's thesis is that private property rights develop to internalize externalities when the gains of internalization exceed the costs. Increased internalization typically results from changes in economic values that follow from changes in technology and from the opening of new markets. His paper has an extremely interesting analysis of the development of private rights in land by American Indians, based on the research findings of two anthropologists. Frank Speck found that the Indians of the Labrador Peninsula had a long-standing tradition of private property rights whereas those of the American Southwest did not. Eleanor Leacock's study of the Montagne Indians (around Quebec) showed that private property rights evolved as the fur trade developed. We concentrate on Demsetz's analysis of Leacock's findings.

Before the fur trade developed, Indians hunted for meat and furs for the hunter's family. An externality was clearly present as each hunt imposed a loss of stock on subsequent hunters, rather as fishing affects stocks in the model considered earlier (section 2.3). Leacock reported that the explorer Le Jeune's record of the winter he spent with the Montagnes in 1633 and a brief account of Father Druilletes of similar experiences in 1647 contained no evidence of private property rights. Both accounts contained evidence of common property.

The fur trade had two consequences. First, the value of furs rose. Secondly, the scale of hunting increased sharply. This meant that gains from internalizing the externality became much higher and the property-rights system began to change towards private rights. Relatively immobile forest animals like beaver dominated in the fur trade so that the costs of enforcing private rights were not as high as in the case of more mobile fish stocks. Leacock reported that by the beginning of the eighteenth century there was clear evidence that territorial hunting arrangements by individual families were developing. The earliest references by travellers indicated a temporary allotment of hunting territories. For example, the Iroquois divided themselves into bands and appropriated pieces of land for each group to hunt exclusively. Interestingly, after ownership of beaver houses had become established a starving Indian could kill and eat another's beaver if he left the fur and tail. By 1723, private rights were well established.

Demsetz (1967) argues that the absence of similar rights among Southwest Indians resulted from the lack of a high-value, contained wildlife stock. On the plains of the Southwest, grazing stocks roamed large distances and could not be economically contained within boundaries. This all changed with the arrival of Europeans with cattle and, later, barbed wire. Demsetz notes that Indians of the Northwest also developed family-based private rights to hunting grounds. Again, forest animals dominated and the area was visited by sailing schooners trading in furs. Recent work on native Indian economies is contained in Anderson (1993).

Demsetz (1967) argues that private property rights with few owners for any piece of property are normal as this minimizes the cost of taking decisions over the future use of the resources involved. Turning to a more modern example, an exception that proves the rule is the joint-stock company. Economies of scale in production and the avoidance of the transaction costs of combining many small firms suggest running a large corporation. However, it is cheaper to raise funds from many equity participants or outside lenders who can diversify their risks. The delegation of authority to a management board overcomes the high costs of decision making that should follow from having so many owners of the modern firm. In addition, limited liability allows investors to be liable for the company's debts only to the extent of any personal investment and helps to diversify risks. In general, it makes sense for property rights to be created over the unit of ownership that best internalizes externalities.

2.6 APPLIED WORK ON PROPERTY RIGHTS: THE 'WILD' WEST

Property-rights analysts have not confined themselves to theoretical work but have also tested their predictions. An interesting laboratory for testing property-rights theories is the history of the development of the American West. In the nineteenth century in particular, property rights and associated institutions evolved in response to clearly observable changes in economic values.

Anderson and McChesney (1994) have analyzed the choice faced by European settlers between attacking Indians and taking their land or negotiating with them for it. They develop a model that is closely related to those about disputants' decisions over whether to litigate or settle a case (Cooter and Rubinfeld, 1989). The basic idea is that negotiation and war have different costs to each side and that each has a different valuation of the property at stake. Thus, it may be in the interests of Indians to overlook small trespasses upon their land if both negotiation and war are costly. There would also be some land of too low a value to interest settlers. Therefore, there will be some tranches of land over which disputes will not arise and a region will exist where conflict is possible. This analysis contrasts with the view that European settlers simply set out to annihilate native Americans as some form of 'ethnic cleansing'.

Figure 2.2 shows the key features of the 'raid-or-trade' model. There is a finite amount of land (L) valuable to both settlers and Indians and initially held entirely by Indians. The value of each unit of land to settlers is shown by the marginal benefit function MB_S and diminishes as more land is obtained. The marginal value to Indians is measured from L and also diminishes as shown by MB_I. Marginal benefit can be measured in terms of the price each group would be willing to pay for exclusive use of the land, assuming the use of force were ruled out. Early units of land given up by Indians (e.g. from 0 to L_1) are of low value to them but are of high value to settlers. Note that if neither side

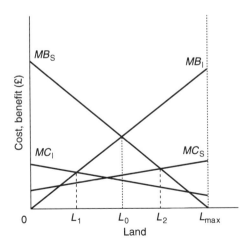

Figure 2.2 Raid or trade? MB_S = marginal benefit of land to settlers; MB_I = marginal benefit of land to Indians; MC_S = marginal cost of land to settlers; MC_I = marginal cost of land to Indians.

could resort to force and if negotiation costs were zero, the settlers would negotiate to take over L_0 units of land as they could easily compensate the Indians for its loss.

However, both sides will possess credible threats of force. The cost of settlers taking additional units of land by force is shown by the marginal cost function, MC_S, in Figure 2.2, whereas the marginal cost of the Indians defending land is shown by MC_I. Marginal costs of force increase for each party, measured from their respective origins in Figure 2.2, as it is harder to attack or defend land that is distant from headquarters. The model demarcates a 'zone of controversy' between L_1 and L_2 within which settlers will find it worthwhile to attempt to take land from Indians and within which Indians would wish to resist them. However, settlers can take up to L_1 units with impunity as the costs of defending exceed the benefits to Indians, who cannot credibly threaten to defend their interests. Similarly, settlers will have no interest in land beyond L_2 because the costs of obtaining it are too high relative to the benefits. The model does not predict that there must be war in the zone of controversy. This will depend on factors that influence the cost of negotiation relative to that of war for the parties. Figure 2.2 does imply that there was never an issue of war to annihilation (no ethnic cleansing) provided marginal benefit and cost functions intersected as shown.

Anderson and McChesney (1994) consider the influences upon negotiation as an alternative to war. To develop this aspect of their model, they assume settlers have trespassed and the issue for both parties is whether to negotiate or fight. In general, negotiation could have many outcomes (e.g. settlers stay, settlers leave or settlers compensate Indians) but for it to be preferable to fighting for both parties we must have:

$$S = S_I + S_S > 0 \qquad (2.1)$$

where S is the surplus from negotiation, made up of S_I for Indians and S_S for settlers. For settlers we have:

$$S_S = CF_S + LF_S - CN_S > 0 \qquad (2.2)$$

where CF_S is the cost of fighting, LF_S is the value of previously taken land lost in fighting and CN_S is the cost of negotiation. The surplus from negotiation increases for settlers as the cost of fighting and the value of lost land increases

For Indians, a similar condition is:

$$S_I = CF_I - GF_I - CN_I > 0 \qquad (2.3)$$

where CF_I is the cost of fighting for Indians, GF_I is the value of land retaken by Indians through fighting and CN_I is the Indians' negotiating costs. The Indians' surplus from negotiation increases as the cost of fighting increases and fall as the gain from fighting increases. For both Indians and settlers, increases in negotiation costs reduce the surplus from negotiation.

Condition (2.1) may be expanded to show a sufficient condition for fighting:

$$S = S_S + S_I < 0, \text{ i.e. } [(CF_S + CF_I) - (CN_S + CN_I)] \\ + [LF_S - GF_I] < 0 \tag{2.4}$$

If we assume that the value of land in dispute is the same (T) to settlers and Indians and letting $CF = [CF_S + CF_I]$ (the joint cost of fighting) and $CN = [CN_S + CN_I]$ (the joint cost of negotiating) then:

$$S = CF - CN < 0 \tag{2.5}$$

governs when fighting will occur. In particular, if the (joint) costs of negotiation are always less than those of fighting, fighting will never happen.

However, it is illuminating to introduce an element of uncertainty into the model. Anderson and McChesney postulate, for simplicity, that there is uncertainty over the prospect of gaining or losing land. Condition (2.5) becomes:

$$S = CF - CN - (P_I T) + (P_S T) < 0 \tag{2.6}$$

where P_I and P_S refer to the probabilities Indians and settlers assign to gaining and losing land valued at T. Now condition (2.6) holds only when:

$$(CF - CN) < (P_I - P_S)T \tag{2.7}$$

or

$$(P_I - P_S) > (CF - CN)/T \tag{2.8}$$

Condition (2.8) indicates that the parties' assessment of their probability of winning land and the relative costs of negotiation versus fighting influence the likelihood that war will ensue. Assuming $CF > CN$, we obtain the simple result that the Indians must be more optimistic than settlers about their ability to win back land for fighting to occur.

Anderson and McChesney (1994, p.54) test their model using the patterns of fighting and negotiation over Indian land that developed during the nineteenth century. The first testable prediction concerns the 'zone of controversy' affecting land. This predicts that disputes will not occur at the first point of contact between settlers and Indians, which appears to have been the case. For example, Anderson and McChesney cite the case of the Pemaquid tribe who acceded 12 000 acres of land to English colonists in 1625 as typical of Indian–settler relations at that time. Bearing in mind the low value that Indians placed on large tracts of land that they did not use efficiently this would be expected. They also argue that two key features of nineteenth-century Indian-land policy are consistent with the details of their model. These were the removal of tribes from the Southeast to Oklahoma and the creation of reservations for western tribes. Both these policies removed

Table 2.1 Indian–settler battles and treaties

Year	Battles	Treaties
1790–99	7	10
1800–09	–	30
1810–19	33	35
1820–29	1	51
1830–39	63	84
1840–49	53	18
1850–59	190	58
1860–69	786	61
1870–79	530	–
1880–89	131	–
1890–97	13	–

Source: Anderson and McChesney (1994, p. 58), based on Federal US data.

Indians to areas of land of comparatively low value and avoided costly conflict.

Even where land was contested, there was an early tendency to settle by negotiation rather than through costly conflict. Early English settlers recognized the value of trade with Indians and in the early nineteenth century US governments made considerable efforts to protect Indian rights and to avoid costly war. This had changed by 1871, when Congress voted to ratify no further Indian treaties. Table 2.1 shows the history of Indian–settler battles and treaties.

The increase in the relative use of violence from about 1840 onwards can be explained in terms of the raid-or-trade model. The principal explanation is the move west by both Indians and settlers. In the West, Indians had a nomadic lifestyle, chasing herds of bison on horseback, even if they were displaced eastern tribes that had originally farmed under some form of private property system. Therefore, Indian property rights were not well-developed and bargaining with Indians over land was more difficult. Also, western tribes tended to have a system of government that made it harder for chiefs to commit individuals to honouring treaties. This increase in the cost of negotiation made fighting more attractive.

In addition, the Indians' assessment of their chances of winning battles probably increased with the move west. The Indians' nomadic existence made it difficult for the settlers to estimate the number of hostiles facing them. A well-documented Indian tactic was to use small raiding parties to decoy settlers or the US Army into a trap where many more Indians lay hidden. George Custer's last stand at Little Bighorn, with just a few hundred bluecoats, was the result of unusually poor information about the true size of the opposing force of over 3000 Sioux and Cheyenne.[5] Information asymmetry could sometimes work in the settlers' favour. In 1867, Sioux losses were exceptionally high at the Wagon Box Fight. The soldiers were equipped with new Springfield repeater rifles of which the Sioux had no experience. The model developed above suggests these costly mistakes would not have happened with better information that would have encouraged the losing side to avoid conflict. At any rate, information asymmetry may have grown from the middle of the nineteenth century onwards, encouraging more conflict.

Anderson and McChesney emphasize that technical change cannot in itself encourage war. In the first place, many technical developments in firearms may have been outweighed by the Indians' excellent guerilla warfare techniques. Anyway, the Indians could eventually obtain the weapons. Generally, the effect of superior weapons is hard to predict: the settlers might have been keener to fight but the Indians might have been deterred. One test of the effect – changes in the ratio of settler to Indian deaths in battle – shows no significant trend over the period 1850–91.

A further explanation of the increase in battles is found in the growth of a standing US Army, particularly after the Civil War of 1861–65. Anderson and McChesney argue that this enabled local citizenry to avoid direct personal costs when incurring conflict with natives, that locals liked an army presence because of the demand for supplies and that officers and army bureaucrats increased the pressure for Indian wars to further their careers. The standing army replaced the earlier English system of militias. Broadly the effect was to reduce the local costs of fighting relative to negotiating for settlers in the West. Anderson and McChesney (1994, p.69) undertake a regression analysis to test the significance of military growth.

One of their tests uses ordinary-least-squares methods to regress the annual number of battles on the size of the US Army and other variables for the period 1790–1897. Their results show that increases in the size of the army have a statistically significant effect in increasing the number of battles. In case it may be objected that causality could run the other way, Anderson and McChesney (1994, p.71) obtain the same conclusion from an equation in which army size lagged by one year replaces army size as an independent variable.

Anderson and McChesney succeed in explaining the raid-or-trade history of the creation of private rights in land for American settlers. Their paper represents a careful application of property-rights theory to institutional development, backed up by empirical analysis. An earlier paper in a similar tradition is Libecap (1978) which explains the founding of the state of Nevada in terms of the evolution of an efficient system for creating and enforcing private property rights as the gold rush developed in the American West. Also of interest is Anderson and Hill (1975) which traces the nineteenth-century move in the West from the open range to private grazing to the invention of barbed wire. Finally in this section, Libecap (1989) recognizes that the costs of reaching agreements over sharing the benefits from creating private rights can stand in the way of privatizing the commons, as illustrated by the case of oil production from common pools in the USA.

2.7 A BRIEF NOTE ON THE COMPARATIVE EFFICIENCY OF PUBLIC AND PRIVATE ENTERPRISE

It is important to distinguish common-property problems from issues concerning the efficiency of public enterprise. Public enterprise is not an example of common property but occurs where the state purchases or takes the private property rights attached to some activity. In the UK, many industries like telecoms, electricity, gas and steel were nationalized after the Second World War until the privatization programme of the 1980s. The history of these industries shows that there were great problems of achieving cost control during the period when private ownership was removed.

Contracting out in the public sector (e.g. refuse collection) shows productivity gains of about 20% (Domberger, Meadowcroft and Thompson, 1986). Pryke's (1982) work comparing similar sectors of private and nationalized companies produced similar findings. A recent research study at the World Bank (Galal, Jones, Tandon and Vogelsant, 1992) examined the post-privatization performance of 12 companies (airlines and utilities) in the UK, Chile, Malaysia and Mexico. The World Bank found net welfare gains in 11 of the cases, with an average magnitude of 26%. They found no cases where workers were made worse off, dismissing the allegation sometimes made that gains for shareholders in newly privatized firms are simply transfers from workers whose wages and conditions worsen.

It is not removing common-property problems that drives such efficiency gains, rather, it is the establishment of incentives to simple cost efficiency. In the private sector, the firms have a residual claimant with an interest in maximizing profits. Profits and general welfare go together under competitive conditions.

2.8 PUBLIC GOODS

We examine the issue of public goods for two reasons. First, the public good must be carefully distinguished both from the nationalized firm, which often produces private goods and from common-property resources, where open access yields private but suboptimal benefits for users. Secondly, some economic problems of law have public-goods aspects and we shall want to refer back to the ideas of this section.

There is a traditional argument that public goods are not suitable for provision through private markets. A pure public good arises when it is not desirable to limit access to the use of some facility. In addition, from a practical point of view, it may be difficult for a private provider of a public good to practise exclusion – although this is not the key defining characteristic. Pure public goods are essentially ones for which consumption is not mutually exclusive for consumers, so that people can be added to the group of consumers without depriving existing members of benefits. It is then efficient to add to the group any

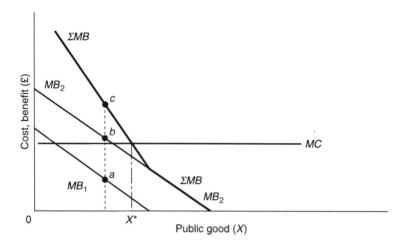

Figure 2.3 Optimal provision of a public good. MB_1 = marginal benefit of consumption for one individual; MB_2 = marginal benefit of consumption for second individual; MC = marginal cost; ΣMB = vertical sum of MB_1 and MB_2; X^* = optimal level of public good.

consumer who would receive some benefit. Classic examples of public goods are said to be services like defence, the police force and the provision of a system of law and order through the courts.

In terms of price theory, the optimal level of provision of a public good occurs where the sum of consumers' marginal benefits equals the marginal cost (Samuelson, 1955). This is shown in Figure 2.3 where MB_1 shows the (declining) marginal benefit of consumption for one individual, MB_2 shows marginal benefit for a second and MC shows (constant) marginal cost. The curve labelled ΣMB is the vertical sum of MB_1 and MB_2, showing the joint benefits from a marginal unit of consumption (i.e. point a plus point b gives point c). The application of the general rule that marginal benefit should equal marginal cost for efficient allocation tells us to provide X^* units of the public good in Figure 2.3.

Consumers have an incentive to understate their preferences to a private firm trying to market a public good as it may not be possible to practise exclusion of non-payers. If we think of trying to market a defence system by asking citizens how much each would buy for the coming year, each individual will seek to free ride and shift the costs by pretending to wish to buy very little – each believing that his neighbour will buy the service anyway and that it will therefore be available. Table 2.2 shows the pay-offs to two individuals, A and B, who receive a benefit worth £4 (for example) to each of them from the provision of the service. Collective provision costs £4 in total, divided equally among contributing individuals. Failure to co-operate forces them to provide their own service at a cost of £3 each. If A and B declare their preferences honestly and share the cost of providing the service, each receives a net benefit of £2. If A contributes but B does not, A incurs

Table 2.2 Public-goods prisoners' dilemma

		B	
		Contributes	Does not
A	Contributes	2, 2	0, 4
	Does not	4, 0	1, 1

(pay-offs: A, B)

the entire cost of providing both with the service. This gives A a pay-off of zero and B a pay-off of £4. If B contributes but A does not, B incurs the cost and receives a zero pay-off but A obtains £4. If neither contributes, each receives a net benefit of £1 (£4 benefit minus £3 cost).

In Table 2.2, the non-cooperative strategy 'does not contribute' strictly dominates for both players, which means it is always better to try and free ride whatever the other does. The difficulty with this is that both will evade contributing and end up at the bottom right of the table, which is the worse possible place to be (the 'joint pessimum'). The table is a public-goods example of the classic problem from game theory known as the prisoners' dilemma, in which apprehended criminals cannot stop themselves from confessing their guilt.[6]

The traditional conclusion is that public goods require the intervention of the state which uses its coercive powers to force individuals to contribute to the provision of public goods (Mishan, 1981). However, it is easy to question this conclusion. In the first place, there are many examples of services that are often cited as examples of public goods that have been successfully provided by private organizations (Benson, 1994; Klein, 1990). These include lighthouses (Coase, 1974; Van Zandt, 1993) which are often cited as classic public goods because of the problem of levying charges on ships. Coase argues that the lighthouse is a particularly bad example of a public-goods problem, having been provided for many years around English shores by a private guild known as Trinity House.[7] These observations are not surprising given that private provision of a public good (for which the term 'collective good' is really more appropriate) could be optimal if the supplier could practise perfect price discrimination by excluding consumers unless each paid his marginal valuation (Demsetz, 1970).

Why were private lighthouses successful? Sometimes the collection of dues was mandated by governments, suggesting that government may not need to provide a public good but that its coercive power may be required. Often though, where lighthouses were provided on the basis of purely voluntary payments, suppliers could rely on a variety of non-legal social and religious sanctions, e.g. a captain could be ostracized for failing to support a local religious order supplying the light. In smaller societies, a close-knit social group may succeed in the voluntary provision of public goods (De Jasay, 1989) which is a point also made by Klein (1990) in relation to historical examples of privately funded turnpike roads. The similar problem of over-exploitation of common-property resources is also sometimes solved by voluntary co-operation, as in the case of meadow land in Switzerland, where the social group is cohesive and informal sanctions can operate.

It is also difficult to find examples of pure public goods. Examples like parks and highways really exhibit publicness only until they become congested. It may be more sensible to think of a spectrum of goods, with the private good and the pure public good as extreme points. The middle of the spectrum is occupied by the 'club good', where an individual's benefits depend on the amount of personal consumption and the number of persons sharing the facility (Buchanan, 1965). Good examples are golf or swimming clubs. It may be that the club good is the best representation of typical consumption.

The coercive power of the state does not really overcome the problem of obtaining a true revelation of preferences for public goods. To be sure, if we knew each individual's preferences, the state could provide the service and levy taxes to pay for it equal to each person's marginal valuation of the service (Lindahl, 1919). But this information is not easily available and special schemes, probably quite costly to implement, would be required (Tideman and Tullock, 1976). Also, it is not certain that 'Lindahl' taxes would always provide sufficient revenue to cover the total cost of the service.

2.9   SOME ASSORTED PROPERTY DOCTRINES

We now examine various legal principles affecting the creation of property rights. These can be linked to some of the ideas on the efficiency of private rights and the undesirability of encouraging rent seeking.

2.9.1   First possession

Unpossessed resources are often claimed under rules of first possession. For example, the US Homesteading Act 1862 enabled citizens over 21 years of age to acquire up to 160 acres of frontier land at $1.25 an acre by residing for six months and making improvements on the land. The Act did not recognize aboriginal practices for this purpose and had the effect of excluding Indian claims to land.

Land claims like this still arise in Australia, although the recent *Mabo* case (1992) in the Australian High Court has raised questions about the extent of property rights gained by settlers and mineral companies (Hulme, 1993). The traditional view was that the Australian continent represented *terra nullius*, or unoccupied land, when European settlement began. In *Mabo*, the High Court recognized the existence of native title for Melanesian tribes living on the Murray Islands off northern Queensland. Native title gives hunting, ceremonial and bush-burning rights. If the *Mabo* ruling turns out to be applicable to mainland Aboriginal claims of native title, it may seriously hamper the economic development of parts of Australia – owing to the widespread legal conflict that may ensue. It is not obvious that it will apply, as the Murray Islanders were a settled people with a gardening culture when they were annexed by the British Crown in 1879, whereas Aborigines were entirely nomadic.

In Canada, New Zealand and the USA, native title has often been successfully claimed by settled tribes that had exclusively used and occupied land for some time at the point when sovereignty was asserted by European settlers. These rights usually refer to some particular form of use of land or an exemption from some statutory control, as in the Canadian case *R. v. Sparrow* (1990) where members of the Musqueam tribe successfully defended their right to use outsized drift nets. These partial rights reflect the movement of settling Europeans past native tribes, with the settlers ceding rights that were not significant to them at the time. Problems may arise, as in Australia, if native rights are suddenly rediscovered and great costs of adjustment are created.

In the case of land, a rule of first possession moves society away from common property and towards enforceable private property rights. This is generally efficiency enhancing, however tough it may be on nomadic indigenous peoples who may never share in the benefits from enclosure. The result contrasts with the effect of first possession for 'fugitive' property, where the prize is the product of a renewable natural resource that cannot be privately owned. Then we have a case like the fishery, where first possession is simply a reflection of open access that never stops. With land, the open access is brought to a halt as possession is obtained.

2.9.2 Water rights

The manner in which water is owned and used in various countries illustrates the effect of scarcity on property rights. In England and in the eastern USA, where water is plentiful, riparian owners (owners of the shore alongside a body of water) have the right to use the flow of water past their land but cannot divert water to the detriment of the flow available to downstream owners of land. In particular, this prevents the diversion of significant amounts of water for irrigation.

However, in the western USA – and in other parts of the USA to which this system has spread – the riparian owner may make 'reasonable' use of the water in any way that does not interfere with the 'reasonable' use of others, where reasonable use can be defined by courts if necessary but is often settled by agreements among ranchers (Anderson and Simmons, 1993). Therefore, the riparian owner can divert surplus water and sell it to a distant property as long as downstream uses are preserved, which leads to greater efficiency over water use and permits irrigation. The subtle distinction is that the downstream riparian owner has no unqualified right to a flow of water but has only the right to enough water for reasonable uses. In the West, water is more valuable and it is worth incurring the costs of determining what is or is not a reasonable use in order to free water for more distant use. In the East, the simple rule not to divert water saves the cost of such argument without unduly imposing on anyone, owing to the more plentiful water supply.

In Australia, statutes arose in the nineteenth century to control river and ground water use. Australian history also illustrates the effects of increased scarcity in changing the efficient solution for property rights. What works in England would be dysfunctional in the Australian outback. Recently, there have been moves towards the sale of irrigation licences in several Australian states (Sturgess and Wright, 1993), which may be seen as encouraging maximum economy over water use.

2.9.3 Adverse possession

Countries typically have statutes of limitations on trespass. If someone occupies land, they can obtain title 'by adverse possession' if the original owner does not sue for trespass within the limitation, which is 12 years in England and differs across states in the USA (but is commonly seven years). Statutes of limitations may be seen as efficient (Merrill, 1986). They suppress claims based on older and less reliable data which may just be too costly to pursue. The rule of adverse possession is efficient if it makes it possible to transfer unused land to a higher-valuing user although this would not be true if the first owner had the highest valuation. The rule is often associated with procedures, such as paying land taxes, that can alert the first owner to the possession. The long period of time that must pass before adverse possession can take effect also helps, as it would be remarkable if someone with a definite interest in the land were to overlook its adverse possession over a lengthy period of years. In addition, adverse possession rules put landowners on notice to avoid boundary errors before improving land, which helps to avoid costly conflicts (Miceli and Sirmans, 1995).

Without limitations on claims, the courts could be overwhelmed by requests to correct ancient wrongs and disputants would incur enormous expense checking title back into the mists of time. Most of the issues associated with such enquiries would have distributional rather than efficiency implications. A line is drawn in the interests of saving costly legal battles over property rights. Interestingly, the Australian High Court has gone against this principle in the *Mabo* decision discussed earlier (section 2.9.1). Notice also that the dispossession of Saxons in England by the Norman Conquest had many of the characteristics of the later settlement of aboriginal lands by Europeans.

2.9.4 Lost property

A problem with lost property is to prevent the devotion of too many resources in finding the original owner which would not typically be efficient relative to the owner's valuation of the property. The danger

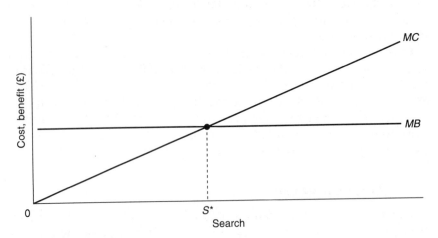

Figure 2.4 Optimal search. MB = marginal benefit of searching; MC = marginal cost of searching; S^* = point at which search activity stops.

with a rule of 'finders keepers' is that people devote too many resources to searching for lost property. A rational person will devote resources to searching if the expected return is greater than or equal to the cost of the effort. Search activity stops when the marginal benefit (MB) is just equal to marginal cost (MC), as shown in Figure 2.4. by point S^*. The marginal benefit of search is shown as constant for simplicity whereas the marginal cost increases owing to the need to search more distantly.

The race to find lost property can be wasteful if people overestimate their chances of finding the property. If ten people each have an equal probability of finding a lost work of art, they should each devote one-tenth of its value to finding it. The search would be efficient because, in aggregate, no more than the value of the work of art would be spent in finding it. But if they overestimate their probability of success at one-fifth, they will devote in aggregate double the value of the work to its recovery. People may well err in the direction of overestimation of their chances of success. There is a link here, as with rules of first possession, with the theory of common-property rights (Mortensen, 1982).

It is also possible to spend too much time and effort trying to locate the original owner of an item. Most countries or states have estray statutes. There is an orderly procedure in which the finder of a valuable item attempts to locate the original owner before claiming the item. The point is to ensure that only cost-effective efforts are made to locate owners in a process that removes uncertainty over title. Estray statutes enable property to be allocated to some valued use.

The law sometimes distinguishes between mislaid and lost property. If property was mislaid, the owner meant to come back but forgot where it was. Title cannot then be claimed by a finder. In fact, this distinction is not sensible if the point of property law is to remove uncertainty over title. Treasure-trove rulings in England are of interest in this respect. If property is judged to have been mislaid (i.e. it was deliberately hidden for future return) the item is declared to be treasure trove and must be given up to the government, although a reward of lesser value goes to the finder. It is thought that this rule dates from the thirteenth century when impecunious monarchs used it to replenish their funds. If an item is judged to have been simply lost or dispensed with (e.g. thrown away on a town dump) then it can become the finder's property. The approach of paying a finder's fee in the case of treasure trove is sensible and could be used more widely. The reward operates to encourage searching but does not encourage the excessive activity that can result when a finder keeps the whole value and is not influenced by the presence of other searchers.

If we knew that n searchers were totally uninfluenced by each other's presence on a search, we would predict that:

$$\text{Total Search Costs} = n \, (\text{Value of Item})$$

which is an excessive level of search. By setting a reward equal to (Value of Item)/n we would reduce the level of search costs to:

$$\text{Total Search Costs} = n \, [(\text{Value of Item})/n]$$
$$= \text{Value of Item}$$

which is efficient.

In the UK in 1994, the Earl of Perth introduced a Bill into the House of Lords with the aim of extending the treasure trove treatment to all discovered items over 200 years old. This seems to be an eminently sensible measure if it is the case that there is too much search activity going on. The motivation for the Bill has come from the growth of amateur treasure hunting. Apparently, in 1994, there were over 10 000 members of the National Council for Metal Detecting in the UK. Museums have found it difficult to acquire items that have not been judged to be treasure trove, e.g. when artifacts were buried in graves.[8] This is another case of technology affecting the desirability of particular property rules. If, however, people underestimate their chances of success, the reduction in the return to finding could reduce search efforts to suboptimal levels.

2.10   INTELLECTUAL PROPERTY

We now consider a less obvious form of property right which has grown in importance in the twentieth century. Intellectual property is mostly the direct product of human creative activity, such as a new invention, design or work of art. Products like these are appropriated by their creators under laws covering patents, design registration and copyright. The main point of these laws is to encourage valuable creative activity by defining a form of future market for the use of the intellectual property. A further type of intellectual property is the business trade mark where enforceable property rights have a useful role to play in communicating information about goods and services to consumers.

2.10.1 Patents

Patents exclude anyone but the patent holder from freely using an invention. The holder may choose to license use of a patented invention in exchange for a royalty payment. In the UK, a patent lasts for a maximum of 20 years, during which time annual registration fees must be paid to keep it in force.[9] The Patents Act (1977) requires that a patentable invention must:

1. be new
2. involve an inventive step
3. be capable of industrial application, and
4. not be an obvious development.

It also must not be excluded from patentability by virtue of being a purely intellectual discovery (such as a scientific theory) or creation (like a work of art) or by being merely a matter of aesthetic outward appearance. The period of 20 years is comparable to the periods used elsewhere, e.g. in the USA a patent lasts for 17 years. In the UK, as throughout the world with the exception of the USA and Canada, a system is in operation in which the inventor who files the first patent for an invention has priority in claiming property rights over it (Ordover, 1991). It is a 'first-to-file' system.

There is a tension in economic analysis between seeing patents as devices that restrict competition and encourage monopolistic pricing of products and seeing them as an essential incentive for invention and innovation (Dam, 1994; Waterson, 1990). An adaptation of an example of Posner's (1992, p.38) shows why patents are needed. If it costs £10 million to invent a better food processor and the marginal cost of production is £50 per machine with anticipated sales of 1 000 000 a market price of £60 is needed. If other companies can freely use the invention, the price of the food processor will be driven down to £50 in a competitive market. As a result, there will be little or no incentive to invent. Patents give a temporary monopoly to the inventor and, by raising market price, increase the incentive to invent.

The current patent law effectively gives a brief monopoly in exchange for full revelation of the invention. Without patent protection, firms would be more tempted than presently to keep their inventions secret. This would hamper further development by other inventors. Patent law can also be seen, therefore, as an attempt to encourage information revelation where this may have benefits that are external to the originating business. It is interesting to note that patents originated with the medieval royal prerogative to grant 'letters patent' to skilled workers. The privilege was widely abused by monarchs and was brought under control by the Statute of Monopolies 1623 but letters patent typically applied to foreign inventors who were required to train the native population in the use of their invention. Patent law has its origins in creating a reward for transferring knowledge.

There is a sense in which, once it is in existence, the invention has the characteristics of a public good. It would seem costless to allow others to use the information. However this argument ignores the cost of disturbing the long-run incentives for invention. When we take this cost into account, it is possible to make an efficiency argument in favour of patents (Demsetz, 1982). Indeed, without patent law, there would be suboptimal levels of research and development because firms would be tempted to free ride on others' efforts, as inventors could not exclude them. Also, invention would be biased towards things that could be kept secret. The patent system makes free riding more difficult by creating appropriate intellectual property rights. There is an optimal patent life, which in principle, is different for each invention. Figure 2.5 illustrates the trade-off between the costs and benefits of extending patent life.

In Figure 2.5, the curve labelled *MC* shows the marginal cost of patenting. Other firms must incur costs from 'inventing around' the patent or paying fees to use it and consumers lose owing to higher prices from monopoly. Increasing marginal cost reflects an assumption that there is an increasing nuisance from extending the patent. The curve labelled *MB* shows falling benefits from extending patent life, in terms of the profit gain to the inventors: as time passes, more people would avoid the patent by successfully inventing around it. An optimum occurs at *L** where the surplus of benefit over costs is maximized. It would be too costly to work out the optimal length of

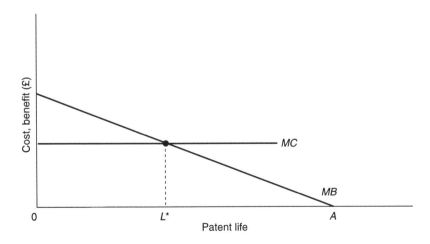

Figure 2.5 Optimal patent life. *MB* =marginal benefit of patenting; *MC* = marginal cost of patenting; *L** = optimal life of patent.

patent protection applying to each invention. The law has to establish a rule that will work on average. The virtue of the model is in showing that patents really ought not be for ever as they impose costs as well as benefits.

In the UK, the fees for maintaining a patent have the effect of facing the inventor with some, although possibly not many, of the costs imposed. In 1992, the fee to obtain a patent stood at a modest £155. The annual renewal fees were based on a sliding scale beginning at £110 in the fifth year of the patent and increasing to £450 for the twentieth and final year. The increasing scale of annual renewal fee accords well with the economic model we have used. Ideally, inventors should be faced with the marginal cost they impose, which increases with patent length, although marginal cost would be very difficult to estimate. As this is not done with precision and since the fees look low, inventors probably feel they would like longer periods – reflecting point A where MB cuts the horizontal axis in Figure 2.5 – for patent life. Other countries have similar systems. Germany has a two-tier system with a full-term patent for major inventions and a three-year patent for minor developments and also has patent renewal fees that rise during the life of the patent. The USA has a complicated fee structure based on a $690 filing fee and a $1130 issue fee, and has recently also adopted an increasing annual fee to maintain the patent (Dam, 1994, footnote 64).

We now consider the danger that patent law may encourage investment in patent blitzing, i.e. speculative investment in research to obtain a patent monopoly and close off a market area. One variant of such behaviour, patent racing, is a bit like treasure hunting and has very clear implications of rent-seeking behaviour (Grossman and Schapiro, 1987). However, as Dam (1994) argues, it is not obvious that rent seeking is as wasteful as some writers believe; also, the law often exhibits devices that work to contain the costs of rent seeking or to reduce the incentives for it.

Any wasteful expenditures on seeking patents broadly encompass two areas: the cost of the patenting system itself and the cost of duplicating effort over research and development. Dam regards the cost of the patenting system as an inevitable cost of the administration of a part of the property-rights system. Unless there is conflict over the property right, the costs are limited to the modest fees of registration and renewal, plus lawyers' fees for drawing up the patent application. Substantial costs arise if there are claims that a patent has been infringed. However, these costs are not unique to patent rights, e.g. land may give rise to costly disputes over ownership. High costs attached to disputes may be more a reflection of high litigation costs rather than of rent-seeking behaviour.

Dam (1994, p.263) argues that even if all research and development activity became encapsulated in patents, it would not follow that duplicative research should be regarded as wasteful. It is a question of making meaningful comparisons. If there exists some other means of generating the same innovation at lower cost, then it would be reasonable to regard duplicative effort as wasteful. By analogy, we do not regard competition between several petrol stations as wasteful even when we know that only one will survive. We accept the cost of competition as the only way to obtain the benefits of competition. Patent races could be of this nature. What are the alternatives? One may be for the government to use competitive bidding to allocate the monopoly right to research into a new drug to the company promising to undertake it at the lowest cost. However, competitive bidding has it own problems (Williamson, 1976). For a start, it is difficult to define the right that would be exclusively allocated. Also, as defence contracting suggests, firms would devote resources to lobbying for the exclusive right. It is not obvious that there would be less waste with competitive bidding, or any fewer problems with any other regulatory framework that might be suggested.

Dam (1994) argues that rent seeking has been exaggerated as a problem and notes that patent law limits rent seeking without notably discouraging desirable competitive activities. He points out that the first-to-invent system of issuing patents in the USA, described by Besen and Raskind (1991), in itself communicates the knowledge that some invention has been captured and favours early registration so as not to run the risk of losing the property right to someone else. This leads to swift termination of other firms' efforts, an effect that is even stronger under the first-to-file rules used to confer patents in almost all other countries, including the UK and the remainder of the EU. Also, the requirement that a patentable invention should not be too obvious eliminates property rights in areas of innovation that might be expected to attract a lot of duplicative effort precisely because they would be the easiest in which to invest.

2.10.2 Copyright

Copyright law protects the property rights of authors, composers and artists as an incentive to creative activity. It prevents unauthorized copying and, in terms of economics, gives the copyright owner a temporary monopoly on the original work. These days, the definition of creative work also encompasses the design of computer software. In the UK the Copyright, Designs and Patents Act 1988 gives protection for the lifetime of the creator plus 50 years in most cases. This is also the position in other countries, like the USA, that have also signed the Berne Convention on mutual recognition of copyright.

Without copyright, the price of some creative work would fall to its marginal cost of reproduction. The qualification is necessary as other factors may restrict the reproducibility of some works, e.g. a Henry Moore work really must be by the sculptor. In many cases, such as the production of novels or textbooks, consumers would be indifferent between the authorized copy and any other. An absence of copyright restrictions would benefit consumers and publishers as prices fell, as illustrated by the competition between Wordsworth Classics and Penguin Classics in the UK in 1994. Wordsworth began to publish cheap paperback editions of classic novels, on which copyright had expired, that sold for as little as £1. This seriously challenged Penguin's market for classic works and they responded with their own line of cheap paperbacks. This benefit to consumers is based on a lack of property rights for the estates of the original authors.

The analysis of patenting in Figure 2.5 could be applied to copyright with suitable amendment of details: there is a marginal benefit to creators from copyright protection that probably diminishes the longer we look into the future and marginal costs to consumers and publishers that will rise with duration. An optimum could, in principle, be found from balancing marginal cost and benefit. It seems that copyright law recognizes the falling benefit to a creator from extending duration in ending copyright restrictions at a fixed number of years after death.

The blanket nature of copyright restrictions has been questioned by Breyer (1970) who argues that the problems attached to allowing copying are not as severe as is conventionally claimed. He focuses on book publishing, which is really the area likely to give difficulty and suggests that the original author has a first-mover advantage of lead time over possible rivals. This may certainly be a valid argument in the case of popular literature, as these books must generally earn profits over their first few months on the market: an example is the book *Princess in Love*, which was a bestseller for just a few weeks in 1994 and is now largely forgotten. By the time a rival publisher realized the value of copying such a work, most of the return would have been earned by the originator. Breyer does not say there is no problem in removing copyright, only that there is not as great a difficulty as is commonly argued.

The limits on copying are even stronger in the case of paintings, sculptures and films. It may be impossible to copy the original, no one may want the copy or other laws of property may prevent copying. However, there is less protection in other cases. It is difficult to see how property rights in textbooks and computer programs could be protected without copyright. Even among more creative products there would be problems wherever lead times counted for little, e.g. the incentives for playwrights would be diluted as professional theatre companies could put on their work without paying royalties. Nonetheless, Breyer's argument that copyright could be less extensive carries some force. It is interesting to note that early copyright, e.g. as in the Statute of Anne 1709 was limited to printed books and lasted for only 14 years. Early copyright law was held to apply to musical composition, e.g. in *Bach* v. *Longman* (1777) – when the composer J.C. Bach sued against copying – and was gradually extended to include plays, sculptures and other works over the course of the nineteenth century. If Breyer's argument is sound, it may be that the lobbying power of creative artists and their publishers was successful in influencing Parliament relative to the more diffused costs imposed on consumers.

2.10.3 Trade marks

Businesses invest large sums of money in developing trade marks which are usually based on an easily identified company logo. Trade marks associate a company name or symbol with a differentiable product or service and are meant to be easily identified indicators of quality. An illustration of this is in franchising, where a company like Burger King (the British-owned international fast-food chain) literally rents out its trade mark in return for royalties from franchisees. The value of the trade mark is in indicating quality to travellers or to others who do not wish to spend much time assessing the quality of restaurants.

Under the Trade Marks Act 1994 in the UK, and in most systems around the world, trade marks can be registered only if they represent a real differentiation of some product. If the name is a generic term for a product it cannot be registered. Furthermore, if the trade mark becomes a general description within the trade for goods of similar description, its exclusive use cannot be enforced and the trade mark tends to disappear. An example of a 'broken' trade mark in the UK is Daiquiri Rum, which was registered in 1922 but was removed from the register in 1969 when it was shown to have become a general term for a cocktail in pubs and clubs. In the USA, broken marks include 'Aspirin' and 'Super Glue'.

It is important for the owners of trade marks to be vigilant in enforcing their exclusive right to use a name or they risk losing it if it becomes too common a currency. The US-owned Coca-Cola company is well known for its vigilance in this respect. In 1994 in the UK, Coca-Cola began legal action to prevent the Sainsbury supermarket chain from marketing its own brand of cola drink ('Classic Cola') allegedly using labelling reminiscent of the 'Coca-Cola' logo. Sainsbury gave an undertaking to redesign their packaging to avoid possible confusion. In the USA, Coca-Cola sues approximately 50 restaurateurs a year for wrongly using its trade name (typically 'Coke') to describe generic cola drinks.

Some economists are keen to see investment in trade marks as supporting monopolies that are against the interests of consumers (Cowling and Meuller, 1978). However, this would seem to ignore the information conveyed to buyers by trade marks (Littlechild, 1981; Demsetz, 1982). It is not enough for firms to produce products or services of a certain technical quality; possible customers also have to receive the information. In addition to developing trade marks, firms also spend money on many other devices to indicate the quality of their service. For example, a bank's expenditure on high-quality fittings on its premises is most likely meant to signal to customers that it is too well funded to be at risk of failure (Klein and Leffler, 1981).

The information-based explanation of trade mark law gains support from the observation that the law does not support trade mark rights where they serve no purpose. The restriction on registering general descriptive terms may be seen in this way. Of particular interest, however, is the prohibition on stopping use of a trade marked business name by another firm in a different line of business. In *Stringfellow* v. *McCain Foods* (1984), the owner of the famous nightclub in London was not able to stop a food company from marketing a product called 'Stringfellow Chips'. From an efficiency point of view this was a correct decision because the chips carried no implications for the efficiency of the quality signal in the nightclub business. A contrasting case is *Levy* v. *McDonald's Hamburgers* (1995), which is current at the time of writing, in which the restaurateur owners of the Route 66 trade mark are seeking an injunction to stop McDonald's from running a Route 66 American-theme promotion in their fast-food outlets. In the Route 66 case, there is arguably greater danger of a quality signal being undermined through confusion.

SUMMARY AND CONCLUSIONS

In this chapter, we have defined a number of systems of property rights and shown how these have implications for economic efficiency. In particular, private property rights encourage efficient use and transfers of resources. Common property is typically associated with over-exploitation of resources, although this argument should be qualified by recognition of the costs of creating private rights. The issues surrounding ownership of resources must be carefully distinguished from those affecting the desirability of public or private provision of goods and services.

We have also shown how economic analysis can throw light on institutional developments. By institutional developments, we mean such things as the emergence of particular systems of property rights and the means of enforcing them. We may also mean the development of particular legal rules over taking possession of lost property or of protecting intellectual property.

ENDNOTES

1. The bell shaped curve actually reflects sustainable yield, but sustainability, although important in the specialist literature on fisheries, is not important in this illustration of common property.
2. For simplicity we assume no discounting of future costs and benefits attached to the fishery. With discounting at a high enough rate, it might be rational for the owner to fish out the entire stock in the current year. The model without discounting is adequate to show the different incentives under open access and private rights.
3. Cultch (*not clutch!*) is the base on which the oysters grow.
4. See 'Fish-war MP urges Navy to send frigate', *The Times* Monday August 8, 1994.
5. E.S. Connell (1984, p.263) cited by Anderson and McChesney (1994, p.59).
6. The classic prisoners' dilemma looks like this:

Table 2.3 Classic prisoners' dilemma

		B	
		Confesses	Does not
A	Confesses	2, 2	0, 4
	Does not	4, 0	1, 1
			(pay-offs: A, B)

The criminals are placed in separate cells and cannot communicate. Each is told that if he confesses and helps to obtain the conviction of the other, the police will charge him with a trivial offence carrying no prison sentence. If he does not confess but a more serious charge can be proved, the court will show no mercy and he will go to jail for four years. If they both confess, the police do not need to be so generous but the court will make an allowance for co-operation and halve the sentence. If neither confesses, the police can only prove a lesser offence carrying a one-year sentence for each. 'Confess' dominates 'does not confess' for each player and they end up going to jail for two years each, which is as bad as things could be.

7. With typical style, Coase (1974) quotes *The Mikado* to suggest the lighthouse is used by economists to provide 'corroborative detail, intended to give artistic verisimilitude to an otherwise bald and unconvincing narrative'.

8. See 'Peer Aims to Save Heritage from Metal Detectors', *The Times*, Wednesday November 2, 1994.

9. There is a parallel system of patent law operating throughout the European Union under the rules of the European Patent Convention (1973).

3 Conflicts over property rights

Property rights often come into conflict as, e.g., when a concrete plant releases dust onto nearby residential property. In economics, such conflicts are examined using the theory of externalities, which were defined in the previous chapter as unintended spillovers between separate economic activities (see 2.5). In law, many externalities can be dealt with by private action to stop nuisance, which is defined as the 'tort of interference with the use of land' (Posner, 1992, p.63).[1] The question in the economics of law is how to settle such conflict efficiently. Although nuisance is technically a topic in tort (the body of law dealing with civil wrongs which we consider more generally in Chapter 6) it is most sensibly examined alongside property-rights issues.

Faced with a case of nuisance, courts may give 'legal relief' and order the defendant to pay damages. Alternatively, they can grant 'equitable relief' and issue an injunction that 'enjoins' (stops) the defendant from generating the nuisance.[2] The traditional approach is for courts to grant an injunction, although they may also order compensation to be paid for existing damages. In much of this chapter, we examine the economic properties of injunctions and legal relief. Courts in the USA have recently moved towards an emphasis on legal relief whereas the English courts have remained more conservative in this respect. Later in the chapter, we look at contractual devices like covenants and easements (see 3.5) and at statutory controls such as planning consent which are further methods of controlling conflict over property rights.

We start by examining the work of Ronald Coase (1960), the 1991 Nobel prize winner in economics, on externality. Coase developed the economic theory of externality by focusing on individuals and drawing in details of the law on nuisance. His work was highly influential in establishing modern law and economics.

3.1 THE COASE THEOREM, EFFICIENCY AND DISTRIBUTION

In his 1960 article, 'The Problem of Social Cost', Ronald Coase argued that bargaining between individuals internalizes many externalities when the cost of bargaining is sufficiently low. Bargaining costs are a form of transaction costs, which are defined as the costs of negotiating and enforcing contracts. In other cases, where transaction costs are high, the law can often be used to correct many externalities, possibly by better defining property rights. Coase's point of departure was a classic nuisance case, *Sturges* v. *Bridgman* (1879), in which a doctor occupied premises neighbouring a confectioner's workrooms, where noisy equipment had operated over more than 60 years.

3.1.1 The Coase theorem and transaction costs

Coase analyzed *Sturges* v. *Bridgman* in great detail. The case resulted in an injunction stopping the confectioner (Bridgman) from using machinery, the noise from which made it difficult for the doctor (Sturges) to treat patients. In terms of economic analysis, the costs and benefits of using the machinery might have looked like Figure 3.1, where the noise nuisance is measured as hours (per day, within working hours) on the horizontal axis. The upward sloping function measures the marginal external cost (*MEC*) of the noise, reflecting an assumption that each extra hour of noise creates a greater cost than the preceding one. This cost is simply lost fee income for the doctor. The downward sloping function showing marginal net benefit (*MNB*), shows the profits (i.e. revenue minus production cost) to the confectioner from extending the use of the machinery.

Left alone, the confectioner would generate eight hours of noise. This is where marginal net private benefit falls to zero, maximizing profits (the area under *MNB*). However, the jointly optimal level of noise is four hours in Figure 3.1. Up to that level marginal net benefit exceeds marginal external cost, whereas beyond it the opposite is true.

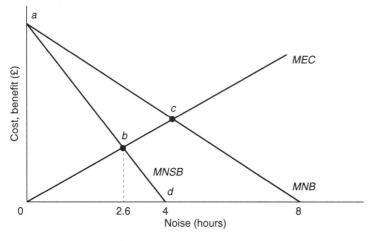

Figure 3.1 *Sturges* v. *Bridgman*. *MEC* = marginal external cost of noise; *MNB* = marginal net benefit of noise; *MNSB* = marginal net social benefit of noise.

If an hour's noise adds more to the benefit from the noise than to its cost, it is worth bearing the nuisance. One way to look at this is to recognize that the confectioner could compensate the doctor for bearing the external cost up to the fourth unit (just) but not beyond. Note that a classic public-policy recommendation for controlling externality (Pigou, 1938) is for the state to impose a charge equal to marginal external cost on the noise polluter ('polluter pays'). This causes MNB to fall to $MNSB$ (marginal net social, i.e. joint, benefit) giving maximum post-tax profits at four hours.

Coase argued that bargaining can make it irrelevant whether the court had found for or against the doctor in *Sturges* v. *Bridgman*. This result follows easily in the case where bargaining is assumed to be costless (zero transaction costs) and is usually referred to as the 'Coase theorem' – although it is not technically a theorem, nor does it fully report the result of Coase's analysis.[3] The court's granting of an injunction assigned the 'entitlement' (Calabresi and Melamed, 1972) to stop the noise to Sturges. The court could have assigned the entitlement to continue with his noisy work to Bridgman by not issuing the injunction. The Coase theorem states that, on the assumption of costless bargaining, the court's assignment of the entitlement is irrelevant for determining the equilibrium (and optimal) amount of the nuisance. This is because the parties can bargain around the injunction or the lack of one. Assigning the entitlement in a case of nuisance creates an additional dimension to an existing property right and will have distributional consequences.

In Figure 3.1, if Sturges has the injunction, he would initially like to stop all noise. However, the marginal profits (MNB) for Bridgman from the confectionery business exceed the marginal external costs (MEC) to Sturges until they reach four hours' worth of the nuisance. Therefore, by paying an amount just greater than the losses, the confectioner can compensate the doctor for putting up with four hours of noise per day. Both parties are then better off than if there were no noise (or compared with any other period of noise). Bargaining, to 'condemn the injunction', automatically leads to the jointly optimal level of four hours' noise.

Now suppose that no injunction is granted. Bridgman would initially create eight hours' noise, which is where marginal profits fall to zero. However, the losses to Sturges exceed the gains to Bridgman over four to eight hours of the nuisance ($MEC > MNB$), which means that Sturges would find it advantageous to bribe the confectioner to reduce the level to four hours per day. Sturges would offer just more than Bridgman's lost profit on each unit of noise (MNB). Both parties would be better off by agreeing to the reduction.

Notice that if it is cheapest to insulate rather than bear the noise or bribe the confectioner to stop, the doctor will do this if he does not have the injunction. Similarly, if the doctor has the entitlement and it is cheaper to insulate than induce him to condemn the injunction, the confectioner will insulate. The example shows that the level of noise is the same whether the confectioner or the doctor has the entitlement. Our example of the Coase theorem shows that allocative efficiency is not affected by the initial assignment of entitlement, which has only distributional impact. All mutually beneficial trade over an externality is undertaken, the final equilibrium is the same whether the polluter is free to pollute or is enjoined, and value of production is maximized.

3.1.2   Assumptions of the Coase theorem

The detailed assumptions of the Coase theorem have been analyzed by several writers. Some of the discussion has resulted in several criticisms of the Coase theorem. These are, in fact, misplaced criticisms as Coase did not intend the case of zero bargaining costs to be a guide to public policy, as we shall see. The following is a list of significant assumptions, adapted from Veljanovski (1982), which are necessary for the Coase theorem to hold:

1. there is perfect knowledge
2. strategic behaviour is absent
3. the courts operate costlessly
4. there are no wealth effects
5. there are no endowment effects
6. the externality does not affect marginal land.

Assumption 3 is a proper statement of the requirement for costless bargaining in the context of a court system and warrants little discussion. Requirements 1 and 2 ensure in a more general way that bargaining costs are zero. It is often alleged that the remaining assumptions are necessary to ensure that assigning entitlement cannot affect the allocation of resources even if bargaining costs are zero.

(a)   Imperfect information and strategic behaviour

Imperfect information, which usually implies information asymmetry, leads to great difficulties in bargaining even when parties are not attempting to mislead each other. Farrell (1987) shows that if some individuals have information when others do not, mutually beneficial trades will not occur. As a simple example, if a seller values a house less than the would-be buyer but erroneously believes there are higher-valuing potential buyers, the house will not be sold and gains from trade are not realized. Similarly, if the victim of a nuisance is unsure of the cost of its impact, it may be hard to reach agreement. Roth and Murnighan (1982) report the results of experiments showing that when people do not know one another's tastes or opportunities, negotiations can be protracted and unsuccessful.

Strictly speaking, information asymmetry cannot affect the Coase theorem because it could not arise in a world of zero transaction costs. The cost of gathering information about a proposed trade is a part of the costs of transacting. Information asymmetry suggests there is information a trader would like to have but which is too costly to gather.

Strategic behaviour would also cause problems. To illustrate these, we continue to assume the mechanics of bargaining to be costless. There is a huge range within which bargaining can take place. For example, assuming Sturges has the injunction and again referring to Figure 3.1, the confectioner would pay up to an amount equal to area $0acd$ (the profit) and the doctor would require at least area $0cd$ (the cost to him) to move to four hours' noise. Even with perfect information so that the confectioner knows the scale of external costs, by holding out, the doctor can increase his share of the surplus from reaching agreement. He has to convince the confectioner of his stubbornness to extract as much as possible. As Mumey (1971) points out, this implies parties would devote resources to developing threat strategies – a form of rent seeking with associated waste of resources.

Expenditures on rent seeking disturb the results of the Coase theorem. With zero transaction costs, making threats would be costless but so would a counter strategy and a process of threat followed by counter threat could go on for ever. Farrell (1987) argues that information asymmetries give an incentive for the devotion of resources to influencing the beliefs of the other party, although this point moves us away from a world of zero transaction costs.

A further type of strategic problem has been described by Regan (1972) drawing on a game-theoretic argument of Schelling (1960). A party may use the threat of irrationally moving to a position that is suboptimal for both parties in order to extract most of the gains from bargaining. If the opponent does not give in, the individual may be forced to carry out the threat if at all interested in preserving a reputation as a tough bargainer for subsequent games. This implies that mutually beneficial trade over an externality may not always occur even when promises are enforceable. However, Regan's claim is vulnerable to a modern game-theoretic argument (Selten, 1978). If the number of repetitions of the game is known with certainty, there exists an end game in which the threat is not credible. Therefore, the threat is not credible in the immediately preceding game or the one before that and so on to affect all bargaining games in which the threatener might be involved. Also, if each party is unsure whether the other might irrationally adopt something like a 'tit-for-tat' strategy (Axelrod, 1984), threats may be deterred.

The problems of strategic interaction would be a powerful criticism of Coase's analysis if the argument really were that costless bargaining can be relied upon to internalize externalities. However, as we shall see below, this is not the interpretation to be put on 'The Problem of Social Cost' – as that would be to take an expository device far too literally. Both Farrell (1987) and Mumey (1971) really only criticize a theoretical simplification. More recent work outside of the case of costless bargaining suggests that legal rules should aim to minimize bargaining costs including those connected with strategic interaction (Epstein, 1993).

The Pigouvian (Pigou, 1938) solution of taxing the externality leads to suboptimally low pollution levels when bargaining is possible. The Pigouvian tax ignores the strategic ramifications of changing a party's costs. In Figure 3.1, if a tax equal to MEC really shifts MNB to $MNSB$ as far as the confectioner is concerned and bargaining is possible, the parties will move to point b (approximately 2.6 hours) rather than to point c. This result is demonstrated by Turvey (1963) and by Buchanan and Stubblebine (1962). The moral here is that it could be reasonable to use a tax when bargaining cannot arise but it is dangerous to do so when bargaining is possible.

(b) Wealth effects

The assumption that there are no wealth effects has a simplifying effect for Coase's analysis. Beneficiaries of changes in entitlements will feel better off after the change, which has much the same impact as an increase in income or wealth for them and may change the marginal value they place on particular items. If this happens, the award of an entitlement by the court is unlikely to be neutral with respect to allocation. For example, giving the entitlement to the victim of a noise nuisance might make him feel better off and increase his demand for noise reduction.

In Figure 3.2, the noise problem characterizing *Sturges* v. *Bridgman* is shown somewhat differently. On the horizontal axis, we measure noise reduction as decibel loss. For simplicity, we assume that it is always cheaper for the confectioner to pay for the doctor's cost of insulation than to cut back the noisy activity. It is also necessary to

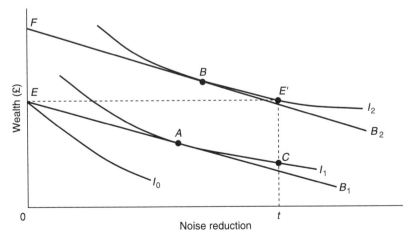

Figure 3.2 Wealth effects from an injunction. I_0, I_1 and I_2 = indifference curves for the doctor; B_1 and B_2 = budget lines for the doctor.

assume that there is some range of noise reduction, falling short of total silence, for which the benefits to the doctor outweigh the cost of insulating. The relevant comparison is then between the benefits to the doctor and the costs of insulation.

The curves labelled I_0, I_1 and I_2 are examples of indifference curves for the doctor. Indifference curves allow us to study changes in the doctor's level of welfare without making an assumption that we can measure utility directly, which is not acceptable. For example, curve I_0 shows combinations of levels of noise reduction and wealth measured in money) that the doctor regards as equivalent and I_1 shows combinations giving a higher level of utility.[4] The convex shape of the curves (they bend towards the origin) indicates a diminishing marginal rate of substitution between wealth and noise reduction: the quieter it gets, the less money the doctor will give up for further unit reductions in the noise level. A line is drawn vertically from point t, reflecting total silence. Similarly, the origin shows the maximum amount of noise.

The line from point E on the vertical axis to B_1, in Figure 3.2, is the doctor's budget line. Point E shows his situation when he has no injunction so that the confectioner is entitled to make the noise. By moving south-east along budget line B_1, the doctor could buy insulation, with the slope of the line reflecting the assumed constant unit cost of noise reduction. The budget line is therefore also an implied price line. Remember, it is always cheaper to buy insulation than to bribe the confectioner to reduce the noise. Point E is on the lowest indifference curve shown, I_0, but by moving along the budget line B_1 the doctor can just reach the higher curve I_1 at the point of tangency, A.

Now suppose that the entitlement changes and the doctor obtains his injunction. Point E moves to E' directly above t, as the doctor can now insist on total quiet. However, we know from our earlier analysis of *Sturges* v. *Bridgman* that the confectioner will want to induce the doctor to tolerate some noise. As a simple (but not unique) solution to the bargaining problem between them, assume that the confectioner agrees to pay the doctor a sum of money sufficient to maintain the doctor's welfare at I_2 after the noisy activity is resumed. The doctor's budget line therefore moves to position B_2 showing the compensation payment as distance EF. The doctor moves from point F to a new optimum at B by purchasing insulation.

Because the indifference curves in Figure 3.2 are not homothetic (vertically parallel) their slopes differ at points drawn vertically above one another, reflecting the doctor's changing marginal valuation of noise reduction as his entitlement (wealth) increases. This means that point B is to the north-east of point A in Figure 3.2: there is a wealth effect, which implies that the court's assignment of entitlement does affect the level of noise reduction even with zero bargaining costs. This result contrasts with the one in Figure 3.1, where the assignment of rights has a neutral effect on allocation.

However, the non-neutrality result in Figure 3.2 emerges precisely because we allow the doctor's taste for noise reduction to change as he becomes richer. In fact, we treat noise reduction as a normal good for which the demand increases as income or wealth increases. This need not be the case if the doctor's demand for noise reduction were determined entirely by the financial impact that noise had upon his practice. He would then buy the same amount of noise reduction whatever the level of wealth. In that case, the indifference curves would be homothetic, B would be vertically above A and the assignment of rights would have a neutral effect upon allocation. As Baker (1975) argues, wealth effects are relevant only where consumer behaviour is involved.

Finally in this section, it is not likely that wealth effects are significant for relatively small changes in entitlements (Hicks, 1943). Coase's (1988, p.174) own comment is of some interest. He argues that although there could be wealth effects from changing the legal entitlement, it is 'inconceivable . . . that this could have any noticeable effect'.

(c) The ask-offer problem and endowment effects

Sometimes the analysis of the impact of changing entitlements in the presence of wealth effects is developed in terms of the 'ask-offer problem' (Kennedy, 1981; Veljanovski, 1982; Fischel, 1995b). The problem arises if an individual is willing to pay a different amount to be free of an externality compared with the compensation required to bear it.

The ask-offer problem can also be illustrated with Figure 3.2. As the injunction is granted, the doctor moves from point A to E'. The confectioner then offers compensation of EF which is enough to buy the insulation required to keep the doctor on indifference curve I_2. The amount (EF) the confectioner must pay before the doctor will agree to condemn the injunction is known as the 'equivalent variation' for the change in entitlement and is also the doctor's asking price for the injunction.

However, if the doctor faced the prospect of paying money to keep the injunction, he would offer less. Starting at E' and bearing in mind that not condemning the injunction implies that the level of noise reduction is constrained to the maximum level t, the doctor's wealth can be reduced by only $E'C$ before his level of welfare returns to the lower level shown by I_1 (at point C). The amount $E'C$ is one form of the 'compensating variation' for the change in entitlement, and is also the doctor's offer price for the injunction.[5]

In a case like Figure 3.2, where more noise reduction is purchased as wealth increases, the equivalent variation exceeds the compensating variation for the injunction. The implication is that the doctor's asking price will exceed his offer price. However, care must be taken in interpreting this result. The ask-offer problem is not responsible for introducing non-neutrality into a simple Coasian bargaining problem. The existence of a wealth effect is really what changes the equilibrium level of noise reduction depending on whether bargaining begins at E

or at E' in Figure 3.2. If there were no wealth effect, the equivalent and compensating variations would be identical. Any ask-offer difference could be a problem for courts trying to ascertain the value of granting an injunction. A lower offer price may not outweigh the losses faced by the generator of a nuisance whereas the asking price would suggest granting it.

As explained earlier (section 3.1.2(b)) when there is no element of consumption attached to a nuisance, the indifference curves will be homothetic and there could be no ask-offer problem caused by movement between indifference curves. A great many nuisance cases will fit this description: often the nuisance is not something of direct value in itself but simply creates a cost. There is then no reason for an individual sufferer's desired level of the nuisance to vary with changes in wealth. We have already noted that wealth effects, when they exist, may anyway be small in cases of nuisance.

Some empirical work has reported experimental evidence of a significant divergence between asking and offer prices when the implied wealth effect is small. Such divergence is usually called an endowment effect (Thaler, 1980). Knetsch and Sinden (1984) distributed lottery tickets to groups of students and then presented individuals with offers to buy back the tickets or demands for payment to keep them. The average compensation required to give up tickets was four times the average offer price to keep them. These experiments can be criticized for embodying an element of risk by using lottery tickets. The ask-offer difference may have picked up a move from risk aversion, when asked to pay, to risk taking when asked to sell.

Knetsch (1989) conducted riskless experiments using market goods and money that support the existence of an endowment effect. In one experiment, when faced with the opportunity to trade, 95% of subjects initially endowed with a good valued it at $1 or more – whereas only 33% of those endowed with money valued the good as highly. Results like this suggest people are reluctant to part with their initial endowments. Similar results were obtained by Kahneman, Knetsch and Thaler (1990). Tversky and Kahneman (1991) see the endowment effect as a manifestation of loss aversion: the generalization that losses are weighed substantially more heavily in the evaluation of prospects and trades. It appears most likely to arise where items are not easily replaceable. Recent experimental work by Shogren, Shin, Hayes and Kliebenstein (1994) questions the existence of the endowment effect and instead relies on movement between indifference curves to explain ask-offer differences.

The endowment effect can be shown theoretically by pivoting indifference curves as shown in Figure 3.3. Points A and B represent different combinations of money and a good that are ranked equally on indifference curve I_0 by an individual. However, if endowed at point A, the individual moves onto the flatter indifference curve, I_A, showing greater reluctance to part with money if asked to do so than is implied by the initial indifference between A and B. If the individual is at B, the

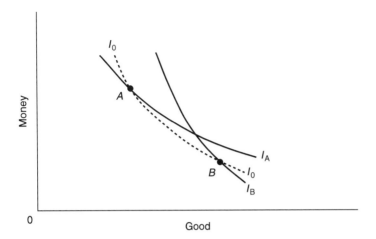

Figure 3.3 The endowment effect. I_0, I_A and I_B = indifference curves for endowment.

move is to the steeper curve, I_B, showing an unexpected reluctance to part with the good if asked to do so. This is a long way from explaining the movement within the indifference map but does describe what may be occurring in experiments.

If endowment effects are of general significance, they would appear to undermine the allocative neutrality of the assignment of entitlement in the simple Coasian bargaining story. It would make a difference to the final level of some nuisance whether the victim or the perpetrator had the entitlement. However, people may not focus well on their preferences when faced with trivial transactions in experimental games carried out in classrooms. The results may not carry over to cases where individuals face large-valued nuisances of great significance to them although wealth effects may then become the problem.

Strictly speaking, the Coase theorem is not undermined by endowment effects since they imply that people have fresh information about their tastes after a change in entitlement has occurred. This in turn implies that perfect information is not costlessly available at the outset which is inconsistent with the Coase theorem. Thus, an endowment effect could not occur under the standard assumptions of the Coase theorem, as it would be completely irrational to have a different *ex ante* valuation of some change when you know (costlessly) how you will feel afterwards.[6]

(d) Economic rent and marginal land

Wellisz (1964), Nutter (1968) and Regan (1972) have asked whether the operation of the Coase theorem depends on levels of economic rent, which refers to the difference between the earnings of a factor of production in its current use and its next best use. In the example used in Figure 3.1 above, e.g., the profit the confectioner earns on every hour up to the eighth hour of noise is economic rent, assuming cost functions embody a normal profit that can be earned elsewhere in the economy (as an opportunity cost). The marginal external cost suffered by the doctor in Figure 3.1 can similarly be seen as a loss of economic rent occasioned by the noise. One way to look at the bargaining result reached in Figure 3.1 is to see it as maximizing the sum of economic rent across the doctor's and confectioner's activities (Coase, 1988, p.165).

To take another of Coase's (1960) examples, imagine a rancher whose cattle damage the crops of a neighbouring farmer. Both the rancher and the farmer earn economic rent in excess of the damage. If the rancher is liable, he pays compensation and continues making the nuisance. If the rancher is not liable, the farmer cannot induce him to stop as we assume the value of the damage is less than ranching rents. Nutter (1968) has interpreted this type of case as one where bargaining makes no impact on the nuisance but just transfers economic rent (from rancher to farmer when the rancher must pay for damage). However, this is not the same thing as the Coase theorem breaking down (Coase, 1988, p.166). The level of the nuisance is unaffected by the assignment of entitlement, as predicted. It is indeed efficient (maximizing joint rents) that ranching should continue. Coase (1988, pp.166–70) considers all the possible permutations of external cost and levels of rents earned on competing activities to show that bargaining with zero transaction costs gives an efficient outcome.

Wellisz (1964) argues that if there is no economic rent on either of the conflicting activities, assignment of the entitlement will have allocative consequences. Suppose that a rancher just covers costs and a farmer would just cover costs if it were not for losses owing to the rancher's damage to crops. If the rancher is not liable, the farmer goes out of business. If the rancher is liable, he goes out of business. Assignment of the entitlement would appear to affect the level of the nuisance. However, this would seem to be something of a special case. Also, efficiency is not affected by the assignment. It is efficient for one of the activities to cease and it does not matter which one. Coase (1988, p.194) accepts the plausibility of Wellisz's argument but believes it to be wrong. The absence of rents suggests that no one would pay for the right to pollute (e.g. if you are driven out of ranching you just costlessly move to another occupation yielding a normal return). Therefore the holder of the entitlement would be prepared to give it up free of charge to the other party. The upshot of this is that each party is equally likely to stay or to leave, which is not affected by the assignment of entitlement.

3.1.3 Experimental tests of the Coase theorem

We have already examined experimental tests of the allocative neutrality of the Coase theorem (section 3.1.2(c)). A number of other experimental workers have directly tested whether bargaining is successful in solving externality problems. The results suggest the Coase theorem is robust in its predictions. Following Regan (1972) the predictions can be summarized as claiming that, in a world of insignificant transaction costs, the parties will agree on a jointly optimal level for some externality and the agreement will be attained by bargaining. Experiments generally use student subjects in an environment created to have very low transaction costs (Roth, 1988; Smith 1989). The subjects may sometimes have private information.

Hoffman and Spitzer (1982) presented people with pay-offs for two or three individuals and allowed one or more to act as 'controller' (analogous to having the entitlement). The pay-offs were chosen so that there were gains from bargaining over an externality. Some experimental conditions were varied to produce repeated games to see if the long-term relationship between players influenced results. In 90% of trials, the gains from bargaining were realized. Deviations from optimality occurred, in some early trials only, when there were three parties and joint controllers and parties knew only their own pay-offs. Hoffman and Spitzer conclude that their results are broadly consistent with Coase's proposition that agents will bargain to reach an optimum under full information and when one party has the entitlement.

Harrison and McKee (1985) report experimental results supporting the view that deviations from Coasian outcomes in Hoffman and Spitzer (1982) were consequences of the relative insignificance of the sums involved. The study by Hoffman and Spitzer (1986) suggests robustness in Coasian results up to groups of 19 individuals. Deviations from optimality turned out to be less likely in both studies if an individual earned property rights in some way, suggesting subjects do not take outcomes seriously if they are obtained by chance in experiment. Harrison and McKee (1985) had the bargainers experience an initial environment in which property rights were not defined. Hoffman and Spitzer (1986) assigned initial rights through a pre-experiment game of tic-tac-toe.

Harrison, Hoffman, Rutström and Spitzer (1987) also found that Coasian solutions to an externality problem were realized, following an initial learning period, in a more complex experimental setting. One aspect of their study was that subjects traded using information that was initially private to them. Nevertheless, Harrison *et al.* (1987) are careful not to overstate the conclusions that can be drawn from their experiments, accepting that they only support the predictions of the Coase theorem in situations characterized by relatively low bargaining costs. They urge the construction of experiments aimed at testing the suitability of bargaining solutions in environments containing significant negotiating costs. A recent study attempting to do this is Shogrun (1993). The work of Roth and Murnighan (1982), which we discussed in section 3.1.2(a), suggests that information asymmetries creat bargaining costs and make it much harder for individuals to negotiate solutions to externality problems.

3.1.4 The significance of transaction costs

'The Problem of Social Cost' is commonly misunderstood. Coase did not argue that costless bargaining would correct all externalities and render government intervention unnecessary. The conclusions of most of his articles are somewhat anti-interventionist but are also firmly grounded in a world of positive transaction costs. As Posner (1993) correctly points out, Coase believes that we live in a world of transaction costs. If this were not so, his work on the nature of the firm (Coase, 1937), in which he regards firms as internalizing some transactions to save costs attached to using markets, would have no subject. The assumption of zero bargaining costs in part of 'The Problem of Social Cost' is purely an expository device and should not be taken too literally. In this sense, the experimental work discussed above (section 3.1.3) misses the point, as do criticisms of the Coase theorem based on analyses of its assumptions. However, the literature on the Coase theorem has developed a life of its own which is why it was necessary to examine it carefully in earlier subsections.

Coase's (1988) later notes on the Coase theorem are of considerable interest:

> The world of zero transaction costs has often been described as a Coasian world. Nothing could be further from the truth. It is the world . . . I was hoping to persuade economists to leave. (1988, p.174).

He is most emphatic that his analysis is grounded in positive transaction costs:

> The same approach which with zero transaction costs, demonstrates that the allocation of resources remains the same whatever the legal position, also shows that, with positive transaction costs, the law plays a crucial role in determining how resources are used. (1988, p.178).

We now examine externality problems in a world characterized by significant transaction costs.

Coase was concerned to show that the interventionist emphasis of much welfare economics was not warranted, not least because it relied too strongly on information that governments are unlikely to have. As discussed above (section 3.1.1) Pigou's (1938) solution for negative externalities was to impose a tax on the creator of the nuisance. Coase pointed out that this was a superficial solution. For example, it might be cheapest for the victim of nuisance to relocate, although a tax-imposing government agency would be most unlikely to realize this. Coase also approved of the fact that the English common-law judges had been examining nuisance cases like *Sturges* v. *Bridgman* in a sensible, comparative-institutionalist manner for years. The courts typically recognize the reciprocal nature of externalities – that the nuisance is in a sense as much caused by the victim being there as by its perpetrator –

and drop questions of causality. They then tend to consider which party should be induced to modify behaviour to solve the problem which does recognize that the impact of the harm is often not reciprocal. In *Sturges* v. *Bridgman*, the doctor had come to the nuisance but this did not stop the court from finding for him, which is correct from an economic point of view as what matters is finding the course of action that maximizes the value of joint production.

In the presence of positive transaction costs, there is no theoretical solution to the problem of externality. It may, for example, still be worthwhile for the affected parties to bargain their way to a solution and it may even remain true that the assignment of rights does not influence the final level of the nuisance. If bargaining is prohibitively costly, the courts may be able to find the solution that would have resulted from bargaining and at a lower cost. In some cases, the court may be able to do nothing more than decide who will benefit the most from the entitlement, knowing that bargaining cannot occur. In still further cases, the optimal solution might well be for government to tax the externality – if it somehow had lower costs than the courts or the affected parties in finding the solution (Coase, 1960). Which is the best approach is a matter of empirical assessment in any particular case. Sometimes it might even be best to do nothing, if all options are very costly relative to the benefits of internalizing the externality, as appears to be the case with the high-seas fisheries discussed in the previous chapter (section 2.3): the grass is not always greener. What is needed is a proper comparison of all feasible alternatives, fully taking into account the cost of each.

Table 3.1 illustrates the solution of one possible problem in a world of significant transaction costs. The table gives details of the case of *Sturges* v. *Bridgman* in the form used in Figure 3.1, where a constant noise level could be varied over the working day. Marginal net benefit again refers to the profits of the confectioner. Social benefit is found by subtracting external cost from profits. We assume that bargaining or operating a Pigouvian tax scheme is prohibitively expensive, as it is for the court to enforce the optimal level of the nuisance. The court is left with the option of assigning the entitlement one way or the other. Its

Table 3.1 The costs and benefits from noise

Noise (hrs)	Marginal net benefit	Marginal external cost	Marginal net social benefit
0	0	0	0
1	14	−2	12
2	12	−4	8
3	10	−6	4
4	8	−8	0
5	6	−10	−4
6	4	−12	−8
7	2	−14	−12
8	0	−16	−16

assignment will have an allocative effect and should be guided by the total net benefit from each possible choice.

In Table 3.1, it is better to assign the entitlement to the victim and award the injunction. The first-best optimum is at four hours' noise, where the marginal net social benefits sum to 24. However, this is unavailable as the court knows it cannot enforce this solution. The second-best solution is to give the injunction and have no noise, which gives a total social net benefit of zero. The alternative of allowing the confectioner to create the eight hours' noise that would maximize his profits gives a negative sum of −16 for the marginal net social benefit column, which is clearly worse. Obviously, different figures could give a different result and there is no general rule. However, the general approach in which discrete comparisons are made between the total net benefits of assigning the entitlement one way or the other is very much the kind of thing a court may do.

3.2 ALTERNATIVE LEGAL RULES AND THE INCENTIVE TO BARGAIN

The choice for courts is not simply between issuing an injunction or refusing it. They may award compensation for damages to victims of nuisance as an alternative to issuing an injunction. Indeed, in more complex formulations they may issue an injunction against future nuisance and order compensation for existing damage or may even require a payment by the victim as part of the settlement. The precise nature of the entitlement that is assigned alters the incentive for bargaining as the following example demonstrates.

Suppose that a ready-mixed concrete plant discharges dust onto a car-sales business, which creates additional costs of £40 000 in preparing vehicles for sale. The concrete plant could fit a filter costing £100 000 or the car business could fit a cover costing £20 000 and either option cures the problem. If the plant fits the filter, the car business makes £60 000 profit. If the concrete business is left free to pollute, it makes £200 000 profit. The optimum is for the concrete plant to be free to pollute and for the car business to fit a cover, as this gives a joint profit of £240 000 (£200 000 to the concrete plant and £40 000 to the car business). The court might grant an injunction to the car business or it might order damages to be paid by the concrete plant.

Assume that transaction costs are sufficiently low to permit bargaining and, for simplicity, let the gains from bargaining be equally divided. Table 3.2 shows the impact of bargaining on the profits of each party

Table 3.2 Pay-offs to bargaining (£000s)

Rule	Initial pay-off	Gain	New pay-off
Compensation	160, 60	20	170, 70
Injunction	100, 60	80	140, 100

under the compensation rule and the award of an injunction. Using the compensation rule but without bargaining, the plant retains £160 000 profit after paying £40 000 damages to maintain the car lot's profits at £60 000. Bargaining enables the parties to move to the optimum and gives a gain of £20 000 (the difference between £40 000 damage and the £20 000 cost of a cover) which is divided equally. Granting an injunction, in the absence of bargaining, causes the concrete business to spend £100 000 on a filter. Bargaining can save £80 000 (the difference between the filter and the cover).

Table 3.2 shows that the assignment of entitlement affects the gains from bargaining. The two rules differ in their distance from the optimum. A corollary of this is that the assignment influences the incentive of each party to bargain. For example, the concrete plant has a much bigger incentive to bargain under the injunction. This suggests that bargaining is more likely to occur when a legal assignment is seriously suboptimal, given modest transaction costs.

3.3 PUBLIC AND PRIVATE BADS AND LEAST-COST AVOIDANCE

Calabresi and Melamed (1972) suggest choosing between remedies for nuisance on the basis of the transaction costs affecting the parties and distinguish two principal routes that courts can take in assigning entitlements. They describe a court that issues an injunction (or declines to do so, favouring the property rights of the injurer) as following a property rule. When it awards compensation for damages, they regard it as adopting a liability rule. Calabresi and Melamed argue that when there are obstacles to bargaining the liability rule should be followed. However, when bargaining can occur it is safe to adhere to a property rule and issue an injunction.

Obstacles to bargaining normally arise when damages are dispersed widely in a population. This case may be referred to as a public bad or public nuisance.[7] With a public bad, it is costly for victims to bargain with the creator of the nuisance (tortfeasor). There is likely to be a free-rider problem, as the individual benefits from negotiation are probably highest if a victim sits back and lets others solve the problem. If all victims feel this way then, analogously to the prisoners' dilemma discussed in Chapter 2 in the case of public goods (section 2.8), the worst outcome occurs as no action is taken. In this case, the cost of keeping the victims' team together would be prohibitively high. Dispersion of damages may also simply make it difficult to gather the necessary information for bargaining. Calabresi and Melamed (1972) argue that in the case of public bads, it is more likely to be worthwhile incurring court costs to assess the level of damages.

Otherwise, obstacles to bargaining are few in disputes involving a small number of people who can easily communicate. This is the case of the private nuisance, or private bad, in Calabresi and Melamed's terms. In fact, *Sturges* v. *Bridgman*, which we discussed in relation to the Coase theorem, is a classic case of private nuisance. There may well just be two people involved, the victim and the generator of the nuisance and we would not expect them to incur high costs in negotiating with each other. Calabresi and Melamed argue that an injunction is the appropriate judicial response to private nuisance, at least on efficiency grounds. By issuing the injunction, the court defines property rights and provides a basis for bargaining to discover the optimal level of the nuisance. This raises questions about the efficiency of the traditional judicial response to nuisance which has been to grant an injunction regardless of the nature of the nuisance.

Calabresi and Melamed's analysis is consistent with an accident-avoidance view of nuisance, which may be illustrated with an example adapted from Stephen (1988, p.70). We examine a public bad. Suppose a power station emits smoke that enters the air-conditioning systems of local factories over some period of time. Each of 200 factories suffers a £1000 loss but can be protected by putting filters on its air intakes at a cost of £500 each factory. The power station makes profits of £300 000 and can stop the damage by changing its fuel source at a cost of £250 000. The relevant options are shown in Table 3.3.

Suppose initially that the court has full knowledge of Table 3.3. With high transaction costs, bargaining cannot occur and option 2. is the most desirable. The court should not issue an injunction – with high costs of bargaining, the power station would change its fuel and there would be a move to 3. rather than 2. Without an injunction, the victims protect themselves by fitting filters and move to 2. – which is the best result. The court is able to use a property rule here because full information is available. The principle for the property rule is: award the entitlement to the highest-cost avoider so that the lowest-cost one does the avoiding.

If the court does not know who is the lowest-cost avoider, there is a problem, e.g. it might not know lines 2. and 3. in Table 3.3. It may know line 1. and might award the entitlement to the power station on the grounds that benefits exceed costs from its operation. This is fine in Table 3.3 as the victims happen to be able to protect at lowest cost. But if the power station had the lowest avoidance costs, this would not do.

Using the liability rule and awarding compensatory damages could work. We could give each of the 200 factories £1000 damages. The power station would still make £100 000 profit and would stay in

Table 3.3 Least-cost avoidance (£000s)

	Power station profits	Factories' lost profits	Net effect
1. Uncontrolled pollution	300	−200	100
2. Fit filters	300	−100	200
3. Fuel change	50	0	50

business. The victims would then protect themselves by fitting filters at a cost of £500 each. There would be a distributional consequence as profits would accrue £100 000 to the power station and £100 000 to the victims of the nuisance (£200 000 compensation minus £100 000 spent on filters).

A variant on the liability rule is to award the entitlement to the injurer but allow victims to buy it out (at a court-determined price so as to reduce transaction costs). Thus, we could allow the factories to buy out the power station's entitlement to pollute if they valued it at more than £300 000. This amounts to 'damages' for the power station. The efficient outcome would then follow: in Table 3.3, the victims would not buy out the power station but would buy filters instead as they are cheaper.

In the case where information is limited, which is likely to be the case for public bads, the liability rule is safer. An approach based on the property rule could work for a public bad as long as the least-cost avoider is known. If the least-cost avoider is not known, but the nuisance is a private one associated with low transaction costs, it is safe to follow a property rule as the parties will bargain their way to an efficient result.

3.4 THE COURTS AND NUISANCE

English courts tend to regard an injunction as an obligatory remedy for nuisance.[8] It is, in fact, a matter of discretion as damages may be awarded (Tromans, 1982). The situation has been under some pressure for change in recent years but it remains broadly true that English judges favour a property rule.

The standard basic case is *Sturges* v. *Bridgman* (1879) which we have already discussed. Two points about the case are worth further comment. First, the court granted an injunction to the doctor to stop the confectioner using the noisy equipment: there was no attempt on the part of the court at carrying out a judicial cost-benefit analysis to decide the optimal level of the nuisance. Secondly, the court did not consider it relevant that the doctor had come to the nuisance; it is a principle of English law that 'coming to the nuisance' is not a defence. Both of these steps were broadly correct from an economic point of view. The injunction could lead to an optimum as only two parties were involved and bargaining costs were probably low (if they wished to bargain). Also, causality is not of economic significance in nuisance. What matters is that the entitlement be owned by the party placing the highest value on it which will happen through bargaining in the case of a private bad, without the court needing to issue detailed instructions. However, it is possible that ignoring 'coming to the nuisance' might encourage strategic behaviour which we consider below in relation to American cases.

The general use of an injunction is supported by many cases. For example, *Pride of Derby* v. *British Celanese* (1953) shows that if the plaintiff proves that the defendant has interfered with private property rights then the court should give injunctive relief except in special circumstances. Those circumstances are clarified in *Shelfer* v. *City of London Electric Lighting Co.* (1895). Damages can be used if the injury is small and can be measured in terms of money if monetary compensation is in every way adequate and if it would be oppressive to the defendant to enjoin. The list implies giving an injunction when the defendant is the lowest-cost abater or best briber (Ogus and Richardson, 1977).

The courts have held rigorously to this principle. In *Pennington* v. *Brinsop Hall Coal Co.* (1877), the plaintiff complained that a mine's pollution of a brook increased costs at his cotton mill. Closing the mine implied a loss of £190 000 but costs at the mill were increased by only £100. An injunction was granted all the same. Similarly in *Attorney General* v. *City of Birmingham Corporation* (1858) riparian owners by the River Tame obtained an injunction to stop the discharge of sewage. The court refused to balance the large cost to the city of Birmingham for stopping the pollution against the small losses to the riparian owners. Providing the Corporation did not incur significant costs in negotiating with the riparian owners, the court's decision in *Attorney General* v. *City of Birmingham* was consistent with efficiency regardless of who was the least-cost avoider of the nuisance. The alternative property rule, of denying an injunction could also work for a private bad as it would also define the rights and give a basis for negotiation. The courts need to have a uniform approach, however, and have settled on granting the injunction as a remedy for nuisance.

Some change may have occurred in *Miller* v. *Jackson* (1977). The plaintiffs sought an injunction against a cricket ground as balls kept damaging their property. Lord Denning argued that in the days of *Sturges* v. *Bridgman* the rights of property owners were more important. But he thought that in modern times there should be an attempt to balance the conflicting interests in a nuisance case. Lord Denning was inclined to refuse both an injunction and payment for damages but as the club did not oppose paying for damages he awarded £400. Subsequent cases, such as *Kennaway* v. *Thompson* (1981), where the plaintiff built a house near a lake used for motorboat racing, have questioned Lord Denning's approach in *Miller* v. *Jackson* and have reverted to an injunction remedy.

In *Miller* v. *Jackson* Lord Denning was possibly trying to assess what makes a nuisance in the context of the social acceptability of certain practices. Courts look at nuisance in terms of what is unreasonable behaviour and are guided in their judgement by such things as the location of the activity (Coase, 1960). As Thesinger LJ[9] commented in *Sturges* v. *Bridgman*, 'what would be a nuisance in Belgrave Square would not necessarily be so in Bermondsey'. This distinction implies that something is a nuisance if a 'reasonable' person would not expect to find it in a particular situation. If Lord Denning had really been inclined towards cost-benefit analysis in *Miller* v. *Jackson* he should have been more receptive to the idea of awarding damages. He was not, which suggests he was arguing that there was no nuisance in a modern context where the value to village life of a game of cricket would be highly ranked by most people and an occasional stray ball would be expected.

An Australian case shows that the legal definition of nuisance, in terms of interference with the reasonable enjoyment of land, tends to be narrower than the economist's idea of an externality which refers to any unpriced spillover. In *Victoria Park Racing Ground Co. Ltd* v. *Taylor* (1937) the defendant erected a viewing tower on his property and overlooking the racetrack, from which he relayed a racing commentary service for wireless broadcasting. The race ground was refused an injunction on the basis that, as Dixon J put it, 'English law is, rightly or wrongly, clear that the natural rights of an occupier do not include freedom from the view of neighbouring occupiers'. Note that Victoria Park was free to bribe Taylor to stop his activity, so the judgement had a distributional rather than efficiency impact. The freedom to view enjoyed by one's neighbours is an example of the law defining 'reasonable enjoyment' of land. A court's focus on 'reasonable enjoyment' allows it to follow simple rules that avoid incurring very high costs in reaching decisions.

The tendency of English courts to issue injunctions against nuisance can be regarded as conflicting with the economic analysis of law. The practice does not recognize the distinction between a private and a public bad. Ideally, we would want the courts to become involved in judicial cost-benefit analysis and award compensation for damages in the case of a public bad, where bargaining could be problematic and reserve the injunction for cases of private nuisance where bargaining should be much easier. However, remember that there are exceptions to the rule on injunctions, such as in cases where it would be oppressive to enjoin, which appear to give scope for judicial cost-benefit analysis where this would be beneficial (Ogus and Richardson, 1977).

The reluctance of English courts to deny an injunction, when there is a balance of benefits over costs from the nuisance, is founded on a belief that to do so would grant licence on payment of damages without statutory authority (*Shelfer* v. *City of London Electric*). This belief overlooks the fact that the injunction gives a basis for bargaining that may lead to its condemnation, in which case the authority of the court also gives a foundation for licensing the nuisance. It may be that public bads, associated with dispersed damages, are an increasing feature of modern life with which the law has yet to catch up. However, the law seems sufficiently up to date in dealing with modern nuisances such as harassment by telephone, as in *Khorasandjian* v. *Bush* (1993), where judgement was influenced by a similar Canadian case, *Motherwell* v. *Motherwell* (1976).

The case law in the USA is broadly similar to England. However, there are two important cases showing that US law has moved away from a property rule and towards the use of compensatory damages.

In *Boomer* v. *Atlantic Cement Co.* (1970), adjacent landowners brought an action against a large cement plant asking for an injunction and damages. They complained of smoke, dust and noise. The court weighed the loss of the plaintiffs against the cost of removing the nuisance. It was not feasible to move the existing plant so the cost to the defendant of moving was the loss of the $45 million investment. The plant employed 300 people. The damage to landowners was small in comparison. The court awarded permanent damages to compensate fully the neighbouring landowners for tolerating the nuisance. One judge (the case was an appeal) dissented, pointing out that paying permanent damages removed all incentive to reduce the harm but the court thought there was no prospect of alleviation anyway. In fact, a long-run incentive did remain: for the adjacent landowners to take steps such as installing double glazing to minimize the nuisance.

The court recognized it was setting precedent as the rule in New York State had been to enjoin nuisance, as in England, notwithstanding any marked disparity in the economic consequences of the injunction and the nuisance. The change was broadly consistent with the literature on the economics of law, as bargaining costs in *Boomer* probably were high given the dispersed nature of the damage. But it is a little odd that the court did not award temporary damages, which would have encouraged Boomer to adopt a cleaner technology to avoid future damage assessments. The court may have wished to avoid the cost of repetitive court action. Also, *Boomer* does set a precedent that encourages other cement companies to avoid pollution, knowing they will be liable for permanent damages. However, the US approach is not consistent with the literature on the economics of law if the courts carry the liability approach over to cases where bargaining around an injunction would not be prohibitively costly.

The second distinguishing case, *Spur Industries* v. *Del E. Webb* (1972), shows that American courts have been prepared to take the reciprocal nature of externality very seriously indeed. Spur ran a cattle feeding operation in Maricopa County, west of Phoenix Arizona, dating back to 1956. By 1967 Spur had grown to the extent that they were feeding 25 000 cattle, which were producing approximately 1 000 000 pounds wet weight of manure daily. Del Webb was a real-estate business that built Sun City, a residential development, in 1960 several miles north of Spur. By 1967, Sun City had expanded to within 500 yards of Spur. Del Webb complained that 1300 plots were unsaleable because of the cattle operation and obtained an injunction at a lower court.

The higher court concluded that Spur created a nuisance but that it was clear that Del Webb had come to it. Some American courts have recognized the defence of 'coming to the nuisance'. However, the court gave Del Webb an injunction on the grounds that many people had been encouraged to purchase houses in Sun City – which implied a high level of damage – but ingeniously made it conditional on Del Webb paying Spur the 'reasonable' costs of shutting down or moving.

From an economic point of view and concentrating on the value of the location in different uses, the defence that Del Webb came to the nuisance does not make sense. If Del Webb valued the local amenity level more highly than Spur, then – without an injunction – it would compensate Spur to move. With an injunction, Spur would fail to compensate Del Webb to tolerate the nuisance. The allocative outcome is the same although the distributional consequences are different. However, Del Webb would be better off by coming to the nuisance and then obtaining an injunction which implies there is a possible problem with ignoring the defence of coming to the nuisance: the court risked being an agent of Del Webb's rent-seeking strategy, incurring court costs when otherwise there would be low-cost bargaining. In the long run, following the rule in *Spur Industries* v. *Del E. Webb*, which was to impose the tortfeasor's removal costs on the victim, removes the incentive for rent seeking through the courts.

3.5   MINOR ESTATES IN LAND

Owners of land can take steps to minimize potential conflicts. They may use easements and covenants to define property rights in a way that anticipates and attempts to control possible external effects. Easements and covenants create minor estates in land: turning a possible spillover into a property right for an external party.

Easements confer the positive right for one landowner to make some use of another's property. Typically, an easement gives a right of access, e.g. a property owner may need to drive vehicles over a neighbour's land to enter his own. In English law, an easement has to satisfy a number of tests before a court would recognize it. Principal among these is that it must 'touch and concern the land', which means it must be a reasonable requirement of someone owning the land. It 'runs with the land', being capable of transfer like any other property right when the land is sold without having to be specifically created each time. Easements can be created over neighbouring land at the time both parcels of land are initially separated for sale. They are not obtained free of charge: the owner of the 'dominant' property buys the easement along with the rest of a property and the 'servient' property is cheaper than it otherwise would be.

In principle, a landowner likely to create an externality could buy an easement. For example, one could be created allowing the emission of smoke over a neighbour's property. This could be bought back if the value of the servient landowner's use of the affected land increased at a later date. An easement defines a property right and internalizes an externality but it requires foresight at some point early on and may be most relevant when a parcel of land belonging entirely to one owner is transferred as when residential developments are built. Easements could cause rigidities if the original relative values of different uses change and there are high bargaining costs. To ease the problem of rigidities, the courts may be asked to strike out obsolete easements. Part of the definition of an obsolete easement is lack of use by the dominant property.

Covenants are restrictions on what owners may do with their land or requirements placed on them to take some kind of positive action. For example, a restrictive covenant may stop a householder from keeping pigs or erecting fences, which gives a number of neighbours freedom from a possible externality. A simple covenant may impose a duty like contributing to the maintenance of common areas in a residential development, which may help to overcome a free-rider problem that would otherwise emerge: at least the other residents have a basis for threatening legal action. Restrictive covenants must meet much the same tests as easements and can run with the land. The difference is that they restrict otherwise legal behaviour. Indeed, the same ends can be achieved by easements and restrictive covenants, e.g. an easement can give an access right whereas a restrictive covenant can require that access is not blocked. Much the same commentary applies for covenants as applies for easements: they may be a low-cost way of avoiding conflict but they require much foresight.

The problem of becoming locked into irrelevant easements and covenants is probably not too severe. If the courts were to award damages for breach of a covenant or easement, breach would occur only when its value to the breacher exceeds the value of the damage. If an injunction is issued against a breach of a covenant or easement, the party that wishes to avoid the requirements can still negotiate with the other affected parties. Both liability and property approaches stop people from simply ignoring easements and covenants when their valuation of the change would not exceed the damage caused.

3.6 STATUTORY CONTROL OF CONFLICTS OF USE

So far we have concentrated on the economics of the private law on conflicting use. We now consider a number of statutory approaches.

3.6.1 Development control

Most countries impose statutory controls on the development of land that can be interpreted as an attempt to control conflicting use. Some of the nuisances that are controlled through systems of planning consent and building regulation may have serious safety implications. The usual pattern is for local authorities to be given powers to specify the type of activities permitted in different areas and to control the technical details of any particular development. In the UK, development control is carried out by local authorities under the Town and Country Planning Acts.[10] Anybody wishing to develop land must obtain planning permission from the local authority which may approve the plans, refuse permission or impose conditions on the developer. There is a system of appeal against decisions. In the USA, the Standard State Zoning Act 1926 accomplishes the same purpose through zoning controls. Similar systems operate in Canada, Australia and New Zealand.

Is development control necessary? There are examples where it is not used, like Houston in Texas which for many years existed without a system of zoning – relying instead on developers' covenants to control conflicting use (Fischel, 1985). Following Calabresi and Melamed's (1972) analysis, we might argue that compensation for damages would control conflicting use when the victims of a nuisance were dispersed and that bargaining would control conflict when there were few affected individuals. There are two possible efficiency reasons why local authorities become involved in development control. First, traditional remedies for nuisance are available to those with neighbouring land interests but would not be available to the wider population of a locality. However, the wider population might well suffer a negative externality if, a development were out of keeping with the rest of a town. Secondly, immediate neighbours may not have much incentive to pursue a nuisance that has a wider impact – perhaps being insensitive to the particular problem. This account of the need for development control follows Shavell's (1993) analysis of the optimal structure of law enforcement.

Development control consists of technical standards and the particular requirements demanded by local authorities. It is enforced by the local authorities' inspectorates. Failure to comply with regulations or development requirements may be penalized by a requirement that an offending development be removed: a costly penalty of 'specific performance'. As Shavell (1993) argues in the context of safety regulation, an inspection-based system is justified when it would be difficult for ordinary citizens to detect problems that could turn into serious nuisances. If detection were easy and temporary nuisance not too severe, it would be easier to rely on a system of fines imposed after nuisances were created as a means of deterrence.

It does not follow that local authorities intervene purely from a wish to maximize the total value of land use. Controls also enable the local authority to extract some of the benefits of any development (Stephen, 1987). This is known as planning gain. A new supermarket may be permitted, e.g. if the builder agrees to put in new access roads that are of wider benefit in the area. Figure 3.4 illustrates a simplified version of Stephen's (1987) analysis of rent extraction by the local authority. The horizontal axis measures increases in the specification of a development which, in this example, is taken to be the amount of road building by the developer. The vertical axis measures the marginal (external)

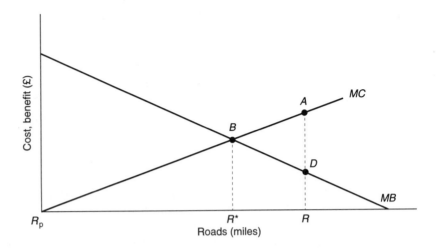

Figure 3.4 Planning gain. MC = marginal cost of compliance; MB = marginal benefit of compliance.

benefit to the local authority and the marginal cost to the developer of the roads.

In Figure 3.4, the origin is labelled R_p, as this is the profit-maximizing amount of road building that would be undertaken by the developer in the absence of controls. The maximum amount that the developer could build before going bankrupt is assumed to be R. Costless bargaining between the authority and the developer would give a jointly optimal amount R^*.

The local authority might insist on a specification level providing R miles of new roads which is the maximum it can obtain without pushing the developer into bankruptcy. The developer would then find it worthwhile to bribe the local authority to move back towards the optimum R^*. The developer will have to pay the local authority at least its forgone total benefits, measured by the area R^*BDR, for the move. If the local authority is a particularly good bargainer, it might extract a higher amount, worth up to area R^*BAR, representing the gain in profit to the developer from the move. For the most part, we would not expect local authorities to accept cash bribes. However, the developer can pay in kind – perhaps offering to undertake particularly attractive landscaping in exchange for a relaxation of the road building requirement.

An alternative strategy for the developer is to appeal against the local authority's specification of R miles of road. In the case of the UK, such appeals are made ultimately to the Secretary of State for the Environment. If the developer were lucky enough on appeal to be permitted to construct only R_p miles of road, the local authority would be faced with inducing him to move to R^*. If the appeal places the specification anywhere to the right of R^*, the local authority can extract planning gain along the lines already described. The attractiveness of an appeal strategy relative to negotiating with the local authority will depend upon its cost.

3.6.2 Compulsory purchase/eminent domain

Most countries have statutes allowing the compulsory purchase of private property, principally land and buildings, by the government (Ogus, 1990; Fischel, 1995a). Compulsory purchase is also referred to as 'eminent domain'. Posner (1992) argues that compulsory purchase is needed because land in a particular position is obviously unique and the owner of the last vital piece of land, e.g. for some public road, could practise hold-up. In particular, the owner could demand at least the entire projected net benefit from the scheme as a selling price and might extract more if there were disruption costs from not going ahead. The price of land would be raised artificially and this would encourage the inefficient substitution of other factors of production. For example, double-decker roads might be built in locations where they would not otherwise be cost-effective.

This argument does not lead to the conclusion that public authorities should be permitted to take land without paying compensation. Apart from the distributional consequences, governments would be encouraged to take land when it was of little public value compared with its value to its private owner (rather as is the case for people's time in a military draft). However, it is also true that a rule of full compensation fails to encourage a private owner to recognize that some private uses may conflict with public developments, e.g. the owner may have no incentive to locate a structure away from a road likely to need widening. No zero-sum compensation rule can give all parties incentives to take care. Existing compensation schemes fall short of full compensation for owners and impose process costs on local authorities which implies that incentives for care will exist.

In the USA, the Constitution limits 'takings' to those of legitimate public use subject to the payment of 'just compensation' where legitimacy and the amount of payment can be defined in the courts. In the UK, similar protection is given by the Land Clauses Consolidation Act 1845 and the Acquisition of Land (Assessment of Compensation) Act 1919. Commonwealth countries like Australia, Canada and New Zealand are in a similar position, e.g. section 51 of the Australian Constitution requires the federal government to pay compensation on 'just terms' for land subjected to compulsory purchase. Compensation is normally for the market value of the property and not for any special valuation placed on it by the owner. This is the current position in the UK and in the USA and corresponds to taking a liability approach over the damage to the owner. Using market value simplifies the calculation of damages.

Knetsch (1983) argues that the market-price approach ignores consumer surplus which is the difference between an individual's private valuation of a thing and the market price for it.[11] The fact that someone has not sold a property suggests he values it more highly than at the market price. Knetsch is correct in arguing that this is something of a problem. If we wish to be sure that the public taking is for a purpose that is more highly valued than that of the owner, we should require the authority to buy at the owner's valuation. More recent analysis has emphasized the ask-offer problem (section 3.1.2(c) above) in arguing for compensation at above market value (Marshall, Knetsch and Sinden, 1986).

Fischel (1995b) concludes that compensation at market value balances the future benefits from eminent domain against the extra taxes that would be necessary if compensation were enhanced beyond market values. Fischel's is a constitutional view but it is anyway difficult to see how to get beyond some rule of thumb to help compensate at above the market price. Attempts to calculate accurate measures of ask-offer discrepancies would increase the transaction costs of public development schemes. The pre-1919 valuation rules in the UK added 10% to market value to compensate for the fact that compulsory purchase did not reflect a voluntary sale. This contributed something to consumer surplus without creating great problems of valuation. Such a rule of thumb is still used in some Commonwealth countries.

Nonetheless, it is puzzling from an economic point of view why compulsory purchase is necessary away from situations where hold-up is likely to be a problem. For example, it could be a reserve power available when almost all land owners affected by some public development have sold out and a small proportion of them choose to hold out for prices way above the market rate. The more general use of compulsory purchase suggests it is more a way of getting land cheaply.

It is important to recognize that public authorities do sometimes use their powers in a manner that has some of the implications of taking land for private purposes. For example, the compulsory purchase of land for the development of a shopping centre or industrial estate may create major benefits for private enterprise partly at the expense of the original owners. This type of thing can be successfully defended by the local authority, if there is a planning appeal, on the basis that the creation of employment opportunities confers a public benefit. Again, the question may be asked why – if the benefits are so great – do we need to use compulsory purchase: why cannot the original owners be induced to sell voluntarily by a combination of the local beneficiaries? Again, the suspicion must be that the local authority wants benefits to come as cheaply as possible.

Finally, in this section, we should also note the existence of planning or regulatory blight (also known as 'inverse condemnation'). The passage of a government regulation, or local-authority approved plan, may blight a property and depress its value. Once any appeal procedures are exhausted by the victims there is little they can do to protect the value of their property. With planning procedures, this would not be worrying if the local authority were obliged to compensate at the victim's property valuation. In cases where regulations change, there may be no obligation to compensate at all, e.g. increases in permitted vehicle tonnages in the UK – announced in 1994 – will impose damage on some residential property but this will not be compensated. Failure to grant planning consent is less of a worry: the 'victim' was simply unable to present a package that would have 'bribed' the local authority into granting consent.

3.6.3 Environmental protection

Most countries have some statutory control of general environmental nuisance and do not rely solely on the private law to regulate conflict over property rights. In the UK, the Environmental Protection Act 1990 lays down fines that may be imposed for creating a nuisance. The Act is particularly noted for controlling noise nuisance in a general way in the UK and we concentrate on this in this section.

A similar justification may be given for environmental-protection legislation as was given for the existence of development laws. The effect of a nuisance may range more widely than just over neighbouring properties and immediate neighbours may have too little incentive to take action. However, note that the Act does not create an inspectorate in contrast to the system of development control outlined above. According to Shavell (1993), this suggests that a nuisance like noise is easy to detect early on and its temporary existence would not be too harmful. The possibility of a fine can then usually be relied upon to deter the nuisance. Ideally, the expected value of the fine should be set to just exceed the value of the nuisance to its creator.

The Act appears to have been a response to changing technology that has made the imposition of a noise nuisance on a neighbourhood an easy matter. In 1993, a fan of the pop singer Whitney Houston was jailed for seven days for playing her hit single 'I Will Always Love You' almost non-stop for six weeks. In 1994, a would-be disc jockey was jailed for three months after playing pop hits and his own commentary at full volume from his bedroom over a powerful sound system for up to 14 hours a day: earlier fines and even the seizure of the equipment failed to end this bizarre behaviour. Again in 1994, according to figures issued by the Institute of Environmental Health Officers, complaints in England and Wales about noisy neighbours were rising at a rate of 20% a year.[12]

Environmental legislation operates in the USA and may be justified in similar terms: some damage is so diffused that a public prosecutor represents an economical way to control pollution. However, a worrying trend in the USA is for statute to undermine possible common-law solutions to cases of nuisance. Meiners and Yandle (1993) have examined the growing dominance of regulators over the common law. One example of this dominance is the Clean Water Act 1972 which forbids interstate lawsuits in matters of water pollution. Federal courts in the USA have repeatedly ruled that interstate suits are superseded by federal regulation of pollution. Although it is possible to justify statutory control of nuisance in terms of cost savings when damages are diffuse, there can be no support for the suppression of common-law solutions when these are possible.

SUMMARY AND CONCLUSIONS

In this chapter, we have looked at the principal methods by which conflicts over property rights are resolved. The economic analysis we have used takes the Coase theorem as its departure point. We have been careful to show that the comparative-institutions analysis of problems characterized by positive transaction costs is the important part of Coase's work. Therefore, criticisms of the assumptions of the Coase theorem are largely besides the point. The work of Calabresi and Melamed (1972) is particularly relevant in stressing the importance of encouraging the least-cost avoider of a nuisance to take evasive steps in the context of particular legal rules. In this respect it is important to distinguish whether nuisances have the characteristics of private or public bads.

There is a considerable range to the law on nuisance. In England, the common law favours a property rule based on awarding injunctions. A liability approach based on paying damages, which is used in the USA, may in fact be safer if damage is likely to be dispersed and the court does not know who is the least-cost avoider although it can lead to unnecessary court costs outside of those circumstances. Statutory efforts to control externalities with a wide impact can be understood partly as unwillingness to rely on immediate neighbours to prosecute nuisance and, in the case of development control, partly as rent seeking by local authorities.

ENDNOTES

1. This is a legal definition of private nuisance. Public nuisance typically arises where a statutory remedy has been attached, as when someone causes an obstruction on the highway. There are also rare instances of prosecution for the common-law offence of creating a public nuisance: see 'Hepatitis Doctor Jailed for "Terrible" Deception', *The Times*, Friday September 30, 1994. We are concerned with private nuisance in this chapter unless otherwise specified.
2. The distinction between the court of equity and courts of law was lost many years ago but the terms persist. Originally, actions in equity appealed to principles of fairness rather than established law.
3. The approach to Coase's work taken here is based partly on discussions with him in May 1994. The term 'Coase theorem' was coined by Stigler (1966, p.113).
4. Indifference curves merely rank different levels of utility without assigning cardinal values.

5. Strictly speaking it is the quantity-constrained compensating variation.

6. If the literature on endowment effects just says that people are irrational, we should give up applying economics to consumer choice. The literature does not appear to urge this. For example Thaler (1980) argues that we need a different economic theory of consumer choice from the traditional one of neoclassical economics.

7. Care must be taken to avoid confusion with the specialized legal use of the term public nuisance (see note 1). The specialized legal use is actually consistent with Calabresi and Melamed's analysis since nuisances with highly dispersed damage imply the need for a public body to act as plaintiff or too little action will be taken. Unfortunately, the law's technical definition of a private nuisance includes nuisances with dispersed consequences, i.e. some are public bads. Given the economics focus of this book, we follow Calabresi and Melamed.

8. We are really discussing the legal category of private nuisance here, i.e. where individuals are affected which may reflect public or private bads in the sense of Calabresi and Melamed (1972).

9. LJ is the standard written abbreviation for 'Lord Justice' and signifies a judge of the English Court of Appeal. Similarly, J signifies a High Court judge in England. Comparable abbreviations are used in other jurisdictions, e.g. CJ and J in the USA. Written use of the title 'Lord' commences for a judge upon promotion to the House of Lords upon receipt of a life peerage.

10. For example the Town and Country Planning Act 1990 for England and Wales.

11. Consumer surplus may be measured by the difference between what a person will pay, rather than go without the item and the market price. In the standard introductory analysis of demand consumer surplus is taken to be the area above a price line and below the demand curve. Note that both the equivalent and compensating variations for a price, or similar, change are alternative measures of consumer surplus.

12. The details in this section are taken from 'DJ next door jailed for blasting road all night long', *The Times*, Friday September 9, 1994.

4 | Contract formation and evolution

Economists have traditionally paid a great deal of attention to contracts. All economic analysis is in a sense based on a view of individuals voluntarily pursuing gains from trade through enforceable contracts, as Trebilcock (1993) points out in his assessment of the welfare properties of freedom of contract. Another important strand in the literature (Williamson, 1985) examines long-term contracts that often have self-enforcement characteristics. Over time, the view of contracts found in economic analysis is becoming richer and more detailed.

In this chapter, we apply economic analysis to traditional legal questions concerning contract law. In particular, we ask what makes a contract and what are the economic implications of the more important rules for contract formation? We also consider several aspects of long-term contracts, including contract renegotiation, which have aroused much interest in economics and in law. We move on to examine the economics of breach of contract in the next chapter.

4.1 THE NATURE OF CONTRACTS

Contract law guides the interpretation of contracts and, in particular, tells traders when promises are enforceable and what the consequences are of breaching contracts. This is essential to business and to most forms of planning. In particular, contracts enable people to move resources to the uses in which they are valued most highly. They are the practical means by which people bargain with one another and realize gains from trade. Predictable contract law implies that people can confidently pursue all transactions that yield gains from trade even when performance occurs over time and not just limit themselves to those embodying an instant exchange. Efficient contracts are enforceable agreements that create gains from trade for all parties.

The time dimension of contracts is also important from the point of view of providing insurance. Agreements often contain express terms specifying who is to benefit or lose from increases or decreases in the prices or costs related to the transaction. But even if there are gaps in agreements, when courts are regular about the manner in which they fill these in people can rely on precedent to specify implicitly the insurance aspect of a contract. Gaps might be left if it is too costly to specify what the parties must do in every contingency. This does not mean that they inevitably end up in court, as the contingencies may not materialize, or the judgement may be so predictable that the parties settle out of court.

4.2 FORMATION OF CONTRACTS

To understand the economic implications of contract formation, we must examine legal principles that largely developed in the nineteenth and early twentieth centuries. These principles are embedded in modern case law and have also influenced efforts to codify contract. In the UK, a number of statutes codify aspects of contract with the Sale of Goods Act 1979, the Fair Trading Act 1973 and the Employment Protection (Consolidation) Act 1978 being particularly important examples. In the USA, the Uniform Commercial Code (UCC) 1958, which has been adopted by virtually all states, codifies much contract law under 11 substantive articles. Also in the US case, the American Law Institute (1981) has published the *Restatement (Second) of Contracts* which is a guide to the general principles of contract case law. We are mainly concerned with principles rather than with statutory details and draw most illustrations from case law.

Traditionally, a promise is enforceable and forms a contract if it is given as part of a bargain. This principle excludes gratuitous promises (unless made under seal) such as an individual's promise to donate a new library to Euphoria University in the event of winning the national lottery. In the traditional doctrine, three basic conditions must hold for a bargain to exist: there must be offer, acceptance and consideration. Some economic support can be given for each of these requirements.

4.2.1 Offer and acceptance

The buyer or seller must have clearly offered to buy or sell the good or service. This need not be in the form of a written document, e.g. a buyer at an auction signals an offer by raising a hand. What constitutes an offer depends upon conventional practices in an industry.

Interesting examples of unwritten formal offers arise with transactions in stocks and shares where people routinely offer to buy and sell shares by telephoning their stockbroker. A note is taken of calls and contract notes are issued which would be taken as compelling evidence of an offer if a dispute arose. In *Entores* v. *Miles Far East* (1955), the Court of Appeal ruled that telex and telephone messages were permissible means of communicating offers. An economic interpretation of special trading routines like this can be given. It is important to be able to act quickly on movements in share prices so the system really needs to operate on the principle of 'my word is my bond'. The gains from this to everyone outweigh the possible increase in costs from having a less certified basis for contract.

The requirement for an unambiguous offer is important from an economic perspective. Contracts normally move resources to more highly valued uses. If a clear offer was not made then we cannot be sure that a promise to sell implies that a seller prefers the monetary price to keeping the good or service or that a buyer really prefers to buy rather than keep the money.

There is a mirror-image requirement for unambiguous acceptance of an offer before a contract can be formed. Again, the requirement for acceptance is also interpreted in relation to standard practice in an industry and may differ from case to case.

An interesting example of offer and acceptance arises in the case of the standard terms used by the De Beers cartel that accounts for 80% of sales of uncut diamonds (Bernstein, 1992). De Beers always sells mixed boxes of diamonds which include both better and poorer stones and refusal to accept these would probably cause De Beers not to deal with a buyer again. Clear acceptance of an invitation to purchase from De Beers carries the implication that the buyer will receive mixed stones. These are well-known standard terms and a buyer could not turn round and demand a refund of the purchase price because he did not like the mix received. Standard terms imply that transaction costs will be saved as there can be less discussion at the time of forming the contract. Courts encourage this increase in efficiency by recognizing standard terms as a basis for acceptance as in *British Crane Hire* v. *Ipswich Plant Hire* (1975) where the terms were those of the Contractors' Plant Association.

Allied Marine Transport v. *Vale* (1985) shows that courts determine objectively whether offer and acceptance has occurred based on the factual evidence. It is not relevant whether a seller misunderstood the buyer's acceptance or did not wish to make the offer. It is necessary that the buyer believes that the offer represents the seller's intentions and was not aware of mistakes the seller may have made. The courts have moved away from what was in theory an older subjective approach of trying to decide whether there was a 'meeting of minds' which is a much harder thing to assess. This move reflects an intention to keep assessment costs within reasonable bounds. Traders are put on notice to incur the lower costs of ensuring clarity in their dealings.

4.2.2 Consideration

A traditional doctrine of common law is that the promisor must receive something valuable in exchange from the promisee for a contract to be formed. This 'consideration' is typically money but could equally well be a service, goods or another promise. Promises lacking consideration are traditionally treated as unenforceable and consideration was treated quite narrowly. On this doctrine, the generous promise to donate a new library to Euphoria University on winning the national lottery is not enforceable as no consideration is present (Kull, 1992).

Posner (1992, p.97) argues that there are good economic reasons for the doctrine of consideration. It reduces the number of inadvertent contracts that might be caused by careless language. Court costs are saved as trivial promises are not enforced and because courts do not have to fill in missing details for vague ones. Finally and most importantly, opportunistic behaviour may be prevented as a result of the requirement.

Posner illustrates the prevention of opportunistic behaviour with reference to an American case, *Alaska Packers' Association* v. *Domenico* (1902). The defendant hired a group of seamen in San Francisco to fish in Alaska. When they arrived, the men demanded more money before continuing with the voyage. The defendant had incurred unrecoverable, sunk costs ('detrimental reliance') and was unwilling to see the voyage end unproductively. Therefore, he agreed to the demands but – upon return to San Francisco – refused to make the extra payments. The court excused him from his promise on the grounds that the modification to the original contract was not supported by fresh consideration.

Any protection from opportunism may, in fact, be slight in the *Alaska Packers'* case. If the seamen had chosen to add fresh consideration, they would have succeeded in enforcing the change, e.g. they could have contracted to sail for an extra day. It may be that consideration protects from post-contract opportunistic renegotiation only to the extent that individuals practising such hold-up tactics are ignorant of the law.

A similar English marine hold-up case is *Harris* v. *Watson* (1791) where Kenyon LJ concluded that to enforce such modified contracts would cause sailors to threaten to sink a ship unless the captain acceded to demands. The modern English authority for the consideration doctrine is *Stilk* v. *Myrick* (1809), where the emphasis shifts from a public-policy approach to the 'pre-existing-duty' rule, which states that it is not possible to make an additional payment for an existing contractual duty (Halson, 1991a). The requirement for fresh consideration effectively rules out simple contract modifications once a contract is entered into, however much the parties wish to make them, which is of great interest from an economic point of view. We return to the issue of contract modifications in a later section as the pre-existing-duty rule has recently been modified (section 4.3.3).

4.2.3 Unilateral contracts

The examples given above are all of bilateral contracting in which buyers and sellers are in direct contact with each other. As long as the terms of a contract are clear and apply to anyone who accepts them unilateral contracts are also possible. In the case of *Carlill* v. *Carbolic Smoke Ball Co.* (1893) the defendant had advertised a smoke ball as a preventative against influenza, and had promised to pay £100 to anyone catching influenza after buying and using it. The plaintiff had complied with all terms and had still caught influenza. She successfully obtained an award of the £100. The company sought to be excused from its promise to pay on the basis that the offer was mere 'advertising puff'.

From an economic perspective, enforcing this type of contract has advantages. Firms may often wish to signal the reliability of their products by advertising compensation schemes that apply if things go wrong. These signals would become impossible to use to any effect if it were known that such offers were unenforceable and could not be taken seriously.

4.3   EVOLUTION OF CONTRACT

Traditional views of contract have been eroded over time. In this section, we look at the economic implications of some of the more interesting developments.

4.3.1   Hard bargains and 'unconscionability'

The law has often enforced a wide range of hard bargains. The traditional outlook reflects a nineteenth-century approach that is still valid in principle but has given way in practice as courts have increasingly interfered with individual choice. Indeed, Gilmore (1986) regards the developments as so extensive that he has written of the 'death of contract'.

A case decided along traditional lines is *Chappell* v. *Nestlé* (1960) where the defendant gave away records of the song 'Rockin' Shoes' in exchange for 1s 6d plus three wrappers from its chocolate bars as a promotion. Chappell owned the copyright and successfully claimed royalties at the rate of 6.25% on the normal retail price for records of 5s,[1] which was rather hard on Nestlé. Before moving on to modern developments, it is important to be clear that cases can still be decided along these lines.

Courts in England have, however, intervened in hard bargains from time to time and US courts have been even more active in this respect following the 'unconscionability' doctrine. It is convenient to examine the doctrine in relation to contract formation although the topic also has great relevance to the later discussion of defences against claims of breach of contract (section 5.2).[2]

(a)   Unconscionability in England

Lord Denning is associated with an attempt to establish an 'unconscionability' doctrine in English courts. In *Lloyds Bank* v. *Bundy* (1975), he argued that although the general rule is that private bargains should not be upset by the courts there could be exceptions to this. In particular, he proposed procedural and substantive tests to decide if the parties had experienced an 'inequality of bargaining power', in which case he argued that the courts should intervene to protect the weaker party.

Lord Denning argued strongly that he could find a general equity doctrine of inequality of bargaining power as a basis for nullifying contracts. This corresponds to the 'unconscionability' doctrine that is more established in the USA where it forms part of the Uniform Commercial Code (section 2–302). The existence of a general doctrine covering inequality of bargaining power in English law is often denied, as by Lord Scarman who, in *National Westminster Bank* v. *Morgan* (1985), confined himself to recognition of limited statutory rules, such as those protecting borrowers in the Consumer Credit Act 1974. Nonetheless, English courts do intervene in cases where a 'poor and ignorant' or otherwise disadvantaged person has entered a contract on manifestly one-sided terms as in *Fry* v. *Lane* (1888). In *Lobb* v. *Total Oil* (1985) Lord Dillon argued that the conduct of the dominant party must also be 'oppressive' or 'unconscionable'.

In *Schroeder* v. *Macaulay* (1974) a songwriter sought to be excused from a contract with a music publisher in which he had assigned the copyright to his songwriting output for five years for 50% of all net royalties on any published songs. The publisher used a standard contract and had the right to extend the contract for a further five years and also could transfer or terminate the contract without the song-writer's agreement. The songwriter had no rights of assignment or termination without the publisher's agreement. The songwriter had become successful and wished to move to another publisher who was offering much better terms. The Court of Appeal and the House of Lords both held that the contract was void as it was a restraint of trade and placed unreasonable restrictions on the songwriter's ability to sell songs.

In *Macaulay*, the courts emphasized that the initial situation was one of unequal bargaining power between a weak, new songwriter, whose work was of unknown market value and a strong, established publisher. It was held that the contract was one-sided and unreasonable between the parties. The courts effectively invoked the equity doctrine of inequality of bargaining power, or unconscionability, to describe the contract as void.

In the UK, the Unfair Contract Terms Act (UCTA) 1977 controls exemption clauses that courts believe to be one-sided. This statute rejects exemption clauses that exclude the liability of businesses to customers or make the enforcement of liability subject to onerous conditions. In general, cases where courts will intervene over the reasonableness of terms often involve standard-form contracts where 'take-it-or-leave-it' offers suggest to some people that monopoly power on the part of the seller is present. UCTA operates in a limited way similarly to the unconscionability doctrine in case law.

In commenting on the judgement in *Macaulay*, Trebilcock and Dewees (1981) point out that nullifying the contract is likely to make publishers less willing thereafter to invest in unknown talent. Promotional expenditure can easily become irretrievably sunk in an insecure contract. They point out that new songwriters might find they must pay to publish their early songs and view this as an unintended, adverse consequence of the judgement that could lead to fewer new writers being published.

Disputes over contracts in show business are common. This is because artists are subject to large, unpredictable changes in their market value and the stakes can be high. In a recent case, *Georgios Panayiotou* v. *Sony* (1994) the pop singer George Michael failed to have his contract with his record company declared void. The singer claimed the contract to be one-sided and a restraint of trade. His particular concern was with the persistence of royalty rates for him of 37p per recording on compact discs even though the rate had been agreed originally for lower-valued vinyl discs. The court effectively required George Michael to stick by his original contract or to buy his way out of it. Critics of the unconscionability doctrine would regard this judgement as efficient.

(b) Unconscionability in the USA

Unconscionability is a ground for declaring a contract void in the US Uniform Commercial Code (section 2–302) and requires:

1. conditions to be grossly unfairly weighted against one party;
2. there to be no evidence that the weighting was deliberately selected as a desired allocation of risk by the parties.

The court may find evidence of 'procedural unconscionability' where the bargaining process – although falling short of violating case law or statutory rules of duress of fraud – is shown to be shady. There may also be evidence of 'substantive unconscionability' where there is a substantial difference between the contract price and the market price. Early concern over imbalanced terms originated with add-on clauses used in credit agreements commonly used between stores and poor people in the USA.

In *Williams* v. *Walker-Thomas Furniture Co.* (1965) the plaintiff obtained a ruling that an add-on making all previous furniture purchases (worth $1800) collateral for a new sale (a stereo worth $515) was illegal. The court argued that poor people were unlikely to understand such a clause and that it worked a particular hardship. However, an efficiency consequence of the unconscionability doctrine is that the poor could find it harder to get credit (and might pay higher interest) if a possible high risk of default cannot be covered by relatively wider collateral.

Unconscionability in the USA now covers wider issues than add-ons. In *Graham* v. *Scissor-Tail* (1981) a musician was able to withdraw from the last two of a series of four concerts. Scissor-Tail, an agency, wanted to offset its losses from an earlier concert against profits on later ones before paying Graham in accordance with a standard contract they had used. The contract also gave details of an arbitration procedure which

Graham lost. The court allowed Graham to rescind on the grounds that it considered the arbitration procedure to be inadequate and therefore to be 'procedurally unconscionable'. The implications here are really the same as in *Macaulay* (section 4.3.1(a)): unknown performers will find it harder to get contracts.

Most commentators point to the adverse implications of the unconscionability doctrine. For example, Posner (1992, p.116) suggests that if courts nullify contracts they consider one-sided, the principle of encouraging market transactions rather than legal surrogates wherever there are low trading costs 'is badly compromised.' He concludes that the unconscionability doctrine is vague and has little or no economic support. Many authors have argued strongly that courts should enforce all contracts that do not generate negative externalities (Epstein, 1975; Schwartz, 1977; Trebilcock, 1993, pp.97–101).

Eisenberg (1982) has made the strongest claims to have found efficiency grounds for the unconscionability doctrine. However, these turn out to be rather special cases. One of Eisenberg's arguments is that a party might be 'transactionally incapable' and this would make enforcement of the associated contract unconscionable. This case is distinct from incapacity, which is a standard excuse for breach of contract, where the party is a minor or is infirm. In this case, an intelligent person is confused by a particular transaction, e.g. when a contract is written in particularly complex terms. Nullifying such contracts puts those drafting legal documents on notice to use simple language which will reduce transaction costs. An obvious criticism here is that an intelligent person could hire a specialist to interpret documents although this may be the (higher) cost that Eisenberg wishes to save.

Eisenberg also claims it is efficient to nullify contracts where the buyer, out of ignorance, has paid a price much greater than the normal market rate which could be regarded as unconscionable. This could not happen in a perfectly competitive market where information is readily available and prices are uniform. Eisenberg effectively argues against enforcing contracts associated with imperfectly competitive conditions. This claim is open to criticism on several grounds. First, the argument suggests nullifying all contracts in the imperfectly competitive industry, not just the one before the court, which would lower social welfare if all other buyers are happy with their terms of purchase. Most worrying, however, would be the removal of the incentive for buyers to search carefully for the best prices. If these search costs are lower than the costs of using the court system to assess the reasonableness of contracts it is best to enforce the 'unfair' contract.

Eisenberg also claims that it is inefficient to enforce contracts where the buyer has been subjected to heavy persuasion. For example, there is often suspicion that some companies exert high-pressure sales techniques over products like time-share properties. If someone's willingness to buy was a temporary phenomenon, we cannot be sure that there are gains from trade from the transaction. However, Eisenberg accepts that if a buyer were merely fickle, the contract should be enforced to encourage more careful decision making and thereby discourage court cases.

Eisenberg's analysis does not undermine Posner's conclusions as the cases that he raises are rather special ones. In general, the unconscionability doctrine is somewhat vague and lacks clear economic justification.

Eric Posner (1995) has proposed a theory which, although not giving an economic justification for the unconscionability doctrine, may explain how the doctrine has come to influence the courts. He argues that restrictions on freedom of contract such as unconscionability can be understood as counteracting distortions to risk taking that result from the activities of the modern state in providing minimum welfare levels for its citizens. In particular, he claims that 'minimum welfare theory' can explain the courts' controversial use of the unconscionability doctrine when they strike down contracts that were apparently entered into voluntarily and that do not involve price disparities or procedural imbalances.

Williams v. *Walker-Thomas* did not involve procedural or substantive unconscionability (the value of the collateral was unconscionable not the price of the stereo). Eric Posner claims that cases like this invariably reveal a poor person (usually a welfare claimant) defaulting on a credit agreement. We have already noted that voiding contracts like *Williams* v. *Walker-Thomas* will reduce the availability of credit to the poor. Eric Posner argues that this is precisely the result required by the welfare state if the availability of welfare benefits is not to create a major problem of moral hazard. There is a danger that people become careless about borrowing money as any impoverishment that arises from a combination of indebtedness and unwise expenditure will be partly relieved by welfare benefits. There is a risk that poor people will become even poorer unless the supply of credit is restricted, which is achieved by restrictions on freedom of contract such as the unconscionability doctrine and, indeed, by interest-rate ceilings that are often imposed on small loans.

It is possible to extend Eric Posner's analysis to encompass substantive and procedural unconscionability. A welfare state concerned to limit the extent to which its citizens became welfare claimants, which could interest the state from altruistic motives or from the perspective of saving public money, would not wish the courts to enforce contracts in which most of the gains from trade went to the wealthier party. Eric Posner does not make this extension nor does he explain how the courts have come to oblige the modern state in this way in the case law. He simply shows that usury laws, the unconscionability doctrine and other laws restricting freedom of contract are best understood as countering distortions to risk taking created by welfare benefits. Eric Posner's argument gives normative support to the unconscionability doctrine only if one supports the aims of the modern state.

In conclusion in this subsection, economic analysis does not generally support the unconscionability doctrine. If one takes the view that voluntary exchange only occurs when there are gains from trade there is no basis for overturning contracts at some later date. It is possible to argue (paternalistically) that weaker members of society may ignorantly enter into contracts that do not then have the characteristics of fully informed voluntary trade or that they may become impoverished and that these contracts might be struck down by the courts. However, the law does not generally seek to protect people from unwise bargains and moving in that direction raises many problems. How do we know where to draw the line over the protection? Should people not be on notice to take maximum care over their actions? The unconscionability doctrine raises major problems.

4.3.2 Gifts

Modern courts will often enforce promises of gifts by taking a creative view of what may comprise consideration. Judges will look for signs that a promisee relied on the promise and incurred costs and may assert that the promisor benefited from giving the promise. Thus, an individual who gives up a job following the promise of a better one could have a case for breach of contract – so would a person who had made serious lifestyle adjustments in anticipation of the promise. Even though no consideration is involved in a narrow sense, the courts have for some years treated the sacrifice of the original job or lifestyle as if it were consideration, as this is viewed as detrimental reliance.

In *Shadwell* v. *Shadwell* (1860) an uncle promised his nephew a yearly income following the announcement of the young man's wedding. Executors of the older man's estate refused payment. The nephew successfully sued and reference was made in the judgement to him having relied on the promise in incurring expenses which were viewed as a detriment to him. Also, the knowledge that the younger man was to become settled was viewed as a benefit to the uncle. It is inefficient to allow promisees to incur costs following an unenforceable promise as this could easily lead to losses from trade which suggests enforcing well-evidenced gratuitous promises. In an American case, *Hamer* v. *Sidway* (1891) an uncle promised his nephew $5000 if the nephew would refrain from smoking, drinking alcohol and gambling until he reached the age of 21. The nephew did this but the uncle died and the executor of his will refused to honour the promise. The nephew successfully sued for the money: again the nephew had forgone opportunities and the uncle could be assumed to have benefited from the behavioural change.

The law does not enforce a promise when it does not serve to change a person's behaviour. In an Australian case, *R.* v. *Clarke* (1927) the defendant informed upon the murderers of two policemen to escape from an unfounded charge that he committed the murders. Before informing, Clarke had seen a notice from the Government of Western Australia advertising a reward for the information but had forgotten it.

He was not allowed to claim the reward because his information was given to escape prosecution and not as consideration for the money. This is efficient as there was no need to create the additional incentive under the circumstances. Failing to give the reward to Clarke would not deter other informers.

Kull (1992) has argued that there are few modern instances of unenforceable gratuitous promises. He shows that the long list of situations where modern courts will enforce these promises has put the common law close to a situation where it may be assumed that enforcement will routinely follow. Kull argues that enforcement is efficient as gift promises are presumptively beneficial to the promisor at the time the promise is made. He attributes the earlier approach to a misplaced paternalism that failed to recognize benefits to the promisor from being able to make enforceable promises.

4.3.3   Recent developments concerning consideration

English courts have recently moved away from the traditional refusal to enforce mutually agreed contract modifications following the case of *Williams* v. *Roffey* (1991). As noted earlier (section 4.2.2), this refusal was based upon the pre-existing-duty rule contained in cases like *Stilk* v. *Myrick* (1809): it was not possible to vary a contract without fresh consideration. The rule had, in fact, been eroded over the years by exceptions, e.g. where courts held mutually agreed changes to be a waiver of the original contract or where the contract was judged to be frustrated (discussed in the next chapter – section 5.2.5) by events.[3] Also, erosion of the pre-existing-duty rule was already more pronounced in the USA where the Uniform Commercial Code (section 2–209) does not require fresh consideration for a binding modification to a sales contract. *Williams* v. *Roffey* is regarded as a significant, although still controversial, change in English law (Halson, 1991b). In this section, we consider whether the move to enforceable contract modifications is efficient.

In *Williams* v. *Roffey* the plaintiff had worked as a subcontracting carpenter for the defendants. Part of the way through the building contract, Williams got into financial difficulty having underestimated the costs involved and was unable to complete the work. The defendants faced a penalty clause for late completion of the work and offered improved payments to the plaintiff to keep him in business. Further work was completed but the defendants went back on their promise and reduced the revised payments. The defendants claimed the price revision was unenforceable as no new consideration had been passed to them.

The court decided that the revision was enforceable as there had been a commercial advantage to both parties at the time it was done which it was inclined to count as fresh ('factual') consideration. It is important to note here that no question of duress was raised by the parties. The subcontractor made a genuine mistake and the suggestion for the revision came from the defendants. This distinguishes the case from 'marine hold-up' cases like *Alaska Packers' Association*. In giving judgement, Glidewell LJ carefully pointed out that the modern doctrine of 'economic duress' (which we discuss in section 5.2.1) would protect a party from hold up and, therefore, it was possible to take an easier line on consideration.

An intuitively appealing argument is that contract modifications should be permitted when they reflect genuinely changed circumstances and should not be allowed when they reflect opportunistic renegotiation by one party. Posner (1977) takes this line in his analysis of contract modifications. On this view we should regard the development in *Williams* v. *Roffey* as an efficient change in the law. This type of argument can be formulated as a proposal to enforce contract modifications that are not unconscionable and do not arise from duress.

Post-contract opportunism can arise in any situation where a party faces sunk costs. Opportunistic renegotiation is aimed at extracting all or part of the value of contract-specific assets that reflect a sunk investment (Klein, Crawford and Alchian, 1978). Sunk investment cannot be moved to another use and this provides the opportunity for hold-up. The investor is entirely dependent on the honesty of a trading partner or on court enforcement of the original contract to recoup the value of the sunk assets through continuation of the contract.

An example helps to distinguish between opportunistic renegotiation by the promisor and renegotiation aimed at correcting a genuine mistake. A firm supplies components to a manufacturer of toys over a period of one year for £50 000, which is an avoidable cost for the manufacturer. There is no alternative supplier. At the start of the contract the toy manufacturer must also spend £50 000 on specialized machinery, which has no alternative use, to assemble the parts. The manufacturer expects to sell the toys for £105 000 at the end of the year which gives a return on the contract of 5%. Therefore:

(Sunk Investment + Avoidable Investment) × (1 + Rate of Return)
= Contract Value, i.e. (50,000 + 50,000)1.05 = 105,000.

We assume that 5% is the normal profit required before any business person would be willing to invest.

The component supplier could adopt the following hold-up strategy: let the manufacturer invest the £50 000 in specialized machinery and then immediately renegotiate to increase the cost of components to £100 000, which gives the manufacturer the normal 5% return on the dearer avoidable investment. The supplier might claim that costs are higher than expected and that the price must rise or the supplier must abandon the contract. Providing this threat is credible and given that the components cannot be purchased elsewhere the manufacturer is better off accepting the revision, as shown in Table 4.1

If the toy manufacturer knew for certain in advance that the supplier would behave like this the manufacturer would not enter the contract.

Table 4.1 Contractual revision

	Investment		Revenue	Loss
	Sunk	*Avoidable*		
Accepts revision	50 000	100 000	105 000	−45 000
Refuses revision	50 000	0	0	−50 000

We know that the contract is of economic value as it yields the normal return to the manufacturer (and generates profits for the supplier). Opportunism discourages otherwise efficient contracts and is a serious matter going beyond mere distributional issues. If courts routinely resist post-contract opportunism by enforcing the original contract, the manufacturer will be reassured and would be more likely to enter into the contract.

Things are different if the supplier made a genuine mistake in initially pricing the contract. Suppose £100 000 is really needed for the components and that the supplier will fail if this is not forthcoming. It might then be argued that the only relevant question is how to minimize the costs of breaching the original contract. This could be achieved in the example by permitting the revision which gives losses of £45 000 to the manufacturer and no losses to the supplier. Abandoning the contract is worse as losses are £50 000 for the manufacturer. On this line of reasoning, the courts need methods to help them distinguish genuinely required revision from the opportunistic kind. If they are capable of making the distinction then, following Posner (1977), they should apparently enforce modifications correcting genuine mistakes as in cases like *Williams* v. *Roffey*.

There are two problems attached to following Posner's approach which are explained by Aivazian, Trebilcock and Penny (1984). First, we require a clear guide for courts as to what constitutes opportunistic behaviour which is difficult to provide. Secondly, enforcing these modifications ignores the insurance aspect of contracts: it might be reasonably argued, e.g. that a fixed-price contract is intended to insure the buyer against increases in costs. There is a danger that a contractor might win a contract by pricing too low, believing that he might succeed in passing risks back to the buyer later through an enforceable contract modification ('underbidding'). A rule of enforceable modifications, as implied by *Williams* v. *Roffey* (1991) or by the US Uniform Commercial Code, may encourage opportunistic underbidding by promisors. The transacting costs of promisees are then increased as they must devise means of protecting themselves, e.g. the toy maker in Table 4.1 might insist on renting the specialized equipment from the component supplier. Aivazian, Trebilcock and Penny (1984) argue for the non-enforcement of contract modifications and for retention of the pre-existing-duty rule, outside of two special cases.

The first case in which contract modifications can be safely enforced is where it is not clear at the start of the contract who is the superior risk bearer. In that case, the parties did not include insurance as part of the contract and proceeded on the basis that risk was not relevant. Secondly, the risk may have been too small to worry about. In both of these cases, enforcing contract modifications cannot encourage opportunistic risk shifting on the part of promisors and allows the parties to adapt to unforeseen or trivial risks.

Dnes (1995) broadly agrees with the analysis of Aivazian, Trebilcock and Penny (1984) but argues that there is an additional case in which it is safe to enforce contract modifications. This is where it was not feasible for the promisor to bear the risks. One indicator of this inability would be if the promisor obviously lacked the financial resources to cover the risks of cost increases, which is often true in cases that come before the courts. In such a case, it must have been clear to the promisee that he could not possibly have been buying insurance and it can do no harm to enforce an agreed contract modification. A lack of financial resources characterized the subcontractor in *Williams* v. *Roffey* (1991) and the move to enforceable modifications probably did no harm in that case. However, enforcing modifications may be questioned as a general principle.

Interestingly, the Court of Appeal in a later English case, *Re Selectmove* (1994), did not follow the rule in *Williams* v. *Roffey* and refused to find good consideration in a promise to pay part of a debt. This opens up a distinction between part payment of a debt (*Selectmove*) and part delivery of a service (*Williams*) which can be regarded as spurious. However, the general principle of enforcing the original contract appears to have been followed in *Re Selectmove* which is what economic analysis suggests.

4.4 MUTUALLY DESIRED PROMISES

Moving away from issues of contractual revision, it would seem absurd not to enforce a simple promise when the courts can easily judge that both parties would have wished for enforcement at the time it was made. Even if a simple promise was made without consideration, it might be to the benefit of both businesses if a promise by A of certain business terms were enforceable by B. The most obvious case fitting this bill is the 'firm offer' which is a useful business device. It encourages the buyer to devote resources to considering an offer seriously and enables the seller to signal terms clearly.

Unfortunately, the firm offer is not enforceable in English courts although the situation is different in the USA under the Uniform Commercial Code (section 2–205). In England, a firm offer is no different from any other promise not supported by consideration. This was established in *Routledge* v. *Grant* (1828) where a revoked firm offer to lease premises was not enforced. A firm offer can be turned into an enforceable option contract by charging for the right to hold the offer.

It might be simpler if the English courts went in the American direction on this one.

4.5 LONG-TERM CONTRACTS

One school of thought argues that the existence of long-term contracts has radically altered the way in which parties and the courts view contractual relationships, compared with the traditional view of the classical contract.

Macneil (1974, 1978) argues that 'classical' contract has evolved through a 'neoclassical' stage to a 'relational' stage. He develops observations made by lawyers and economists on the incomplete nature of contracts. It is impossible in all but the simplest (classical) cases to specify all contingencies in a formal agreement. Many aspects of a relationship will necessarily be left to be sorted out as events unfold. Indeed, this is precisely how courts often come to be involved in contracts. Macneil argues that as contracts become more complex and more prone to containing gaps, courts become increasingly involved in intervening in them as a form of third-party governance – reflecting neoclassical contracting. If a contractual relationship reaches a high level of complexity, perhaps involving a very long association and frequent interaction between parties, even neoclassical governance may prove inadequate. The parties then have an incentive to set up their own private governance system perhaps using specialist arbitrators to settle disputes. Arbitration is very common in franchise, procurement and engineering contracts. Relational contracting relies predominantly on the value of the long-term economic association for governance of the parties. Interestingly, the practices of relational contracting often show up well in activities, like organized crime, where the participants cannot rely on the legal system (Gambetta, 1993).

In relational contracting the emphasis is on overcoming short-term problems to preserve a valuable continuing relationship. An implication is that courts should look at the whole relationship as it has evolved over time, rather than just the original agreement, when they become involved in the governance of a long-term contract. Macneil's analysis may be linked to the work of Gilmore (1986) who argues that courts are often so little guided by formal agreements that this implies the 'death of contract' in traditional terms. A contrary view is put forward by Schwartz (1992, p.317) who points out that parties choose the original terms of an agreement to condition subsequent renegotiations: therefore courts should enforce terms that are subject to information flows that were either known or envisaged by the parties when they entered into the contract.

Macneil's argument should anyway not be taken to imply that the study of classical contracting rules, from an economic or indeed any perspective, has somehow lost its relevance. The classical rules, with their piecemeal amendments, represent a starting point in studying contracts. There are still many short-term contracts in which repeat business is not an issue and the identity of parties is largely irrelevant. However, the idea of relational contracting alerts us to the fact that long-term contracts are different and raise many additional issues.

Hviid (1995) shows how some of the complex issues surrounding relational contracts may be understood with the aid of a little game theory. Relational contractors may be thought of as being bound together in a sequence of moves in repetitions of a game which offers returns to them both from co-operation. At any time they might stop trusting each other and lose the gains from trade. Table 4.2 illustrates the benefits from one game in a hypothetical relational contract. Party A decides whether to trust B who in turn decides whether to respect or abuse A's trust. Neither party knows what the other has chosen. The pay-offs reflect purely ordinal rankings of outcomes, showing the greatest individual benefit from a trusting relationship and some benefit to B from abusing A's trust.

If the game in Table 4.2 were played just once, trust would never emerge. Abusing A's trust is a dominant strategy for B, which makes him better off if A is trusting (30 > 20) and at least as well off if A is distrusting (0 either way). Given this prediction, A would distrust B, which gives a pay-off of 0 to A rather than −10. The bottom right cell with a zero pay-off to each party is the 'iterated-dominant strategy equilibrium' for this game.

Trust can emerge if the game in Table 4.2 is repeated. A needs a mechanism to punish abuse of trust by B. Hviid (1995) points to two possible effective punishment strategies. The first is an extreme case known as the 'grim strategy' in which A co-operates until B abuses the trust, whereupon A refuses to co-operate thereafter. Alternatively, A can punish B long enough to at least wipe out the opportunistic gains B made (e.g. by not co-operating for two rounds, A deprives B of a possible 40 pay-off). The latter 'carrot-and-stick' strategy is less costly to A. For a punishment strategy to work it is important that the number of repetitions of the game is not known with certainty or punishment is not a credible threat in the end game and, by backward induction, nor is it in any earlier stage.

Williamson (1985, 1993) recognizes Macneil's work on relational contracting as a major influence on his development of the economic analysis of organizational questions. Williamson regards an organization, such as the business firm, as a nexus of contractual relationships. He follows Coase (1937) in arguing that organizations develop to minimize

Table 4.2 Trust in a relational contract

		B	
		Respect A's trust	Abuse A's trust
A	Trust B	20, 20	−10, 30
	Distrust B	0, 0	0, 0
			(pay-offs: A, B)

the costs of transacting and he gives an account of the factors affecting transactions costs. Contracting takes place in an environment characterized by uncertainty. For there to be interesting contractual problems, according to Williamson, three things must be present: bounded rationality, opportunism and asset specificity. If any one of these three were removed, contractual problems disappear.

People suffer from 'bounded rationality' when there are limits on either the information at their disposal or on their capacity to process it (Simon, 1957). Bounded rationality implies that contracting will be incomplete. Opportunism has already been discussed in this book and refers to the propensity that people have to pursue 'self-interest, with guile' (Williamson, 1985, p.30). Asset specificity has also already been encountered and refers to investment that cannot be moved to alternative uses, reflecting sunk costs. As we know from section 4.3.3, asset specificity makes individuals vulnerable to hold-up strategies. Bounded rationality makes it difficult to deter opportunism over sunk assets.

Without bounded rationality, contracting is simple because parties have full information and are able to write fully contingent contracts. Opportunism does not then matter because the contracts can be written to ensure that it always pays for a party to behave honestly. Similarly, a cleverly written contract ensures that no one wants to take advantage of asset specificity. Williamson (1985, p.30) refers to this as a world of 'mechanism design'.

If we assume there is no asset specificity, it does not matter that people are opportunistic or that they are boundedly rational. No party is locked into a contract and, if someone begins to cheat, it is easy to find an alternative trading partner. Williamson (1985, p.31) refers to this as a world of 'competition'. Interesting contracting questions only arise, therefore, in small-numbers bargaining situations.

Taking away opportunism means that parties can simply agree to adapt to all contingencies in a jointly profit-maximizing fashion when required. It is then easy to cope with bounded rationality and asset specificity. Williamson (1985, p.31) refers to this as a world of 'promise'.

The real world is characterized by complex transactions with bounded rationality, opportunism and asset specificity usually in place. Williamson emphasizes the need to protect specific assets from opportunism while economizing on bounded rationality, which emphasizes the costs of controlling hold-up problems (section 4.3.3) as the main driving force in creating transaction costs. This contrasts with earlier work (Williamson, 1975) where the emphasis was more on the measurement and information costs attached to transactions.

Williamson (1985, p.168) argues that the economic equivalents of hostages are widely used to effect credible commitments. The simplest example of a hostage arises when a contractor undertakes to pay a penalty if it fails to complete work on time. The 'hostage' reassures a buyer that money would be available to offset disruption costs if the contractor failed to deliver and the buyer had to find someone else. Without the hostage, the contractor might be tempted to try and increase contract charges, claiming costs had risen, knowing that the buyer faced the costs of either finding another contractor or enforcing the original contract in the courts. Hostages can be more implicit than in the example just considered, e.g. one party may be reassured over making a highly specific investment if he knows that the other party is also incurring sunk costs. Hostages lower the costs of contracting by reassuring parties that contractual performance is more likely. However, threats and commitments must be credible (Raub and Keren, 1993).

Williamson (1985, p.177) makes some suggestions concerning the selection of hostages which should be unattractive to hostage takers. An ideal hostage is like an 'ugly princess': the medieval king with two equally cherished daughters was better off posting the ugly one as a hostage as she was less likely to be appropriated by the captor. In practical terms, a business is best advised to offer in-kind (implicit) hostages which are less vulnerable to opportunistic appropriation by trading partners compared with pecuniary bonds.

Dnes (1993) has undertaken case-study analyses of UK-based franchise systems, using a transactions-cost approach and focusing on hostage issues. A number of common observations emerge from the cases. First, franchising increases the specificity of investment for the satellite business compared with independent operation. As an example, leasehold improvements are trade marked and therefore harder to adapt to other uses. Also, lump-sum fees are typically small in relation to sunk investment for the franchisee and appear to be linked to the franchisor's costs of establishing the franchisee (training and launch advertising). The increase in the specificity of investment has hostage properties for the franchisee (if he is not successful the investment is lost) but avoids posting upfront monetary bonds that might attract a franchisor to contrive reasons for terminating the agreement.

SUMMARY AND CONCLUSIONS

In this chapter we have examined a series of issues concerning the nature of contracts. Beginning with the traditional 'bargain' approach to understanding contract formation, we examined the requirements for enforcing promises in terms of offer, acceptance and consideration. We then quickly saw that contract law has evolved with the courts becoming more interventionist over time. Furthermore, intervention, e.g. in hard bargains, has strong economic implications. Finally, we examined the economics of long-term contracts in terms of transactions-cost analysis. Modern transactions-cost economics has been used to explain a wide variety of organization-cum-contractual questions and is increasingly taking on an empirical dimension.

ENDNOTES

1. There were 20 shillings (s) to the pound and 12 old pence (d) to the shilling prior to decimalization in the UK.
2. There are 'formation' defences.
3. The doctrine of estoppel also allows courts to enforce contract modifications when the promisee has reasonably relied (incurred irrecoverable expenditure) on the promise.

Breach of contract 5

In examining breach of contract, our first question concerns the appropriate attitude courts should take towards breach. We shall see that the courts should not seek to enforce every agreement regardless of the events that have intervened since promises were made. In much of this chapter, we consider the economic implications of standard defences against actions for breach of contract. We also examine remedies for breach of contract.

5.1 OPTIMAL BREACH

Lawyers and economists agree that it is not a purpose of law to enforce the terms of an agreement rigidly. Rather, the legal convention is to allow breach of contract providing the promisor pays damages to the promisee. As Lord Diplock put it in *Photo Production* v. *Securicor Transport* (1980), 'The . . . obligation on the part of the contract-breaker . . . is to pay monetary compensation to the other party for the loss.' Only in very special circumstances do courts require specific performance of a contract. The economic justification for this approach is that the law should encourage efficient breach. If circumstances change after the contract has been agreed, it may be desirable to allow breach so that resources can be moved to higher valued uses.

Suppose that a car manufacturer orders 5000 pressed-steel bodies for a new model but, after taking delivery of 500 bodies, realizes that demand is poor and it would be best to close down production. The manufacturer contacts the supplier and cancels the order, apologizing for the breach of contract. It would be wasteful if the supplier could insist on specific performance which requires the delivery of the original order for the agreed price. Resources would be used to make products that were not in demand. It is better that the car maker be allowed to withdraw from the contract (buyer's breach) but be required to compensate the supplier for any lost profit. The resources saved by not producing the bodies can be used elsewhere in the economy. Interestingly, under the doctrine of 'mitigated damages' the law will not compensate the supplier for losses incurred after notice of breach is received, which helps create the correct incentives.

It is tempting to argue at this point in favour of uncompensated breach. In terms of the previous example, it is enough that the car maker could in principle compensate the supplier and still be better off from the breach, without actually requiring him to make the payment.[1] The same efficiency gain occurs with uncompensated breach. However, this argument overlooks the fact that we cannot be sure that a given sum of money creates the same utility for different individuals. A net gain in money terms for the defaulter need not reflect a net welfare gain. We can only be sure that there is a net gain from breach if the car maker actually compensates the supplier. The car maker is better off from the breach and, since the supplier is as well off as before, there must be a net welfare gain. The legal doctrine that adherence to contracts is typically not compelled, but that compensation must be paid for breach, is generally efficient.

In special cases, courts order specific performance by the breaching party. This normally arises when the good or service under contract is unique, implying that money compensation would be very difficult to calculate and might not be adequate. For example, a contract may relate to a piece of antique furniture or to an original oil painting for which a disappointed buyer could find no market alternatives. It is usually also required that specific performance should not involve the court in high costs of monitoring performance.

We consider further economic implications of compensation for breach and specific performance after we have analyzed some of the classic defences against actions for breach of contract.

5.2 DEFENCES AGAINST ACTIONS FOR BREACH OF CONTRACT

Defences against actions for breach of contract fall into the formation or performance categories. A formation defence is a claim that the contract was improperly constructed at the start and is therefore void or – in some cases – voidable by the adversely affected party. A performance defence claims that the contract cannot be completed for some reason and is therefore voidable.

5.2.1 Duress

Courts do not enforce contracts based on threats of physical, mental or economic harm. This is sensible from an economic perspective since gains from trade can only arise for sure on voluntary trade. Duress is a formation defence for breach of contract. Originally the doctrine was confined to threats of physical harm but of most interest from an economic perspective is the doctrine of economic duress that has developed since the 1970s.

A recent English case, *Dimskal Shipping* v. *International Transport Workers' Federation* (1992) illustrates a defence of economic duress rather well. Dimskal owned the merchant ship known as the *Evia*

Luck, which stopped in the port of Uddevalla in Sweden during a voyage in 1983. It was then boarded by officials of the International Transport Workers' Federation (ITF) who threatened to stop members of the union from working with the ship unless the *Evia*'s owners entered into ITF contracts with the crew and gave them back pay totalling £50 000. The union also required payment of ITF entrance and membership fees, payments to its welfare fund and certain costly bank guarantees, which together added up to a further £20 000. The *Evia*, which had a largely Filipino crew made up of non-union labour, would have been unable to continue its voyage if its owners had resisted the demands as union labour at the port was needed for towage and berthing. Clearly, the union was concerned that non-union ships would undercut shipping costs of vessels using dearer union labour and indirectly undermine the union's monopoly power.

The *Evia*'s owners agreed to the contractual revisions, continued the voyage and then sought to have the revisions overruled in the English courts and to reclaim the additional expenditure. Having determined that English courts had jurisdiction because the original contract was drawn up under English law, the House of Lords supported the lower court of appeal and nullified the contractual revisions owing to economic duress even though the duress was not against the law of the country in which it occurred.

Continuing with a nautical theme, the legal principle that duress cannot be the basis for contract lies behind the Admiralty Court's rules of salvage. A contract made after a ship gets into trouble, usually for saving the whole ship or cargo, is not held to be binding. A rescuing ship cannot extort a high fee based on its windfall monopoly power as the only tow rope available. If the master of the sinking vessel disputes the fee later the courts can revise the figure downwards. A sensible economic principle is to leave the reward for salvaging just greater than the costs incurred by the assisting vessel which maintains an incentive for passing vessels to assist those in distress. There is no efficiency gain from setting it any higher. The same principles apply to the fees that may be charged by rescuers on land (Landes and Posner, 1978).

If rescuers were permitted to extract very high fees, it would deter travellers and adventurers from their activities. As things stand, a traveller of any kind balances the expected benefits of the trip against its costs including the risk of total loss (of life, or a ship or other property). The costs are reduced if rescuers receive reasonable fees rather than extortionate ones. This is a clear economic justification for the duress defence in rescue cases.

As noted in the previous chapter (section 4.3.3), the doctrine of economic duress has become more important in very recent years since the courts have become more sympathetic to enforcing contract modifications as in *Williams* v. *Roffey* (1991). This move requires the ability to distinguish hold-up situations from cases of genuine mistake. The doctrine of economic duress supports the nullification of opportunistic revision.

5.2.2 Incapacity

The courts do not enforce contracts entered into by lunatics, juveniles and similarly mentally infirm or immature persons. Such people are not capable of making carefully considered economic decisions. They may be unable to understand the full extent of their contractual obligations or the true nature of the benefits to them. Again, non-enforcement is supported by economic reasoning as we cannot be sure that such contracts generate gains from trade for both parties. Incapacity is another formation defence against a claim for breach of contract.

In *Nash* v. *Inman* (1908) a Cambridge undergraduate, at that time a minor, spent over £145 on clothing that included 11 fancy waistcoats. The plaintiff was not permitted to recover the money on the grounds that he should not have entered into such a frivolous supply contract with the immature young man.

If the courts routinely do not enforce such contracts it puts competent, sane traders on notice to check the 'contracting credentials' of those they deal with. This encourages the least-cost checking of ability to contract intelligently. Finally, there is a deterrent to those who would take advantage of the infirm as they might worry about incurring costs only to have contracts routinely set aside by the courts.

5.2.3 Mistake

Both English and US courts allow use of a limited doctrine of mistake as a formation defence against an action for breach of contract. As Rasmusen and Ayres (1993) point out, judicial excuse for mistake is rare and there is some confusion over the circumstances in which it is allowed. There is a tendency for writers to generalize that certain types of mutual mistakes are more readily accepted as excuses for breach of contract compared with cases where the mistake was made by one party although this generalization may be questioned.

(a)   Mutual mistake

English, other Commonwealth and US courts will declare a contract void if it can be shown that each party thought differently at the time of contract formation about the nature of the contract obligations. They were at cross purposes and there was 'no meeting of minds'. This type of problem is sometimes (confusingly) called 'mutual mistake' and describes a classic case of 'misunderstanding' which is illustrated by *Raffles* v. *Wichelhaus* (1864). From an economic perspective, if both parties misunderstand the nature of what is being traded we cannot be certain that gains from trade exist.

In *Raffles* v. *Wichelhaus*, the plaintiff sold the defendant 125 bales of cotton to arrive on the ship *Peerless* from Bombay. The ship departed in December and when it arrived the defendant refused to take delivery on the grounds that he thought his cotton would have been on another ship called *Peerless* departing from Bombay in October. It seems the ships were not peerless after all. The defendant obtained judgement.

The ruling was efficient as we can be fairly sure that basing the contract around the later voyage generates a net loss from trade. As the defendant did not simply take the bales rather than end up in court, taking the bales implied a significant loss. We effectively have an 'accidental' delivery of cotton to clear up at lowest cost. It seems likely that the shipping agent would have been better placed to sell the bales as he was in regular contact with a number of potential users. This is not to argue that the agent faced no losses from this need to sell the cotton as, clearly, he also preferred to go to court. Assuming that the agent was better placed to sell the consignment, the court ruling led to the minimization of losses. This argument assumes there was nothing to choose between the plaintiff and defendant on distributional grounds.

Even if the agent had not been the lowest-cost seller, the ruling may still have been efficient. This is because it defined obligations which needed to be settled before a bargaining solution to the 'accidental' delivery could occur. Once liability was assigned, the agent could offer to pay the defendant a fee to sell the cotton if this were the least-cost option. However, prior to the ruling, neither party had much incentive to bargain. The ruling in *Raffles* v. *Wichelhaus* also puts shipping agents on notice to take the utmost care in getting the details of their shipments right. This will reduce the number of cases of cross-purpose mistake. Cases of mistake reflect costly errors and deterring the underlying negligence is probably the strongest support for the ruling in *Raffles*.

In England, 'shared or common mistake', where the parties were labouring under a shared mistaken belief at the time of contract formation concerning facts affecting the contract, does not make the contract void unless it makes it impossible to complete. 'Shared mistake' is also sometimes referred to as 'mutual mistake'.[2] In this type of case, the parties are not at cross purposes and clearly understand the contractual obligations. This legal distinction is spurious from an economic perspective. Much the same economic logic can be applied to common mistake as in the case of mutual misunderstanding based on cross purposes.

US law does recognize common mistake, for which it reserves the term 'mutual mistake', as an excuse for breach of contract. The US position is summarized in the *Restatement (Second) of Contracts* (American Law Institute, 1981).[3] Mutual mistake allows the adversely affected party to treat the contract as voidable unless he can be shown to have assumed the risks associated with the mistake.

A much commented upon US case of common mistake is *Sherwood* v. *Walker* (1877) in which both seller and buyer believed a cow, Rose of Aberlone, was barren. Rose was in fact pregnant and worth ten times the selling price so the seller cancelled the sale. The court upheld the cancellation on the grounds that the common mistake, discovered subsequent to the formation of the contract, gave an excuse for non-performance. An English court would probably have done the same as pregnancy makes it impossible to transfer a barren cow.

The ruling can be seen as efficient although it is tempting to argue that a distributional issue is at the heart of the case. Given the appreciation in the value of the cow, the buyer could resell to a higher-valuing user which could also include selling back to the original seller who might have the highest valuation. Clearly, the resource can move to its highest-valuing user. It seems to be a question of who appropriates the gains from trade. Similarly, with a depreciation in value, the buyer might object to the contract and the main question seems to be who suffers the unforeseen loss.

Posner (1992, p.102) argues that the case can be viewed more fruitfully by asking how the parties would have allocated the risk of common mistake had they foreseen it. He argues that it would be better to make the seller bear the risk as he is likely to be the least-cost assessor of the cow's characteristics. Posner regards the judgement as inefficient: leaving liability with the seller as a general rule in these cases would encourage adjustments to be made earlier which would save court costs. The parties might have taken more care over the allocation of the risk in the contract which could have given the seller the right to extra payments if Rose turned out not to be barren.

(b)   Unilateral mistake

The general position is that unilateral mistake, which refers to a mistaken belief by one party, is not a valid defence against an action for breach. Courts allow people to trade on superior information although only when this is entrepreneurial in nature and increases wealth. For example, a person who discovers a cheaper production process is allowed to continue selling at the old product price. We would not expect the courts to interfere with such highly profitable contracts as intervention would destroy the incentive for innovation.

Where one party is mistaken and the other knows it at the time of entering into the contract, English courts will not enforce contracts. In *Hartog* v. *Colin and Shields* (1939) the defendants were released from a contract in which they had offered to sell animal skins at about one-third of the normal price. It was held that the mistake ought reasonably to have been known to the plaintiff and the court declined to let him trade on his purely redistributive information advantage. It is difficult to see an economic justification for this approach unless it puts parties on notice not to invest in gathering purely redistributive informational advantages. The approach effectively treats this type of unilateral mistake as misrepresentation. Nullifying these contracts may also remove the mistaken party's incentive to search diligently for the best price.

The position in the USA over unilateral mistake is broadly comparable to English and Commonwealth cases. *The Restatement (Second) of*

Contracts (American Law Institute, 1981) states that unilateral mistake allows the disadvantaged party to avoid a contract if the other party knew of the mistake or if it would be unconscionable to enforce the contract. We discussed unconscionability in Chapter 4 (section 4.3.1). It is difficult to obtain excuse for unilateral mistake.

Insider trading relates to unilateral mistake and is covered by statute in the UK, USA and other countries. The insider in a company or in a consulting group of financial specialists may have advance knowledge of a takeover that might affect the share prices for the target and bidding firms and cannot legally buy shares until that information has become public. It is difficult to criticize insider trading on efficiency grounds. Whenever someone uses private information to buy shares they necessarily communicate the fact that those shares are now more valuable which can be seen as efficient (Manne, 1966).

A US case illustrating unilateral mistake is *Laidlaw* v. *Organ* (1817). The defendant knew before others that the British had ended their blockade of New Orleans and bought tobacco at a war-depressed price from Laidlaw. The next day the treaty became public knowledge and tobacco prices increased. The lower court set the contract aside which is what an English court would do since Organ knew of Laidlaw's mistake. However, the Supreme Court reversed this and enforced the contract. The issues here really seem to be distributional rather than allocative although Posner (1992) argues that Organ was usefully communicating information.

It is very difficult to find economic logic to justify the distinction that courts draw between mutual and unilateral mistake. Cooter and Ulen (1988, p. 258) suggest that American courts, at least, use the distinction as an *ex post* rationalization for their actions: calling a case 'mutual mistake' if the general facts lead them to excuse the defendant from performance of the contract. They suggest drawing a distinction between productive and redistributive information: if trading on asymmetric information would allow more productive use to be made of resources then the contract should be enforced. However, if the mistake merely redistributes wealth, it should be grounds for the disadvantaged party to treat the contract as voidable. This approach would deter people from investing resources in acquiring information that gives them a trading advantage but does not lead to increased production: a form of rent seeking.

Kronman (1978) argues that in cases of unilateral mistake, the contract should be set aside if a party obtained an information advantage casually. If the information was acquired deliberately, by the party with the contracting advantage, the contract should be enforced. This distinction preserves the incentives for individuals to gather commercially valuable information. Kronman uses a welfare standard that focuses on the impact of a legal rule on a representative individual from a group that it affects. Kronman argues that a representative trader will be better off if courts follow his distinction between casually and deliberately acquired information. Trebilcock (1993, p. 109) regards Kronman's conclusion as speculative.

In recent game-theoretic work on mutual and unilateral mistake, Rasmusen and Ayres (1993) follow the two principles of avoiding negative gains from trade and creating an incentive for cost-efficient care to avoid mistakes. Whether it is desirable to enforce contracts based on mistake depends on the facts of particular cases. However, they do succeed in demonstrating that the traditional approach of enforcing contracts in cases of unilateral mistake, but not enforcing in cases of mutual mistake, is not justified. There are some cases of unilateral mistake where enforcement would lower the joint welfare of the parties.

Rasmusen and Ayres (1993, p.334) cite *M.F. Kemper* v. *City of Los Angeles* (1951) as an example where unilateral mistake would be best dealt with by rescission of the contract. Kemper successfully bid $780 305 for a contract to build a piping system having overlooked a cost of $301 769 in the estimates. When the error was discovered, before work had started, Kemper wished to be released from the contract. The City refused on the grounds that a clause stated that bidders would not be released from obligations 'on account of errors'. The court released Kemper nonetheless. Rasmusen and Ayres regard the court's action as efficient because the costs of recontracting were low for the city which could just turn to the second-highest bidder. The benefits of avoiding losses from trade in this case outweigh the benefits from encouraging greater care among bidders that would follow from enforcing the contract.

5.2.4 Misrepresentation

Misrepresentation allows the victim to treat the contract as voidable and to claim damages for any losses. An economic justification is not hard to find. The liar positively invests resources in misleading the other party. It is inefficient to encourage this as the resources could be put to a more productive use. The option of damages instead of nullifying the contract gives a penalty for relatively minor misrepresentation where the victim still has positive benefits from the contract.

English common law interprets misrepresentation fairly narrowly. It used to treat it very narrowly so that only fraudulent misrepresentation – where the liar had recklessly made a statement knowing it to be untrue – counted. Fraud also carries criminal penalties. The general doctrine is now covered by the Misrepresentation Act 1967 and requires that the liar took steps to communicate an unambiguously false statement that drew the victim into the contract. This includes active concealment of defects, as in *Gordon* v. *Selico* (1986) where a contractor deliberately covered up dry rot in a property. However, mere silence about some problem is not generally misrepresentation. An economic justification for this exclusion is that courts would incur high costs in distinguishing innocent silence from silent misrepresentation. In addition to fraudulent misrepresentation, there is negligent mis-representation – where the liar was careless in checking facts – and innocent misrepresentation – where the misstatement is made in true ignorance of the facts. All three categories lead to possible rescission of the contract and to a claim for damages aimed at restoring the situation before the contract was made – a form of 'reliance' damages. We discuss reliance further below in the sections on damages for breach of contract (section 5.3.2(b)).

It is not necessary for harm to befall the ignorant purchaser for there to be an efficiency argument in favour of controlling misrepresentation. The cheat makes gains from trade when the victim cannot assess the value of the contract. Even if the victim gains from the fraudulent contract, it is not clear this was the best option for him at the time, which is not a problem as long as the innocent party can choose to avoid the contract when misrepresentation is discovered. Also, the argument that fraud causes a wasteful devotion of resources to misleading the innocent is quite independent of the true allocation of costs and benefits to each party. Encouraging proper disclosure also allows defects to be remedied as swiftly as possible (think of a defective car that injures an ignorant buyer). The seller is in the best position to know of defects and is usually the least-cost revealer.

In English law there is a positive duty to disclose possibly unfavourable facts in contracts of 'utmost good faith'. The most significant example is the insurance contract where the purchaser must reveal all information likely to have a bearing on the risk borne by the insurer. A questionnaire is an important source of information for the insurer. Without the penalty for misrepresentation by the buyer, insurers would revise their estimates of risks upwards to be on the safe side, which would drive up insurance premiums. It may be that the large values often involved in insurance contracts make it worthwhile for courts to attempt to distinguish innocent silence from silent misrepresentation. This process has gone further in the USA, where, many states have statutes requiring the accident history of used cars to be reported and where there is a positive duty in common law to reveal known defects when selling houses as in *Obde* v. *Schlemyer* (1960).

5.2.5 Frustration

Frustration is a performance defence against an action for breach. Impossibility of completion is the traditional and straightforward frustrating circumstance and is well illustrated by *Taylor* v. *Caldwell* (1863). Taylor leased the defendant's concert hall for £100 per night for four nights. The hall burnt down after the first concert and Taylor asked for the costs of preparing for the last three concerts. The defendant successfully pleaded impossibility as an essential input was lost.

It is not physical impossibility but an insurance issue that lies at the heart of the impossibility doctrine (Posner and Rosenfield, 1977; Goldberg, 1988; White, 1988; Posner, 1992, p.104). In the absence of explicit contractual details covering who is to bear risks, the courts should decide who would have been the least-cost insurer. In *Taylor* v. *Caldwell*, the defendant could have insured the hall against damage but would have found it difficult to assess consequential losses to promoters. However, Taylor could insure himself against specified losses and was in the best position to assess the extent of these. Therefore, allowing the defendant to claim impossibility encouraged efficient insurance arrangements in other cases. English courts appear to understand the importance of the insurance issue and will not intervene in cases where a risk was foreseeable and the parties could have provided for it. In *Davis Contractors* v. *Fareham UDC* (1956) the court declined to overrule agreed prices that left the plaintiff with losses after unanticipated, but foreseeable, labour shortages increased building costs.

It is common for parties to insert *force majeure* clauses in a contract specifying that it will terminate on some contingency which is usually the outbreak of war. This removes all ambiguity about who bears certain risks. Thus, if a driver refuses to continue with a trip without extra payment because war erupts and the journey is more risky, it makes sense to nullify the original contract if it did not explicitly assign this risk to the employee. The employer is probably in the best position to assess such a risk and insure against it. However, if the prospect of war was well known before departure, it would seem that the risk was implicitly borne by the driver and that the original contract included a reward for this and should be enforced.

Care must be taken in unravelling the insurance aspect in a frustration case. In *Tsakiroglou* v. *Noblee Thorl GmbH* (1962) the plaintiff contracted to sell peanuts to the defendant on terms including 'cost, insurance and freight' (c.i.f). A standard contract required a two-month extension of delivery time followed by cancellation for *force majeure*. The Suez Canal, the normal delivery route, closed from November 1956 to April 1957 and the sellers claimed impossibility. The buyer successfully claimed the contract was not impossible but just more costly for the seller to complete. Note that the contract was c.i.f., implicitly assigning risks on shipping costs to seller. Anyway, the seller, with local knowledge, was likely to be the lowest-cost insurer.

5.2.6 Commercial impracticability

In the USA, the courts have moved to a standard of commercial impracticability rather than impossibility (Sykes, 1990). The Uniform Commercial Code (section 2–615) states that failure to complete is not a breach if it is made impracticable by a contingency that was not a basic assumption in the contract. The rather sweeping nature of commercial impracticability in the USA is limited in practice by three requirements. First, the contingency really must be unforeseen. Secondly, the risk of failure must not have been assumed directly or indirectly by the party seeking to be excused. Finally, the defendant cannot be the cause of the events that form the excuse. Nonetheless,

the commentary attached to the Uniform Commercial Code emphasizes the flexibility of the impracticability doctrine in relation to its
purpose of preventing performance of a contract from leading to
business failure. English courts have largely resisted the doctrine of
commercial impracticability.

In practice, severe shortage of raw materials, owing to the closure
of suppliers, to war or to crop failure, is accepted as a basis for
impracticability. The implication is that replacement materials may be
so costly that the contract would make losses. But rises or falls in
market conditions are outside of the scope of impracticability. The
contracts are presumed to be the means of covering price variation in
either inputs or final outputs.

One of the best-known US cases of commercial impracticability is
that of Westinghouse, analyzed by Joskow (1977). In the 1970s,
Westinghouse sold nuclear reactors to electricity generating utilities
with an attached fixed-price contract to sell uranium at $10 a pound. By
1975, Westinghouse had a commitment to supply 60 000 tons of
uranium but only had supply lines covering 20 000 tons and the price
had risen to $30 a pound: Westinghouse would have incurred losses of
$2 billion. By the end of the year Westinghouse announced that it
would not honour the contracts and claimed commercial impracticability.
Joskow suggests that Westinghouse had subscribed to a minority view
that prices would fall as military stockpiles were sold off.

In fact, the Uniform Commercial Code would probably not have
supported Westinghouse as its problem resulted from a rise in the
market price of uranium which was widely foreseen. Most of the
utilities filed claims for breach which were settled out of court with
losses on the contracts being shared. The settlements probably re-
flected the value of the long-term association with Westinghouse. The
utilities would have been unwilling to push Westinghouse to the limit.
As a postscript, note that by 1982 the price of uranium had fallen to $8
a pound.

The defence of commercial impracticability has no basis in economic
analysis because fears of business failure and associated unemployment
overlook the long-term implications of reallocating resources. Firms
get into difficulties because they are unable to adjust to changing
economic conditions. If they fail, their assets and workers might be
better used by other firms. However, as in the Westinghouse case,
contracts can be adjusted to overcome problems of a purely short-term
nature.

Commercial impracticability creates several problems. First, firms
may be tempted to practise creative accounting and claim impracticability
when it does not really exist. This opportunism might give some
leverage with customers or suppliers in attempts to renegotiate more
favourable terms after a contract has been entered. Impracticability
encourages the wasteful devotion of resources to fraud and to its
detection. Also, fear of post-contract opportunism might in itself deter
people from entering otherwise efficient contracts. Finally, firms have

less incentive to practise careful management if they can always escape from the consequences of their incompetence. Critics of the defence of commercial impracticability ask whether it is really a good idea to keep firms in business regardless of how inefficient they are.

5.3 REMEDIES FOR BREACH OF CONTRACT

There are three possible remedies for breach of contract. First, the parties may have stipulated remedies in the contract, perhaps specifying an arbitration procedure or a schedule of penalties for delayed delivery. Secondly, a court may grant legal relief and award compensation for damages. Finally, in some cases a court may grant equitable relief and make an order for specific performance. All of these devices have clear economic implications.

5.3.1 Party-designed remedies

These can include liquidated damages, performance bonds and arbitration procedures. Courts are traditionally reluctant to enforce stipulated damages that contain a punitive element, as in *Jobson* v. *Johnson* (1989) where a penalty clause affecting delays in the purchase of shares was not enforced. Judges argue that compensation should be limited to the damage caused which is the basis of liquidated damages. There is some conflict with economic reasoning here as a punitive element may be needed to support a contract.

Goetz and Scott (1977) give two good reasons for supporting punitive clauses. First, someone may have paid well above the market rate for a service to obtain an unusual level of compensation should the service fail. In their example of the 'anxious alumnus' who charters a bus to follow his college basketball team, the psychic loss is very high for the alumnus if the bus breaks down. The bus company may be the best underwriter for this insurance as it is in a good position to assess the risks of breakdown and to provide back-up vehicles.

The second example involves signalling. A supplier may be willing to post a high bond (a 'hostage') to signal that the service is reliable. This signal may be especially useful to a new supplier that knows it is the lowest-cost and most reliable firm but must convince a sceptical market. In general the benefit to a buyer from a contract is:

$$\text{Expected Net Benefit} = E[B] = p.b - (1 - p)(c - d)$$

where p = probability of successful completion; b = net benefit from successful completion; c = costs caused by failure; d = penalty payment (bond) from failed supplier. If the buyer believes the firm to be less reliable than others, p is taken to be lower. If d were set equal to c(compensatory damages) the low value for p depresses the expected net benefit. The supplier can compensate for this by increasing d to yield a higher net benefit and win the contract. If the supplier is the most reliable firm, it is desirable that it should win the contract. It needs to be able to offer a punitive bond as part of the stipulated damages in order to do this.

An alleged inefficiency of enforcing stipulated damages is that it encourages completion of a contract when breach would be preferable, e.g. the stipulated penalty is £10 000 but the benefit of completion is just £3000 to the buyer. The supplier has an incentive to spend up to £10 000 apparently to avoid a cost of failure of just £3000. But this ignores the risks borne by the buyer. The higher compensation payment reflects a part of the package offered by the supplier to obtain the contract in the first place. The penalty of £10 000 and buyer's loss of £3000 are compatible with the following contract (in £s):

$$E[B] = 13\ 500 = 0.5(20000) - 0.5(3000 - 10000)$$

where, b, the benefit of successful completion to the buyer, is £20 000, and p, the probability of success is 0.5. We assume that the £13 500 expected net benefit is required to undercut the next-best contract offered to the buyer. If the supplier cannot complete the contract, the bond (£10 000) should be enforced or the reliability of this type of contract will be undermined. Undermining bonding would imply that efficient new firms would not be able to compete with inefficient established ones by offering higher bonds.

In the UK, the legal presumption against punitive bonds has probably deterred some firms from competing for contracts for government services. It has become common practice for consultants engaged in advising clients on contracting out services to emphasize investigation of the contractor rather than the use of performance bonds. In view of this, there may be no way for a relatively new firm to overcome the superior reputation of established suppliers. Contracting out has become very important since the UK passed legislation in 1988 requiring the market testing of most government services. Tendering to supply these services might be more competitive if more severe bonding practices became more legally acceptable.

Arbitration clauses in a contract reflect competitive contracting conditions. Such clauses can reassure a buyer or seller that they will not become involved in costly litigation if there is a conflict at a later stage in the contract. Courts should be supportive of arbitrated decisions, by this reasoning, if a dissatisfied party takes legal action. The consequence of not supporting arbitration is the discouragement of contracting in cases where it would be found useful.

5.3.2 Legal relief

There are four possible bases on which to award damages to the victim (promisee) of a breach of contract:

1. expectations loss – the promisee's lost gain from the contract;

2. reliance loss – the costs a promisee incurs in reasonable anticipation of the promise;
3. restitution damages – the promisor's profit from the breach;
4. consequential loss – flow-on losses from the breach for the promisee.

Each of these may have a role to play in particular cases. We examine them in turn.

(a) Expectation damages

The normal practice of courts is to award expectation damages. The authority for this is *Robinson* v. *Harman* (1848) in which Lord Parke said: '. . . where a party sustains loss by reason of a breach of contract, he is, as far as money can do it, to be placed in the same situation . . . as if the contract had been performed.'[4] The following example shows that expectation damages encourages efficient breach only. A consumer promises to buy a product from a manufacturer at price *p* but then considers whether to breach the contract. The manufacturer makes specific investments in anticipation of (in reliance upon) the sale which means he incurs sunk costs, e.g. a manufacturer of custom-built furniture would use up tools and materials in making the item.

From the point of view of both parties, completion of the contract is efficient if:

$$CS + P - C - S > -S, \text{ i.e. } CS + P - C > 0 \qquad (5.1)$$

where CS = any consumer surplus on the transaction; P = manufacturer's revenue; C = manufacturer's variable costs; S = manufacturer's sunk (unavoidable) costs. Note that $P - C - S$ equals the manufacturer's profits and that for simplicity the buyer has no costs. Consumer surplus measures the difference between what the consumer pays and the maximum price he would be prepared to pay rather than go without the item, as explained earlier (section 3.6.2, note 11). Sunk costs are irrecoverable expenditures on specific assets, as also explained earlier (section 4.3.3). The manufacturer's sunk costs therefore measure detrimental reliance, which in this case comprises the tools and materials used up.

Condition (5.1) tells us that completion is efficient if the contract has a surplus over costs, excluding sunk costs – which are incurred with or without completion. For simplicity, prices and costs are assumed to be unchanged from the start of the contract. However, consumer surplus may be lower than expected as clearly something must have changed to make the consumer contemplate breach, e.g. the product may have become more cheaply available elsewhere.

English courts expect breached-against parties to minimize their losses. This is the doctrine that the victim has a 'duty to mitigate damages' as developed in *British Westinghouse* v. *Underground Electric Railways* (1912). However, the courts recognize unavoidable (sunk) costs incurred by the victim prior to breach. These sunk costs, or reliance expenditures, are included in an expectation damages assessment. Thus, if a seller expected a price of £10 and had sunk costs of £4 and avoidable costs of £5, the cost of the breach is £5 and not £1 (£4 sunk cost plus £1 lost profit). It would not do just to award 'lost net profit' in the presence of sunk costs. In *Hydraulic Engineering* v. *McHaffie, Goslett & Co.* (1878) the plaintiff was allowed to claim for sunk expenditure plus lost net profit. On this basis it is fair to say that expectation can include reliance. The courts sometimes put this as allowing claims for 'wasted' expenditure and lost net profit, as in *Cullinane* v. *British 'Rema'* (1954).

A little algebra shows that the practice of the courts encourages efficient breach only. With expectation damages, the supplier in our example must be made indifferent between the buyer completing the contract and refusing to buy. Therefore, the supplier receives lost profit plus any incurred sunk costs as damages:

$$(P - C - S) + S = P - C = d_e \tag{5.2}$$

where d_e is the expectation damages if the buyer does not buy. It follows that the supplier receives:

$$-S + d_e = P - C - S \tag{5.3}$$

if there is breach, which is the same as the profit from completion.

The consumer completes the purchase if:

$$CS > -d_e \tag{5.4}$$

where the change of sign on d_e reflects the fact that the consumer pays it as a cost if he breaches. It follows that:

$$CS + d_e > 0, \text{ implying } CS + P - C > 0 \tag{5.5}$$

which is the earlier condition for optimal completion. This shows that the customer completes under expectation damages when it is optimal to do so.

A further numerical example also helps to clarify the issues surrounding expectation damages. This time we take a seller's breach and assume for simplicity there are no sunk costs. Suppose a firm agrees to sell a building for £200 000 but suddenly realizes that it will lose £20 000 on the deal. It therefore wishes to breach. However, the buyer cannot find a replacement building for less than £250 000 and consumer surplus therefore equals £50 000. Under the rule of expectation damages, the seller must pay the buyer the extra £50 000 and will be deterred from breaching, preferring to suffer the £20 000 loss. This is efficient as it is cheaper for the seller to lose £20 000 under the rule than for the buyer to lose £50 000 without it.

Courts generally use market prices in calculating the victim's expectation. However, if work has been partly completed when a contractor stops work, the only way the victim can be given his expectation is if he is awarded the cost of completion by another contractor. The 'cost of cure' is a standard procedure in such building cases. However, if the cost of completion is disproportionate to the market value of the work, courts may intervene on a market price basis. A US case, *Jacob & Youngs* v. *Kent* (1921), in which the plaintiff specified a particular make of copper for pipework but the defendant used another of identical quality, illustrates this. The court refused to award cost of cure and only gave the nominal difference between the cost of the different makes of pipe. However, courts do not use market prices if a specific benefit is required, as in *Radford* v. *De Froberville* (1978) where the cost of a wall was allowed as contracted for but not that of a cheaper structure like a fence. It is a question of where a court chooses to draw the line over how reasonable it is to require a particular subjective benefit. *Jacob & Youngs* v. *Kent* may be seen as too interventionist, or, alternatively, as courts saving the costs of assessing the subjective benefit of a particular brand when this was far from obvious.

From an economic perspective, expectation is probably the best measure of the real loss to the promisee, as it measures the lost opportunity for the victim. There is one problem, however, which is that expectation damages may encourage overreliance by the promisee in situations where this is possible. We return to this issue after we have considered reliance as a damage measure.

Friedman (1989) argues that expectation damages can be too generous if there is an element of monopoly profit in the victim's loss. In that case, the prospective defaulter will compare his benefits from completion with damages including the monopoly profits, rather than with the cost of the breach in a competitive market for the goods or service. A buyer would complete with a monopoly supplier when he would not if markets were more competitive and profits were lower. Monopoly profits may be 'monopoly rents' that have been gained at the consumer's expense and should not in such cases be counted as an additional loss from the breach. A possible criticism of Friedman is that not all monopoly profits are rents (i.e. pure surpluses) but might be necessary to maintain an incentive for high levels of innovation, in which case it is appropriate to regard lost profit as a real loss. Littlechild (1981) gives a good account of the welfare aspects of monopoly profits.

(b)   Reliance damages

Under a reliance rule for damages, the victim is put into the same position that would have been enjoyed if the contract had never taken place (Shavell, 1980a, p.471). Compensation is for any sunk costs incurred and any payments made in reasonable anticipation of the completion of the contract. English courts give the victim the option of claiming reliance where the expected net profit from the contract is too speculative to establish, as in *Anglia Television* v. *Reed* (1972) in which an American actor withdrew from an agreement to make a television play. An interesting Australian case is *McRae* v. *Commonwealth Disposals Commission* (1951) where the plaintiff agreed to salvage an oil tanker that turned out not to be at the indicated location. Loss of net profit was not permitted as it was regarded as too speculative and the compensation was confined to reliance loss.

If reliance damages were used generally for breach inefficient breach would be encouraged. Using the example of the previous section, where a buyer might breach, reliance damages can be defined as:

$$d_r = S \qquad (5.6)$$

which is less than $P - C$, the expectation measure, because $P - C - S > 0$. The reliance measure is therefore less than the expectation measure of damages when we consider the data upon which the contract was based and would encourage an excessive number of breaches of contract.[5]

The algebra also indicates that it is safe to use the reliance measure of damages if net profit $(P - C - S)$ is zero. This is implicitly how the English courts proceed. The rule is to use reliance when net profit is too speculative to calculate, which is to regard it as effectively equal to zero.

Figure 5.1 illustrates the impact of reliance, taken generally, and expectation damages on the number of completed contracts. The horizontal axis shows the number of a certain type of supply contract that a manufacturer offers whereas the vertical axis shows the benefits from them. Each contract has the same price, variable costs and sunk costs. Consumer surplus falls with each additional contract which is best thought of as involving separate consumers. The line labelled CS' shows the original consumer surplus from the contracts. The original number of completions would have been X', all of which contracts would have been associated with positive profits for the supplier as well as positive consumer surplus for buyers. Some shock then caused

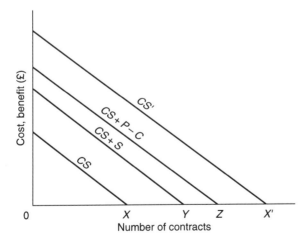

Figure 5.1 Damages and breach. CS = any consumer surplus on the transaction; P = manufacturer's revenue; C = manufacturer's variable cost; S = manufacturer's sunk costs.

benefits to fall to the line labelled CS implying that $X' - X$ of the original contracts could be breached.

With no damages to pay, the buyers would complete X contracts, which is where consumer surplus becomes zero. We then add a constant amount $d_r = S$ onto CS to reflect reliance damages, causing Y contracts to be completed. Expectation damages are shown by moving to the line labelled $CS + (P - C)$, which causes Z contracts to be completed. The optimal level of breach is $X' - Z$ which we deduced algebraically above.

Note again, that if net profit $(P - C - S)$ is treated as zero the line $(CS + P - C)$ cannot be established separately from the one labelled $(CS + S)$. This corresponds with efficient use of reliance damages as derived above.

(c) A further comparison

It is useful to compare the general principles of expectation and reliance damages using indifference curves (section 3.1.2(b)). Figure 5.2 shows the trade-off between damages (on the vertical axis) and gains or losses in a contract for a buyer facing possible breach by the seller. Consider the owner of an unreliable car who hires a mechanic to fix it. Unfortunately, the mechanic makes it worse so that it becomes reliable for only 50% of the time on average. Before it was 'fixed', the car was reliable 75% of the time. The owner was hoping for an improvement to 100%.

The indifference curve, labelled I_1, shows the owner's level of welfare before entering the contract. It shows the amount of compensation required for giving up some of the existing reliability level of 75%

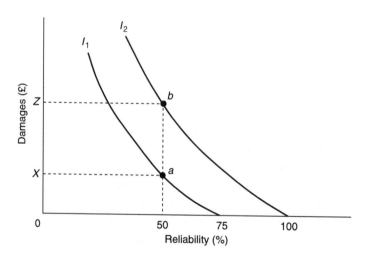

Figure 5.2 Expectation and reliance. I_1 = owner's level of welfare before entering contract (reliance damages); I_2 = owner's level of welfare if contract is completed (expectation damages).

so as to keep the owner's level of welfare constant. The convex shape of the indifference curve reflects diminishing marginal utility for successive increments of money compensation. Compensation has to grow as more equal losses of reliability occur if the consumer is to be kept at the same level of welfare. The upper indifference curve, labelled I_2, shows the level of the owner's welfare if the contract is completed by the mechanic so that reliability increases to 100%. I_2 therefore shows the amount of compensation required for giving up some of the improved reliability.

The mechanic makes things worse, giving just 50% reliability. A reliance rule of damages puts the owner back to the same level of welfare that he had before the contract. The mechanic pays £X damages to the owner, taking the owner to point a on I_1. The loss of reliability for the owner plays the same role as sunk costs in our earlier examples. An expectation rule requires £Z damages to take the owner to point b on I_2 which gives the same level of welfare that would have been enjoyed after the successful completion of the contract.

(d) Restitution damages

Under the restitution measure, the defaulter returns any payments received before the breach (Shavell, 1980a, p.471). This form of damages is most easily studied in the case of seller's breach with payment having been made in advance. An increase in the costs of completing the contract might lead the seller to contemplate breach. This case can be fitted into the analysis used to study reliance and expectation. The damage payment owed by the seller under the restitution rule is:

$$d_{re} = P \tag{5.7}$$

The optimal condition for completion remains the same as before ($CS + P - C > 0$) and is not affected by the fact that payment has been made in advance. In general, having received payment, the seller completes if:

$$\text{profit from completion} > \text{profit from default,}$$
$$\text{i.e } P - C - S > P - S - d \text{ or } d - C > 0 \tag{5.8}$$

where d = damage payment of whatever kind.

Under expectations damages, the defaulting manufacturer would be required to compensate the buyer for his lost consumer surplus and also to return the price paid:

$$d_e' = CS + P \tag{5.9}$$

Therefore, under the expectation rule, the seller completes if:

$$CS + P - C > 0 \tag{5.10}$$

which is the condition for efficient completion. Expectation damages are also optimal in this case of seller's breach.

Under the restitution rule, $d_{re} = P$, and since:

$$CS + P > P \tag{5.11}$$

damages are too low under restitution (unless $CS = 0$) and there will be excessive breach.

Note that restitution damages are relevant whenever courts order the return of money paid prior to the breakdown of a contract. This applies to nullification of contracts for misrepresentation as discussed in the previous chapter. Restitution may also be part of a damages award that is really based on expectation. For example, the court may return the price paid plus the extra required to buy a replacement item. In this case, restitution is part of a settlement that discourages inefficient breach.

(e) Consequential damages

Consequential damages include compensation for flow-on effects from the breach but are not generally allowed. The courts follow the rule in *Hadley* v. *Baxendale* (1854) where the plaintiff, a mill owner, failed to recover lost profits after a mill shaft was delayed while in the care of the defendant, a haulier. The reasoning was that the damage was too remote and did not 'arise naturally'. Lord Alderson commented that consequential damages should not be awarded unless there were special circumstances that were known to both parties at the time they made the contract.

From an economic point of view, this means the plaintiff was not permitted to use the haulier as a supplier of insurance without his consent. Liability for consequential damages requires, e.g., that a haulier is made aware of the losses from delay before promising a delivery date. This ensures that the parties will only select the haulier as insurer if this is the least-cost form of insurance. Otherwise the transporting party is left to bear the risk or buy insurance from a third party.

In terms of the comparisons made for the other rules, and again using seller's breach, liability for consequential damages is defined as:

$$d_c = P + CL \tag{5.12}$$

where CL is the consequential damage, and we assume that the price for the failed service is either not paid or is returned. The supplier completes if:

$$d - C > 0 \tag{5.13}$$

as before. This implies that:

$$CL + P - C > 0 \tag{5.14}$$

which only corresponds to the condition for optimal completion $(CS + P - C > 0)$ if $CL = CS$.

The consequential loss (CL) equals consumer surplus (CS) if the buyer purchased insurance against consequential loss as an integral part of the contract. This is because the contract price then includes insurance and saves the buyer from bearing all connected risks. Otherwise, consumer surplus is limited to something like the saving of transport costs compared with another contract. If consequential loss exceeds consumer surplus but the supplier is liable for consequential loss, the supplier will complete contracts when this is not optimal. We can ignore the case where consequential loss is smaller than consumer surplus as no buyer would then make it the basis of a claim.

The buyer's intention to purchase insurance as part of the contract must have been communicated to the seller or it must be obvious as in *Koufos* v. *Czarnikow* (1969) – where the plaintiff recovered damages for a difference in sales price caused by a shipping delay. The communication is essential or the buyer could not have bought the integral insurance.

If consequential losses were awarded to a buyer who had not contracted to cover them, it would be a matter of conferring a windfall gain at the expense of the supplier. Conversely, if they are awarded when contracted for, the buyer obtains the expected gain from the contract and the supplier gains a return on the insurance side of the business considered over all contracts.

5.4   OPTIMAL PRECAUTION AND RELIANCE

We have considered breach of contract and its consequences as if it completely depended on factors outside of the control of the parties. In fact, the choice of remedy affects the promisor's incentive to take precautions against accidents that might encourage breach. Similarly, the remedy influences the promisee's expenditure in reliance on the promise.

The promisor can often take steps to reduce the probability of events likely to encourage breach, balancing the costs against the benefits of this. For example, a builder might put the roof on at an early stage to minimize the risk of bad weather holding up the construction of interior walls. But doing so makes the interior less accessible and increases construction costs. Incentives work efficiently when the promisor receives the full benefit (the value of the associated reduction of risk) of precautionary expenditure. Court remedies are important here. Under the rule of expectation damages, the promisor internalizes the full value of any reduction in risk that he achieves.

Figure 5.3 illustrates optimal precaution. The vertical axis measures the costs and benefits of precautionary expenditure by the promisor. The horizontal axis measures the amount of precaution (this can also be measured in money if necessary). The horizontal line measures the marginal cost (*MC*) of precaution, which is assumed constant for simplicity.[6] The negatively sloped line shows the marginal benefits (*MB*) of precaution: moving from left to right, this shows the value to the promisee of additional reductions in the probability of contract

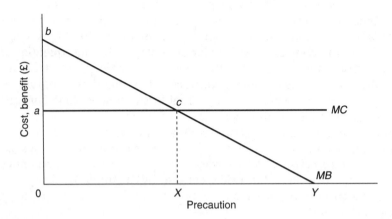

Figure 5.3 Optimal precaution. MC = marginal cost of precaution; MB = marginal benefit of precaution.

failure as the promisor spends on extra units of precaution. The entire area under MB ($0bY$) equals the expected value of the damage from the breach with no precautionary expenditure (i.e. the sum of all the savings).

An optimum exists at a level of precaution X, below point c, where marginal benefit and marginal cost intersect. To the left of c, the benefit of a unit of precaution exceeds its cost. To the right of c, cost exceeds benefit. As long as the courts use the expectation measure of damages, the promisor will be led by self-interest to undertake the optimal level of precaution. This in turn means that the expected damage from breach is reduced to area XcY, because the probability of breach falls to the level associated with X.

The promisee can also influence the extent of the harm from breach by varying expenditure in reliance on the promise. Suppose a builder is constructing a new gym in a fitness club. The club's profits are higher if the builder performs to schedule and the gym opens on time. The owner of the club will spend more on staffing and equipping the club if the gym opens on time.

Figure 5.4 examines the incentives for reliance. It measures revenue and costs on the vertical axis, against membership on the horizontal axis. Two total revenue (TR) functions are shown depending on whether completion of the gym is certain ($p = 1$) or whether it is certain not to be finished ($p = 0$). Each total revenue function is convex reflecting the assumption that price must be reduced to attract more members. There is, in fact, a whole family of total revenue curves – one for each value of the probability of completion – but most of them are omitted from Figure 5.4 for simplicity.

Reliance expenditure (equipment and staff) is higher if performance is regarded as certain. We make the simplifying assumption that all

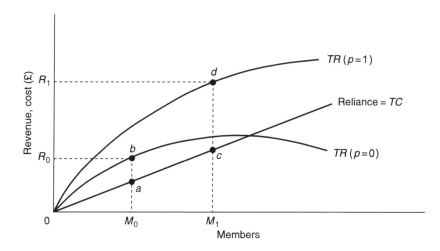

Figure 5.4 Reliance and performance. TR = total revenue; TC = total cost.

costs are sunk for the club (they must be incurred at the start of the year). On the further simplifying assumption that cost per member is constant, total cost (TC) is a straight line from the origin. If the club were certain of completion, it would spend R_1 in reliance, as this is where profit (distance cd) is maximized (comparing the upper total revenue function with total cost). If it knew for certain that the gym would not be finished, it would only spend R_0 and maximize profit (ab) on the lower total revenue function. Any other level of risk of non-performance will cause the club to spend between R_0 and R_1 in reliance.

The problem is to get the club to take an efficient amount of reliance, given the probability of breach. In particular, if the promisor is simply liable for all of the promisee's expectation, the promisee will over-rely. He may as well spend R_1 and be compensated for the profit and cost difference between membership levels M_1 and M_0. But if the promisor is liable for none of the promisee's expectation, the promisee will carefully assess the probability of failure and only undertake the associated (efficient) level of reliance.

There is a paradox here but it is one that can be solved. Efficient precaution is obtained by making the promisor liable for all of the promisee's expectation but efficient reliance is found by making him liable for none of it. The solution is to use the expectation measure of damage in a qualified manner. Courts can impose damages for 'reasonable expectation' where this includes 'reasonable reliance'. They would state that lost profit (or consumer surplus) plus reliance is the basis for expectation damages but that reliance expenditures must be appropriate to the probability of failure experienced. The courts can form a judgement about the probability of failure (in an average case) from the precaution undertaken by the promisor when he knows he is liable for 'reasonable expectation'. In principle, the problem can be solved although the practical difficulties may be severe. Still, courts should be able to approximate this procedure with the careful exercise of judgement. The solution copies one that can be applied to the contributory negligence standard in the law of tort which we examine in the next chapter.

5.5   EQUITABLE RELIEF: SPECIFIC PERFORMANCE

An order for specific performance requires the promisor to carry out the obligations of the contract. It is a discretionary remedy that is not commonly used for breach of contract, sometimes taking the form of an injunction preventing breach of a clause in a contract. Its basis is in equity rather than in common law although it is also codified in section 52 of the Sale of Goods Act 1979 in the UK. There is a general presumption that compensatory damages should be awarded unless there is a particular reason why they are considered inadequate.

Damages are considered inadequate, if it is not possible for the victim of breach to replace the promised good. This is the case of unique goods although uniqueness should not be interpreted too literally. The key fact is whether the good can be replaced. It might be a piece of antique furniture or an old master. Equally, it could just be that market conditions prevent replacement. Thus, in the case of *Sky* v. *VIP* (1974) the plaintiff had agreed to buy the petrol for all its filling stations from the defendant at fixed prices for a period of ten years. After three years, the defendant tried to terminate the contract (claiming breach by Sky). The oil crisis of 1973 made it unlikely that Sky could find an alternative supplier and it sought an injunction to prevent withholding of supplies. The court held that this amounted to an order of specific performance but was justified as supplies were essential to the plaintiff's business and money to buy alternative supplies would be inadequate compensation.

From an economic perspective, the fixed-price contract suggests that VIP was intended to bear the risks of market changes. The award of specific performance then makes this form of insurance contract reliable from the point of view of those wishing to use it. VIP could always buy out the injunction from Sky if it wished to avoid specific performance. This would enable Sky to extract compensation for its full losses, which it intended to insure against through the fixed-term contract and which would have been difficult – if not impossible – for the court to assess. We could view awards of specific performance as an attempt to define entitlements as a basis for bargaining in situations where the court cannot easily discover the value of the harm done by breach.

Specific performance is not awarded in cases where the court would encounter difficulties of supervision. The modern version of this principle emphasizes problems of defining the service in the contract, rather than the mere presence of supervision, as in *Posner* v. *Scott Lewis* (1987). The economic analysis of this is straightforward. If a court cannot easily ascertain the details of the contracted service, it would incur major costs of enquiry and supervision – not all of which would be borne by the parties – possibly making the welfare effects of the cure worse than the disease.

Also, specific performance is not usually awarded for breach of a contract for personal services where the court judges that the supplier would then have no option but to perform the services. It is commonly said that this is because to enforce performance would be an infringement of liberty but there may be more to this. In the case of *Page One Records* v. *Britton* (1968), the defendants, the pop group known as 'The Troggs', were permitted to leave the management of Page One on the grounds that it would have been wrong to make them employ a manager in whom they had lost confidence and they needed a new manager to be able to work.

A problem of economic inefficiency is at the bottom of this case. The relationship between The Troggs and their manager was one of principal and agent which is to be understood in this instance in terms of economics rather than law. The general issue is that an agent may come to pursue his own sub-goals over time instead of properly serving those of the principal although the precise details of failure may be difficult to pin down. After a pop group has become successful, its manager might take to the quiet life and rest content with commission payments from earlier work. This would be manifested in the group losing confidence in the manager. To insist that the contract should hold would give the manager considerable bargaining power to extract a healthy compensation payment for ending the relationship. In principle, the manager could extract his own expectation from the contract, plus the benefit the group expects from changing managers, as an exit fee. This is not only a distributional issue: if managers cannot obtain specific performance, they are limited to pursuing court-governed compensation for breach which is less than they could extract under specific performance. This makes contracts less valuable for managers who are inclined to pursue the quiet life, discouraging such behaviour. In general, agency problems may be reduced by avoiding orders for specific performance in cases of breach of contract for personal service. A recent case that is similar to *Page One Records* v. *Britton* is *Warren* v. *Mendy* (1989) in which the court refused an injunction to stop the boxer, Nigel Benn, from changing his manager.

Injunctions are often obtained to enforce negative covenants where courts judge this will not force the defendant to perform a service. Normally, these covenants are highly specific and of short duration. In *Warner Brothers* v. *Nelson* (1937), the Hollywood actress Bette Davis was required to observe an undertaking not to work for another company in the UK for a period of one year. In giving the injunction, the court argued it did not force Miss Davis to work for Warner Brothers as she had the option of not working as an actress. This seems to be a spurious distinction, as no one is really forced to perform services by an order for specific performance, since they might buy out the injunction. Clearly, Miss Davis must have been dissatisfied with Warner Brothers as her employer in the UK. The question was how she was to get out of her contract with them: by sacrificing more under an order for specific performance or less under a court-governed compensation payment. The case has mainly distributional questions as a relationship of principal and agent is not involved in the way it was in The Troggs' case.

Some writers have questioned the limited use of specific performance as a remedy for breach. For example, Ogus and Veljanovski (1984, p.81) point out that the avoidance of specific performance in contract remedies contrasts with the normal rule in cases of nuisance which is to award an injunction to the victim in cases involving few parties. The normal situation in contract is that there are few parties and, therefore, bargaining costs should be low. An injunction, or order for specific performance, defines entitlement and gives the basis for parties to bargain their way to an optimal solution of their conflict, following the Coase theorem (section 3.1).

Ulen (1984) argues for the extension of specific performance as a remedy, claiming it could encourage efficient breach, efficient precaution and efficient reliance. He also uses the argument that there are usually few parties involved in cases of breach and therefore bargaining costs are low. Making an analogy with the treatment of nuisance, he argues that court costs should be avoided by only assessing and awarding money damages where post-breach bargaining costs are high for the parties. Otherwise the promisor can compensate the victim to waive the right to specific performance whenever he gains more than the victim loses from breach which is efficient. Furthermore, this has the advantage of more accurately assessing the victim's subjective losses.

Ulen also claims that a requirement for specific performance would encourage efficient precaution because the promisor would save the costs of bribing the victim to forgo specific performance. This saving gives an incentive to avoid damages whenever marginal costs of avoidance are below marginal savings of losses. There is no difference between court-awarded damages and negotiated compensation in this respect. Furthermore, if specific performance were the routine remedy, parties could still write conditions into their contract to select court-awarded damages as a remedy for breach whenever special factors suggested doing so.

Finally, Ulen claims that a specific-performance rule would provide an incentive for the victim to mitigate losses and would induce efficient reliance. It is often claimed that specific performance makes the victim indifferent between completion and breach of the contract. He may then be thought likely to take no steps to mitigate his losses, which implies over-reliance – especially if some of the steps are best taken in anticipation of a possible breach. This is not the case because the parties will have an incentive to bargain around the specific-performance rule.

Suppose a buyer breaches a contract to take delivery of a used car and the supplier obtains an order of specific performance rather than the award of expectation damages commonly used in 'used-car' cases like *Thompson* v. *Robinson* (1955). It may seem that the car dealer has no incentive to mitigate the loss by finding a substitute buyer as the original one is compelled to take the car. But, if the dealer is really better placed to resell the car, the buyer will buy out the order of specific performance by offering the dealer his reselling costs and any difference between net profits on the two sales, which is precisely what a court would order under the expectation rule, and damages are mitigated.

Posner (1992, p.131) criticizes this line of reasoning. In terms of our example, the dealer may not take compensation on the basis of reselling costs plus expectation. Rather, he may practise 'hold-up' and extract a sum equal to the much higher reselling costs faced by the buyer, possibly plus some of the benefits the buyer expects from the breach. There is really a pure bargaining situation here, the outcome of which is difficult to predict. Anyway, taking a simple case where the seller can extract all of the buyer's (higher) resale costs but where the buyer retains his expected benefits from breach, the buyer completes if:

$$R - B > 0 \qquad (5.15)$$

where R is the buyer's cost of resale and B is his benefit from breaching. The efficient condition for completion is:

$$d_s - B > 0 \qquad (5.16)$$

where d_s is the seller's (lower) cost of resale plus any lost profit. If $R > d_s$ there will be excessive completion. Ulen's (1984) conclusion depends upon an absence of strategic behaviour by the victim over the promisor's costs of complying with specific performance.

It is interesting to consider cases involving land, where specific performance is routinely used, to examine seller's breach under specific performance. Land is treated in the law as necessarily a unique good and contracts for the transfer of land are strictly enforced. In instances where the seller wishes to default, the buyer can insist upon completion. It is tempting to argue that this is efficient because the buyer probably enjoys consumer surplus on uniquely sited land, particularly in the case of house purchases. If the court were to award damages, it might have difficulty in assessing the loss of expectation to the buyer and would probably be sceptical of claims of a large surplus over market price. Under-compensation would lead to too much breach by sellers. The argument may work fairly well for seller's breach. The seller no doubt wants to breach because he has discovered a better use for the land. The buyer can therefore bargain to extract the seller's anticipated gain from breaching and will permit breach if the gain exceeds his own loss of consumer surplus – which is efficient. Although as Posner (1992, p.131) points out, bargaining costs may be high enough to prevent an efficient bargaining solution.

The case of buyer's breach over land is identical to the case already examined for the used car. The seller can force the buyer to complete and thereby extract the buyer's compliance costs – and possibly deter an efficient breach. The use of specific performance remedies for contracts involving land is likely to be efficient only if court's attempts to assess damages always run into excessively high costs of administration.

Some of the special defences available to the breaching party when the plaintiff seeks specific performance make sense although some do not. First, the defendant may claim impossibility. If it really is impossible to complete, the promisor may have to hand over his entire wealth to buy out the order for specific performance. This may over-deter breach. Secondly, if there is difficulty of supervision, courts may incur excessively high costs in enforcing the order. If A undertakes to paint B's portrait and the court enforces the contract, how can it be sure that A will paint well? It may very well find the parties back in court with A arguing that B deliberately painted badly. Rather than have a dispute run and run, it may be better to award damages. Contracts for personal services are particularly affected by problems of supervision.

Other special defences are permitted such as claiming unilateral mistake or that there was inadequate consideration (implying a hard bargain). These make no economic sense and were considered in the previous chapter in connection with defences for breach of contract and unconscionability (section 4.3.1).

SUMMARY AND CONCLUSIONS

For the most part, defences against actions for breach of contract make economic sense. Defences based on commercial impracticability and on mistake appear to be exceptions to this. Misrepresentation is another area where legal doctrine could benefit from more attention to economics.

In this chapter we have examined remedies for breach of contract. The general procedure of awarding expectation damages has been shown to be efficient. Exceptions to the general rule represent efficient departures in the main as courts contend with special factors. However, several commentators have made strong arguments in favour of greater use of the specific performance remedy. We have seen how the approach taken by courts to defining and remedying breach of contract can help in the creation of a reliable trading environment for individuals.

ENDNOTES

1. This is the Kaldor-Hicks criterion for a welfare improvement, and asks whether the gainers from change can compensate the losers and still have something left for themselves. See Mishan (1981) for further details.
2. There are therefore two types of mutual mistake in English common law: one where the parties have both made mistakes but these differ (cross purposes) and another where they share the same mistake.
3. The *Restatement* is not a statute, but is an effort by the American Law Institute to give a guide to the practices of the courts.
4. Also see Shavell (1980, p.471).
5. Posner (1992, p.120) has an example where reliance exceeds expectation. This can occur if the profit (or consumer surplus) has become negative which is implicit in Posner's example ($60 000 outlay to level land which then has a market value of $12 000 after land values fall).
6. If precaution is measured in money then the marginal cost line has an intercept just £1 up the vertical axis.

6 Tort

Tort[1] is the part of the common law concerned with the redress of civil wrongs. It embraces negligence, nuisance, product liability and intentional torts such as trespass or defamation. Nuisance has already been considered in an earlier chapter. The intentional torts, although of considerable interest from a legal point of view, have been subjected to very little economic analysis. Therefore, we simplify the discussion in this chapter by concentrating on negligence, manufacturers' product liability and related issues.

The victim initiates an action in tort and normally seeks compensation for damages although, as we have already seen, an injunction is a common remedy in cases of nuisance. In negligence cases, the law of tort deals mainly with accidents and has three main roles. First, liability for damages may encourage a possible initiator of an accident (the tortfeasor) to take precautions. Secondly, payment of damages compensates the victims of accidents acting as a form of insurance. Thirdly, the law may encourage potential victims to take care. Historically, tort law was mainly concerned with compensation, which is a tendency that has reasserted itself in recent years. However, there has been growing concern with deterrence of accidents in the contemporary law and economics literature.

The standards of responsibility in tort law have developed considerably over time. Until the nineteenth century, causing injury implied strict liability for damages. This principle gave way, in most cases, to a negligence standard in which the injurer (tortfeasor) is liable for negligent acts. In turn, the treatment of negligence has been refined into standards of contributory and comparative negligence. The traditional view of contributory negligence, in which the victim is held partly to blame for an accident, was that it formed a complete bar to recovery of damages. Common-law jurisdictions have moved more recently towards a comparative-negligence standard in which responsibility for the accident is apportioned between the tortfeasor and victim and damages are reduced for contributory negligence on the part of the victim. Comparative negligence is the American term for the modern approach which is still called contributory negligence in England. We examine the efficiency of various standards of responsibility in tort law below.

6.1 WHAT CREATES A TORT?

Before examining the economics of tort law, it is necessary to have some idea of the factors that create a tort. In this section we examine the principal elements of a tort, again focusing on negligence.

6.1.1 The duty of care

Harm need not be intentional to create a tort. Rather, the victim must show that the tortfeasor breached a duty of care for which the principal requirement is that damage to the victim was foreseeable. For example, a manufacturer of a faulty and consequently dangerous product breaches a duty of care to the user. Similarly, the speeding motorist breaches a duty of care to a pedestrian who is run over. Liability in common law is separate from any liability that may exist under statutes (consumer protection legislation and traffic laws, respectively, in the examples). The judgements of the courts in a wide range of cases have given a reasonably clear picture of the circumstances in which a duty of care exists. However, it is important to note that the courts do extend the list of circumstances over time, e.g. the list was extended by *Donoghue* v. *Stevenson* (1932) to include a duty of care by manufacturers towards all users of their products for whom possible harm was foreseeable. At one point, the English courts looked as though they had adopted a general guide to future extensions of the duty of care. Following *Anns* v. *Merton London Borough Council* (1978), a two-stage procedure was suggested for defining a duty of care by asking:

1. if there is a sufficient degree of proximity between parties to make possible damage foreseeable?
2. if so, are there countervailing considerations of public policy making it undesirable to impose a duty of care?

Anns implied that the courts could be creative in extending the duty of care to situations not previously recognized by tort law.

However, more recent cases have shown a retreat from *Anns*. In *Yuen Kun Yeu* v. *Attorney General of Hong Kong* (1988) the Court of Appeal refused to recognize a duty of care allegedly owed by the licensor of deposit takers to individual investors in a deposit taker. Similarly, in *Hill* v. *Chief Constable of West Yorkshire* (1989) the Court of Appeal refused to hold the police authority liable for failure to apprehend a murderer who had already committed 12 murders. In both cases, the Court of Appeal refused to apply the foreseeability test to areas not already recognized by tort law – a conservative decision relative to *Anns*. From an economic perspective, if extension of the scope of tort law would deter injury in a cost-effective manner then it would be worthwhile. However, the two cases just cited do not look very promising areas for extensions. Imposing liability for the acts of unapprehended criminals upon the Chief Constable would not alter the likelihood of apprehension by much. Imposing liability for financial failure on the public licensing authority for financial institutions could be counter-productive if it led individuals to be careless over their investments.

In assessing whether there has been a breach of a duty of care, the standard of negligence is judged in terms of the care to be expected of a 'reasonable' person of average characteristics under the circumstances. Lawyers regard this as an objective standard although it clearly involves no absolute definition of care and requires the court to exercise judgement. Still, courts are likely to be fairly predictable over what is regarded as reasonable care in particular circumstances. Some regularities are very clear, e.g. special care would be expected when handling dangerous chemicals. Posner (1992, p.167) has argued that the reasonable-care standard is interpreted by courts in terms of whether the tortfeasor or victim faced the lowest cost of taking care. We can easily interpret an English case in terms of Posner's claim. In *Haley* v. *London Electricity Board* (1965), the contractor was expected to take care in excavating to guard against the special risks to blind persons. The costs to the blind of avoiding an accident might involve staying indoors if there were unguarded holes in the pathway whereas the contractor faces the lower cost of erecting effective barriers. The reasonable-care standard saves both parties the court costs of investigating the defendant's true capacity for care.

6.1.2 The nature of damages

We now examine several issues related to the assessment of payments for damages.

(a) Tangible and intangible damages

There must be measurable damages before there is a cause of action over breach of duty.[2] This requirement is relatively easily met in cases where an individual has suffered a physical injury or damage to property. Things are less straightforward in cases where the victim suffers mental trauma. The law is traditionally cautious in awarding damages for intangible damage to the plaintiff who must have incurred a recognizable psychological disorder as the result of a personal accident. Following *Bourhill* v. *Young* (1943) a mere bystander cannot sue for grief at the sight of an accident. However, the case following on from the Hillsborough Stadium soccer disaster, *Alcock* v. *Chief Constable of South Yorkshire Police* (1992), allows for damages for mental trauma following the witnessing of injury to a close relative. The economic principle at work here appears to be the avoidance of high costs in establishing the extent of the damage. The increased receptiveness to awarding damages for some mental trauma could reflect reductions in the costs of measuring damage as modern psychology has developed. In a recent case, *Vernon* v. *General Accident*

(1995) the plaintiff was awarded a highly significant £1.1 million for recognizable mental disability caused by the nervous shock of witnessing the death of close relatives.

Writers on the economic analysis of law differ on whether it is a good idea to award damages for intangible losses. Some argue that lack of compensation for pain and suffering was a shortcoming of tort law (Landes and Posner, 1987, p.187). Others argue that it is difficult accurately to compensate intangible losses, and that therefore tort law should avoid imposing liability for pain and suffering: risk bearing could be controlled through the provision of information (Schwartz, 1988). Cook and Graham (1977) point out that when preferences depend upon whether or not one is injured, recovery for non-pecuniary loss may be inconsistent with the insurance function carried out by tort law: product prices will be higher if producers must cover intangible losses which may reflect insurance that people do not wish to buy. Calfee and Rubin (1992) argue that measurement difficulties can easily lead to over or under compensation of pain and suffering and urge a return to the use of contract law to cover this area of liability.

(b) Economic loss

The law also imposes limits on the extent to which pure economic loss can be recovered. Economic losses such as loss of earnings following injury to the victim's property or person can be recovered. However, it is not possible to recover damages in tort following the breakdown of a contractual relationship, such as when a partner withdraws from a business, because remedies may be available in the law of contract. English law is also particularly restrictive over the ability of dispersed victims to claim damages for pure economic loss, following *Spartan Steel* v. *Martin and Co.* (1973), where the defendants negligently cut through a public-supply power cable and where Lord Denning argued that it was most efficient for the likely victims of such accidents to insure themselves against the consequential losses.

US law is similarly tough over economic loss, as in *Rickards* v. *Sun Oil Co.* (1945), where the owner of tourist businesses that lost revenue after a bridge was damaged could not recover damages, following the *Robbins* doctrine (*Robbins Dry Dock* v. *Flint* (1927)). This bar to recovery stands in the way of modern litigants hoping to recover damages following the Exxon *Valdez* oil spill (Goldberg, 1994).

In some Commonwealth countries, the courts are more willing to allow recovery of economic loss on a case-by-case basis, as in *Canadian National Railway* v. *Norsk Pacific Steamship Co.* (1992), where the plaintiff recovered the additional cost of re-routeing trains after the defendants damaged a publically owned bridge. In the *Norsk* case, McLachlan J argued that by checking for 'proximity' in either physical or causal terms between the plaintiff and defendant, courts could award damages for economic loss without opening a floodgate of claims, which has always been an important legal issue in economic-loss cases.

The typical tort case involving pure economic loss is described by Feldthusen (1989) as 'relational economic loss'. Commonly, the accident results in an interruption of business and if the court bars recovery, which mostly happens, it leaves the victim bearing the cost of the risk of interruption. However, it may not be possible to impose liability for relational losses upon the tortfeasor without overstating the losses to society.

A common argument in the law and economics literature is that compensating relational economic loss leads to excessive compensation of the damage following an accident (Landes and Posner, 1987, p.251). Losses from interruptions to some businesses (e.g. hotels whose beaches are polluted by an oil spill) will be offset by gains to other businesses (e.g. increased demand for hotels elsewhere along the coast). This argument is illustrated in Figure 6.1, where the marginal cost of the contracting (MC) and expanding (MC_1) businesses are equal and the demand shift in D_1 and d_1 are identical. The expansion of demand for the second hotel ($q_2 - q_1$) exactly matches the decline in demand for the first hotel ($Q_2 - Q_1$). There is no net effect on welfare: the loss of consumer surplus shown by area $abcd$ for the victim is exactly compensated by the gain of area $efgh$ for the second business. The damage to the first firm is a pecuniary externality (i.e. one with purely distributional effects).

The argument for not compensating relational loss is problematic even when gains and losses clearly are offsetting (Bishop and Sutton, 1986). Requiring the tortfeasor to compensate for a pecuniary externality imposes excessive costs upon him and would encourage too high a level of precaution. However, not compensating the victim would lead him to take excessive precautions, e.g. a vulnerable hotel might invest in costly protection against oil spills whereas liability for relational loss would cause tankers to re-route at lower cost. Also the argument against compensation could be carried over to claims for loss of earnings by accident victims: if there are unemployed persons who could fill the jobs there is no social loss. However, courts do compensate the (private) loss of earnings.

If either the marginal costs or demand effects differ between the two businesses shown in Figure 6.1, there could be a net relational loss. If marginal cost for the expanding hotel were given by MC_2, the demand shifts would not lead to offsetting changes in the levels of demand or consumer surplus. Demand for the expanding hotel grows only to q_3 and the increase in marginal costs reduces the growth in consumer surplus (by $eh'h$ compared with expansion along MC_1).

Net relational loss can be cited as an explanation of an exception to the rule excluding recovery of economic losses. Landes and Posner (1987, p.252) suggest that the award of damages in cases where fishermen lose some or all of their catch, e.g. in the (American) oil-spill case of *Union Oil* v. *Oppen* (1974), can be understood as clear examples of net loss. Fish are actually destroyed and there are no offsetting gains elsewhere. This suggestion makes sense although it is

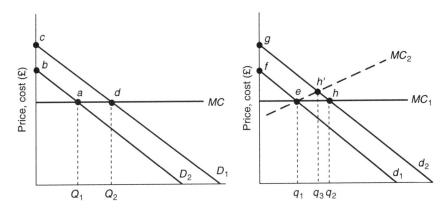

Figure 6.1 Relational loss. *MC* = marginal cost of business; *D* = demand.

also possible that the courts simply wish to treat fishermen favourably (Goldberg, 1994, p.4).

Goldberg (1994, p.36) argues that the exclusion of claims for relational economic loss is an imperfect but sensible rule that limits the liability of tortfeasors. Even though offsetting gains may not fully compensate pecuniary losses, to ignore them would overstate the damage to society. On this basis, *Norsk* would appear to have been wrongly decided. Corollaries of Goldberg's argument are that courts cannot make cost-effective detailed enquiries in each case and that costs are saved by not opening up a floodgate of claims.

(c)   Victim heterogeneity

The tortfeasor takes the victim as given from the point of view of liability to pay damages. Once a duty of care has been shown, the tortfeasor is liable for the true damage caused and cannot plead that the victim was especially susceptible to injury. This is the 'eggshell-skull' principle: if a victim of head injury has an exceptionally thin skull, he is to be compensated for his unusually severe injuries and not for the injuries the tortfeasor might have expected based on average cases. Such cases can be complex. In *Robinson* v. *Post Office* (1974), the Court of Appeal held the defendant liable for damages associated with an allergenic reaction to treatment of the plaintiff's injury. In *Stephenson* v. *Waite Tileman Ltd* (1973), the New Zealand Court of Appeal held the defendant liable for damages from a virus entering the victim's wound. In the US case of *Vosburg* v. *Putney* (1891), the tortfeasor was held to be liable for exacerbating an existing condition of which he was ignorant.

The eggshell-skull principle encourages economic efficiency. If above-average and below-average damages must be compensated accurately, then expected liability equals actual damage caused in an average case. As Landes and Posner (1987) point out, if damages were limited to the average case, thin-skulled potential victims would take excessive precautions whereas the thick skulled would not take cost-effective safety measures as accidents would be profitable to them.

6.1.3 Causality

The victim must show that the tortfeasor breached the duty of care by some action. Therefore, it is necessary that the action be shown as a cause of the injury. The courts distinguish between the 'cause in fact' and the 'cause in law'. The cause in fact is sometimes examined in terms of the 'but-for' test which asks: but for A would B have occurred? If the answer is no, and B could not have occurred without A, then A is the cause in fact for B. The test establishes whether the defendant's act was a necessary condition for the plaintiff's injury. Unfortunately, it is not always a decisive test, as there may be simultaneous candidates for the cause in fact. Two cars may simultaneously hit and kill a pedestrian in which case each driver could claim under the 'but-for' test that he was not a cause in fact as the other car would have killed the victim anyway. Also, the 'but-for' test cannot distinguish between differing degrees of remoteness. A defendant could claim that his parents were to blame for his negligence: but for their meeting and his birth, he would not have been there to 'cause' the injury. However, in many cases the 'but-for' test will succeed in ruling out a possible cause or in showing a causal connection without raising problems, e.g. in *Barnett* v. *Chelsea and Kensington Hospital* (1969), the plaintiff's husband was judged to have faced certain death anyway as he had been poisoned for some time, making the negligence of the hospital to which he was admitted irrelevant.

If the defendant's action is shown to be a cause in fact, the next question is whether it is a legally significant cause. If so, then it is said to be the cause in law and is held to be a sufficient condition for the defendant to have caused the injury. In the USA, for the plaintiff to recover damages, the defendant's action must be not just the cause in fact but also the proximate, or direct, cause of the injury. The world-famous US case is *Palsgraf* v. *Long Island Railway Co.* (1928), in which Mrs Palsgraf failed to recover damages after a railway guard, in helping a passenger to board a moving train, dislodged a package of fireworks which exploded causing scales to fall on her: Cardozo CJ held that the guard's actions were too remote to be the legal cause of Mrs Palsgraf's injuries.

In England and the Commonwealth, proximity has been ousted as a test for legal causation by the decision in the Australian case (on appeal to the Privy Council) *The Wagon Mound (No.1)* (1961), in which the defendants had negligently spilled oil into Sydney Harbour from the SS *Wagon Mound*. The oil had spread causing foreseeable but minor damage to the Sheerlegs Wharf. Later welding operations set fire to the oil causing considerable damage to the wharf. The Privy Council allowed an appeal by the defendants on the grounds that the ignition of the oil was not foreseeable. The foreseeability test for legal causation is consistent with the requirement that damage be foreseeable for there to be a duty of care.

The requirement for either a direct or a foreseeable causal link has much the same effect from an economic point of view. Rather as in contract, where remote damages are not recoverable, the law suppresses costly arguments over tenuous links. In addition, a direct or foreseeable causal link is a basic test of whether there is an externality.

6.2 THE ECONOMIC ANALYSIS OF ACCIDENTS

Calabresi (1970) has argued that an aim of accident law should be to reduce the sum of the costs of accidents and the costs of avoiding accidents. Strictly speaking, we would wish to minimize this joint cost. Calabresi's analysis suggests allocating the cost of accidents to the activities that could avoid the accidents most cheaply. This approach is an application of the principle of least-cost avoidance which has already been discussed in connection with nuisance (Calabresi and Melamed, 1972). Calabresi applies the Coase theorem, arguing for a system that would allocate costs to activities that an initial bearer of accident costs would find it worthwhile to bribe to reduce accident rates. Calabresi's approach is formalized by Diamond (1974).

Calabresi's analysis is normative in that he seeks to construct guides for a rational system of tort law. The approach is illustrated in Figure 6.2, which shows the costs and benefits of precaution against a certain type of accident. For simplicity, we assume that a single source generates the accidents and that precaution against accidents is possible at the source. Precaution could refer to something like a bus company taking longer routes on quieter roads to avoid traffic. The marginal cost (MC) of precaution is shown as the constant amount W. The marginal

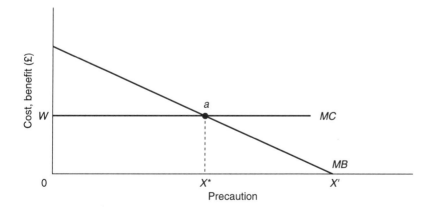

Figure 6.2 The costs of accidents. MC = marginal cost of precaution; MB = marginal benefit of precaution.

benefits (*MB*) of precaution refer to the savings in the direct costs of accidents and are assumed to fall as precaution increases. The optimal amount of precaution is X^* since marginal benefit exceeds marginal cost up to point *a*. Thus $0X^*$ precaution is taken and X^*X' accidents are incurred. Total cost is $0WaX'$ and is minimized.

The least-cost-avoidance principle suggests that courts should expect people to take only cost-efficient precautions. It really gives us a standard for judging negligence. In the above example, if a bus company could show that it had lengthened journeys to point X^*, it should not be held liable for the costs of the accidents, X^*X', that do occur. Some writers argue that the courts do operate many tort rules as though economic efficiency were the objective (Posner, 1972, 1973; Landes and Posner, 1987). Conversely, Dworkin (1980, 1986) has argued that economic efficiency is not an appropriate aim for the law although he has also derived a 'market-simulating' approach to accident law based on egalitarian considerations.

6.3   STANDARDS OF RESPONSIBILITY

As mentioned at the start of this chapter, the standards of responsibility in tort law have developed considerably over time. We now examine the efficiency of the standards under the assumption that the courts have full information concerning the risks faced by and the actions taken by the parties.

6.3.1   Strict liability

Until the middle of the nineteenth century, causing injury implied strict liability for damages. The entitlement lay entirely with the victim, who needed to show that he had been injured but did not need to show negligence on the part of the tortfeasor. Strict liability can be an efficient rule as shown in Figure 6.3, which has the same benefit and cost functions as Figure 6.2 and where we assume one tortfeasor and one victim for simplicity.

Since the tortfeasor pays damages shown by the marginal benefit function (*MB*) for any accidents that occur, he has an incentive to take precautions up to point X^* on the horizontal axis. The tortfeasor then pays X^*aX' damages to the victim which is cheaper than incurring the cost of additional precaution (X^*acX'). Strict liability can result in least-cost avoidance of accidents.

One problem with strict liability, however, is that it will not encourage efficient precaution in cases where the victim's behaviour affects the likelihood of the accident. Since the victim is fully compensated (in principle at least) he does not care whether the accident happens or not. If the victim could take cost-efficient steps to avoid the accident and bargaining costs are too high for the potential tortfeasor to bribe the victim to take precautions, then strict liability is not an

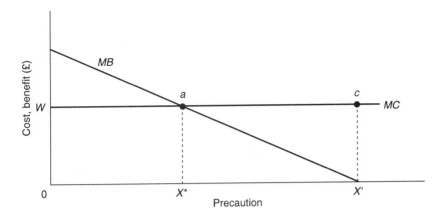

Figure 6.3 Strict liability. MC = marginal cost of precaution; MB = marginal benefit of precaution.

efficient rule. Victims' incentives can be improved by allowing the injurer the defence of claiming contributory negligence by the victim as a complete bar to recovery (section 6.3.3).

Strict liability persists in three important respects. First, following *Rylands* v. *Fletcher* (1868), where a reservoir flooded a mine, people are strictly liable for the results of hazardous activities. Secondly, in England, the Commonwealth and the USA, people are strictly liable for damage caused by dangerous animals that they own. These examples of unusual threats to the ordinary person are dealt with efficiently by strict liability as it is most unlikely that the victim would be in a position to take cost-effective precautions. For example, if a Black Mamba escapes from its owner's apartment and kills a neighbour, it is unrealistic for the owner to claim that the victim should have made his house snake proof. No one would anticipate this type of danger. It is therefore the owner who is the least-cost avoider and who should be made to pay damages if he chooses not to avoid the accident.

The third area of strict liability is in the modern law of product liability in which manufacturers are made liable for certain categories of injury caused by defects in their products. The law of product liability has provoked a great deal of criticism from economists, particularly in the USA, where strict liability for product defects has been the rule for many decades. As this is such an important area, we consider it in a separate section below.

6.3.2 Negligence and the 'Hand' formula

Under a negligence standard, the tortfeasor pays damages if he did not take reasonable care. Common-law jurisdictions moved to a negligence standard in the middle of the nineteenth century which some suggest was a result of the growing importance of railway accidents (Landes and Posner, 1987, p.2). Earlier tort law was little concerned with accidents and was more concerned with intentional harms like assault. The implication of a negligence standard is that the costs of some accidents (where the injurer was not negligent) will be borne by the victim.

The negligence standard is efficient. Indeed, it performs better than strict liability in cases where the victim can also take precautions. With reference again to Figure 6.3, as long as the courts interpret 'reasonable care' in terms of cost-effective care, the injurer will be expected to compensate for all accidents beyond the efficient level X^*X'. Therefore, the injurer will take $0X^*$ precaution which is efficient and victims will bear the cost (X^*aX') of unprevented accidents. The fact that victims bear accident costs encourages them to take any cost-effective measures available to them to prevent accidents.

The courts do indeed tend to interpret reasonable care in terms of cost effectiveness. This proposition is summarized by the 'Hand formula', which arose from the comments of Learned Hand J in *US* v. *Carroll Towing Co.* (1947). This American case is an illustration of the type of judicial cost-effectiveness analysis that tends to occur when courts are assessing the nature of reasonable care in particular cases. In discussing the liability for damages of the owner of an unattended barge that broke its moorings, Hand J said that the owner's duty was a function of three things:

1. the probability that the boat would break away;
2. the gravity of the resulting injury;
3. the burden of taking adequate precautions.

Algebraically, the three points give the following formula, which shows negligence if:

$$B \leq pL \qquad (6.1)$$

where B = cost of avoidance; p = probability of harm; L = value of harm. Strictly, the Hand formula should compare the marginal costs of avoidance with the expected value of marginal harm from some action. However, since courts can only identify the effect of discrete changes in precaution by a defendant, the Hand formula is implicitly marginal in its approach.

Several cases provide additional illustration of the Hand formula at work. In *Blyth* v. *Birmingham Waterworks* (1856) the defendant was not liable for damage from shallow-buried pipes that burst as the frost was judged to be unusually severe – implying that p was low in condition (6.1). The defendant in *Adams* v. *Bullock* (1919), another US case, was not liable for injuring a boy who touched a trolley-car wire, as Cardozo J held it would be unreasonably costly to prevent the remote possibility of contact (high B coupled with a low p). In the *Wagon Mound (No.2)* (1967), an Australian case on appeal to the Privy Council,[3] Lord Reid argued that a reasonable person 'would weigh the risk against the difficulty of eliminating it'. These examples support the claim that the Hand formula summarizes the practices of the courts.

If everyone were aware of the duty to take reasonable care under a negligence standard, it might be thought that there could be no accidents for which the victim could win damages. The implication would be that all cost-effective care would be taken by potential injurers who would not be liable for the efficient level of accidents that remained. However, the observation that victims do win damages in court does not discredit the Hand formula as the estimates are for reasonable care by the average person in the circumstances. Therefore, if the benefits of avoidance are £100 and average avoidance costs are £50 there is a legal duty to avoid an accident; but if a particular tortfeasor faced avoidance costs of £110 it was efficient that he imposed the injury even though he will be found liable for damages.

The law saves costs by concentrating on cost-effective care by an average person in the circumstances and does not generally distinguish differential levels of care in particular cases. However, differential levels of care are distinguished where it is of low cost to do so. For example, a blind person would not be held to the normal standard of care but would be held to a standard applicable to the blind as a class. Similarly, children are not generally held to the adult standard of care as shown by *McHale* v. *Watson* (1965–66) in which the High Court of Australia did not find a child of 12 liable for an accident arising from play with a discarded welding rod. Another group subject to a lower expected standard of care are the insane. In *Buckley* v. *Smith Transport* (1946) the Ontario Court of Appeal allowed an appeal by a mentally ill truck driver against liability for a collision with a tram in Toronto. The common theme in these cases is low costs of exercising judgement over the care to be expected of particular classes of injurer.

However, a negligence standard may provide no incentive for the injurer to limit the scale of an activity (Shavell, 1980b). A bus company driving 100 000 miles a year is ten times more likely to incur an accident compared with one driving 10 000 miles but if it never drives negligently it always escapes liability for accidents and has no incentive to curtail the scale of its operations. Under strict liability, the tortfeasor is always liable and has an incentive to control all variables that affect the probability or amount of damage. The rule of strict liability is superior to negligence whenever the injurer's activity level is important. However, a negligence standard is better at controlling the victim's activity level: as long as the bus company is not negligent, the victim has an incentive to control all factors that expose him to risk.

6.3.3 Contributory negligence: a traditional view

The traditional view of contributory negligence, in which the victim is held partly to blame for an accident, was that it formed a complete bar to the recovery of damages. Common-law jurisdictions now generally follow a comparative-negligence standard in which responsibility for an accident is apportioned between the tortfeasor and victim and damages are reduced for contributory negligence on the part of the victim. Comparative negligence is the US term for the modern approach which is still called contributory negligence in England. We follow the American practice of referring to the modern approach as comparative negligence and the earlier view as contributory negligence. This subsection is concerned with the earlier view in which contributory negligence was a complete bar and which still holds in some American states (Landes and Posner 1987, pp.83–84). We examine the modern approach in the next section.

Contributory negligence can be illustrated using an example from the American law covering damage caused by railway engines.[4] In *Leroy Fibre Co.* v. *Chicago, Milwaukee and St Paul Railway* (1914), sparks from a locomotive had ignited a pile of flax located near the tracks: the issue was whether the railway should have taken more care over sparks or whether the owner should have moved the flax. Holmes J argued that each party had a right to expect reasonable care from the other. It can be shown that a rule of contributory negligence can cause each party to take cost-effective precautions in a bilateral-care case, which is efficient. We now give a game-theoretic exposition of this conclusion based on the data in Table 6.1, which refer to the costs to the railway and to the owner of the flax of particular combinations of bilateral care. The example that follows is a development of the treatment of railway cases in Landes and Posner (1987, p.89) and is a simplification of the approach in Chung (1993). The same example will also be used to examine comparative negligence in the next section.

In Table 6.1, the owner can leave the flax by the tracks, move it 50 feet or move it 100 feet. The railway company can exercise no care and allow sparks to fall on the flax, fit a spark guard or fit a more effective track guard. The damage to the flax, if it occurs, is worth £100. The track guard, on its own, will stop all damage but is expensive: the entries in the third row of Table 6.1 show a cost of £50 for the railway regardless of the action taken by the owner of the flax whereas the owner's costs vary according to the distance moved. However, the most efficient solution is for the cheaper spark guard to be fitted at a cost of £25 and for the flax to be moved 50 feet at a cost of £12, giving a combined cost of £37. This cost is lower than the cost (£55) of moving the flax 100 feet. The remaining cells in Table 6.1 will be explained shortly.

Both parties will adopt their components of the least-cost method of care providing the courts follow Holmes J and define reasonable care in

Table 6.1 Costs of bilateral care (£)

		Owner (flax)		
		0 ft	*50 ft*	*100 ft*
	No care	0, 100	100, 12	0, 55
Railway	Spark guard	25, 100	25, 12	25, 55
	Track guard	50, 0	50, 12	50, 55

(pay-offs: railway, owner)

terms of the care to be expected as long as the other party takes reasonable care. This proposition implies that we expect the flax to be moved 50 feet and for the railway to fit the spark guard. Consider the first row of the table. In the top left cell, the railway is negligent but pays no damages if the owner did not move the flax, since contributory negligence bars recovery: the owner simply incurs the loss of £100. However, if the owner moved the flax 50 feet, there is no contributory negligence and the railway is liable: the owner paid £12 to move and the railway must pay £100 damages. In the top-right cell, no damage occurs but the owner paid £55 to move the flax 100 feet. The bottom row of the table has already been explained as has the least-cost combination in the centre cell. In the left cell of the second row, the railway company paid £25 to fit the spark guard and was not negligent: the owner therefore simply incurs £100 damage to the flax. In the right cell of the second row, the £25 cost to the railway combines with a £55 cost incurred by the owner moving 100 feet and there is no damage.

The centre cell in Table 6.1 shows the pure-strategy Nash equilibrium, defined as the point from which neither party would choose to move providing the other stays put, for this bilateral-care game. The railway will not wish to move to the top row, taking no care, because this would make it liable for £100 damages given the location of the flax 50 feet from the tracks (centre top cell). Neither will it wish to fit the track guard and move to the third row as this incurs unnecessarily higher costs of £50 (bottom centre). Similarly, the owner will not wish to move to the leftmost column, as £100 uncompensated damage will be suffered, given that the railway is exercising due care in fitting the spark guard (left centre). The owner will not move the flax 100 feet as this incurs unnecessarily higher costs of £55 (right centre).

Each party will move to the Nash equilibrium shown in the centre cell and stay there, knowing that the courts define due care in terms of least-cost bilateral care. The railway will never fit the track guard as the costs from fitting the spark guard are always lower (£25 < £50). The owner can therefore concentrate on the first two rows of Table 6.1 and will move the flax 50 feet which is cheaper (£12) than either not moving (£100) or moving 100 feet (£55). The railway then minimizes its costs by fitting the spark guard as fitting taking no care is more costly given the liability for damage (£100). The iterated-dominant strategy equilibrum for this due-care game moves the owner and railway to the Nash point.[5]

Contributory negligence came to be seen as a harsh rule in common-law jurisdictions. If the victim were just a little negligent this would be a complete bar to recovery even though the tortfeasor had been outrageously negligent. The courts tried to mitigate this effect through the doctrine of the 'last clear chance' in which the plaintiff is only contributorily negligent if he had the last clear chance to avoid the accident. In *Davies* v. *Mann* (1842), the plaintiff was allowed to recover for the loss of an ass he had negligently tethered in the road as the defendant, who had been driving negligently at great speed, was judged to have had the last clear chance to avoid the accident. In the twentieth century, the move has been towards some form of comparative negligence, to which we now turn.

6.3.4 Comparative negligence

The move to a rule of comparative negligence was formalized in the Law Reform (Contributory Negligence) Act 1945 in England. The underlying idea is that the courts reduce a plaintiff's damages for contributory negligence in proportion to his assessed liability for the accident. The position in England is typical of Commonwealth jurisdictions for which Ontario led the way in 1924. In the USA, the move to comparative negligence has occurred over the last 20 years although some states still follow a traditional rule of contributory negligence. As mentioned at the start of this chapter, we will follow the American practice of referring to the linking of damages to the apportionment of blame as a rule of comparative negligence although in England we refer to the practice as following a modern rule of contributory negligence.

It is relatively straightforward to show that a rule of comparative negligence results in the tortfeasor and victim adopting cost-effective precaution. Following Posner (1992), assume that the rule is that contributory negligence reduces the victim's recovery of damages by 10% which is a tough rule for the tortfeasor and does not act as a total bar to recovery. Using the same underlying data as Table 6.1, the new pay-off matrix is shown as Table 6.2. Only the top left cell has changed to reflect the 90% recovery of damages which implies that fitting the spark guard and moving the flax 50 feet is still the iterated-dominant strategy (and Nash) equilibrium.

Table 6.2 is a very simple illustration of the conventional wisdom on comparative negligence: providing the legal standard of care is set at the efficient level and given full information for the court, any form of negligence rule provides a full incentive for efficient precaution by both parties (Cooter and Ulen, 1986; Haddock and Curran, 1985; Landes and Posner, 1987; Chung, 1993). Under these circumstances, concern for a more sympathetic treatment for plaintiffs does not incur an efficiency loss.

Comparative negligence has grown in importance relative to other rules for apportioning responsibility for accidents which implies that the courts emphasize the insurance aspect of the tort system. It is as though they place greatest importance on obtaining compensation for

Table 6.2 Pay-offs with comparative negligence (£)

		Owner (flax)		
		0 ft	*50 ft*	*100 ft*
	No care	90, 10	100, 12	0, 55
Railway	Spark guard	25, 100	25, 12	25, 55
	Track guard	50, 0	50, 12	50, 55

(pay-offs: railway, owner)

the victim. As Posner (1992, p.177) points out, this is puzzling as separate insurance markets have grown in size and sophistication throughout the twentieth century. This approach may be due to the courts avoiding having the victim place demands on state-run welfare systems by ensuring that as much private compensation as possible is paid.

Empirical work suggests that the move to comparative negligence in the USA has been associated with an increase in the number of road accidents. White (1989) compares road accidents in the 37 states using comparative negligence with road accidents in the 13 states (plus the District of Columbia) still using traditional contributory negligence. There appear to be more road accidents under the comparative rule after controlling for other influences. It does not follow that comparative negligence is less efficient. For it can be shown that traditional contributory negligence encourages excessive precaution among possible victims when the assumption of full information for the courts is relaxed (Cooter and Ulen, 1986; Chung, 1993). Uncertainty about the court's assessment of a party's level of care will lead risk-averse[6] people to take excessive precautions as they would give themselves a margin of security to avoid being found contributorily negligent and thereby barred from recovering a loss. The incentive to over-precaution by potential victims is less under the comparative-negligence rule as losses from courts' mistakes over the proper level of precaution are shared.

6.4 DAMAGES AS A REMEDY FOR TORT

An action for damages is the remedy pursued in the majority of tort cases. We concentrate on damages as our focus is primarily on negligence cases. The fundamental approach in awarding damages, following *Livingstone* v. *Rawyards Coal* (1880), is for the court to place the victim in the same position he would have been in had the accident not occurred. This is equivalent to the reliance measure of damages discussed earlier (section 5.3.2(b)) in relation to the law of contract. The basic task faced by the court is to find a money sum that is equivalent to the loss experienced by the plaintiff. The logic involved in compensation is illustrated in Figure 6.4 which draws on the indifference-curve analysis introduced in Chapter 3 (section 3.1.2(b)).

In Figure 6.4, which measures wealth on the two vertical axes and health status on the horizontal axis, the victim is assumed to suffer personal injury. Health status shows the condition of the injured element of the victim's health (e.g. a damaged limb or perhaps impaired mental health). Before the injury, the victim is faced by budget line *WY*, which reflects his existing wealth and the cost of health improvement (medical and related facilities). The origin *O* shows the individual's health status, before injury, in the absence of any expenditure. Point *a* on indifference curve *U* shows the initial optimal combination of retained wealth and health status.

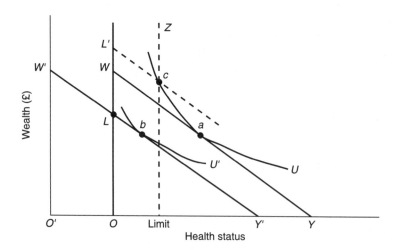

Figure 6.4 Compensating a loss from tort.

After the injury, the indifference map in Figure 6.4 must be rescaled. The origin of the figure shifts to O', taking the budget line with it to $W'Y'$. The movement of the origin reflects the lower health status available following injury if there is no expenditure. The movement of the budget line shows that a lower health status ($O'Y'$ at most) results from any given expenditure on health improvement compared with the pre-injury case. Indifference curves do not shift as they show the victim's preferences rather than the feasible possibilities. Faced with budget line $W'Y'$, the new optimum is at point b on the lower indifference curve U'. The victim's welfare is clearly lowered by injury.

The court must try to estimate the compensation required to restore the victim's previous level of welfare on indifference curve U. In Figure 6.4, the required amount is shown by the distance LW, which is the 'compensating variation' for the injury-induced shift in the budget line. Increasing the victim's wealth by LW will shift up the budget line back to its original position and restore the original optimum at point a. The analysis so far assumes that expenditure on health care can fully correct an injury.

If expenditure on health care cannot completely restore health, the court needs to award a larger amount of compensation. In Figure 6.4, the vertical line labelled Z shows the limit of improvement to the injury that is possible through buying health care. The line cuts through indifference curve U at point c. Therefore, given the limit on health status, the budget line must be shifted up by LL' to make it cut through point c. The victim's (corner solution) optimum is then at point c, giving the same level of welfare (on indifference curve U) as before the accident.

Figure 6.4 illustrates the general principles of awarding compensation for injury. The analysis can easily be used to show compensation for damage to property or for other forms of loss. In practice, the courts cannot operate with great precision in each case as it would be too costly to estimate accurate indifference maps for victims. Over the years a 'tariff' has emerged in which particular frequently encountered injuries attract compensation for suffering based on the assessment of average cases, with adjustments for clear cases of above or below average suffering. Compensation for loss of earnings, which is a relatively straightforward calculation, tends to be assessed on more of a case-by-case basis by estimating the capital sum that must be invested to replicate a victim's expected career earnings.

Carter and Palmer (1991, 1994) have argued that calculations for the loss of an expected future flow of income can be simplified in both principle and practice by recognizing the 'offset rule'. They argue that on average the expected growth (from changes in labour productivity) in a person's income will equal the rate of interest so that both may be ignored in calculating the equivalent capital sum. If this offset is valid, the present value of a stream of lost earnings is simply a person's current earnings multiplied by the number of years for which the loss occurs.

To illustrate the offset rule, assume a simple case in which there is no price or wage inflation. The individual's earnings are expected to grow because of labour productivity growth, but we ignore the effects of possible promotion. To keep the calculation of the present value (PV) simple, assume that the loss occurs over two future time periods. Then:

$$PV = D[(1 + w) / (1 + i)] + D[(1 + w) / (1 + i)]^2 \qquad (6.2)$$

where D = current annual earnings; w = annual growth rate of labour productivity; i = rate of interest. If $w = i$, then condition (6.2) simplifies to:

$$PV = 2D \qquad (6.3)$$

In general under the offset rule, the present value will equal current earnings multiplied by the number of years of loss.

Carter and Palmer have presented empirical evidence for the USA (1991) and for Canada (1994) that supports the use of the offset rule. The evidence suggests that interest rates and labour productivity growth cancel out after allowance is made for inflation. Posner (1992, p.196) similarly notes that calculations can be simplified by deducting inflation from both earnings growth and nominal interest rates.

Arguments arise in assessing loss of earnings concerning the choice of an appropriate rate of interest and in estimating earnings growth. The offset rule allows this task to be considerably simplified. The courts can multiply current earnings by the relevant number of years as a benchmark, average case. Then, an adjustment can be made for above or below average expected earnings growth in compensating the particular victim. We must of course compensate victims as we find them, or the incentive for precaution by the victim will be disturbed (section 6.1.2(c)).

6.5   NO FAULT ALTERNATIVES TO TORT

Most Canadian provinces, several Australian states and about half the American states have enacted no-fault compensation schemes for road accidents. These schemes provide limited compensation for the victims of road accidents, without requiring proof of fault and with the money being paid by insurance companies or by a public agency. These insurance mechanisms are strictly liable for damages once a causal connection is shown between the tortfeasor and the victim. The schemes differ in detail and may or may not permit a victim to bring a separate action in tort. The original models for such schemes were workmen's compensation regulations, such as the National Insurance (Industrial Injuries) Scheme of 1948 in England, which also compensate victims without requiring proof of fault and without deducting money for contributory negligence.

An extreme development of the no-fault approach is the Accident Compensation Commission (ACC) in New Zealand which awards compensation payments for personal injuries from levies on risk creators like employers and motorists and from general taxation. The ACC does not even require that a causal connection be proved between the tortfeasor's actions and the injury: if there is injury then there is an entitlement to compensation. In the New Zealand case, tort liability for injuries following accidents has been abolished and the compensation system has effectively become social security. A further modern example, but outside of the common-law jurisdictions, is the system of insurance against medical misadventure operating in Sweden.

The no-fault alternative to tort is an attempt to provide an insurance scheme incorporating considerable elements of a social-security system. The idea is to avoid lengthy and costly litigation and to ensure that victims are not impoverished because they cannot win a case in tort. The downside of this is that a no-fault system may encourage potential victims of accidents to take inadequate precautions. There is an element of moral hazard attached to any insurance system, e.g. a car owner is likely to be less careful over locking a car if it is fully insured against theft. Under no-fault accident insurance, less care will be taken to avoid accidents if potential victims regard the compensation payments as adequate.

If a no-fault system is in place, it is necessary to rely on the likely inadequacy of compensation, or the possible simultaneous operation of the tort system, to deter excessive risk taking. Nonetheless, policy makers in many countries appear to believe that the cost savings attached to these schemes make them worthwhile. In the UK, proposals were put forward by the Royal Commission on Civil Liability and Compensation for Personal Injury (Pearson Commission, 1978) to introduce no-fault elements into accident law. The Commission noted that the tort system in England had operating costs that were over three-quarters of the value of the annual awards paid. In contrast, the social-security system in the UK pays out benefits on injuries worth over twice the annual figure for tort damages and has operating costs equal to just 10% of the benefits. However, the Commission's proposals did not lead to significant changes in English law.

It is not really appropriate to compare tort law with no-fault systems in terms of the benefit-to-cost ratios as the tort system also creates deterrence, the value of which is difficult to quantify. Also, a great many tort cases are settled before going to court because the system is predictable for tortfeasors and victims. The Pearson Commission estimated that, of 250 000 tort cases, 86% were settled without legal proceedings and over 13% were disposed of without a court hearing which leaves just 1% to be judged in court.

6.6 VICARIOUS LIABILITY

Certain categories of people are vicariously liable for the torts of others. The best example of vicarious liability is in the case of the employer who is strictly liable for the torts of an employee. In *Jefferson* v. *Derbyshire Farmers* (1921) a young employee of the defendant caused a fire, which destroyed a garage workshop, by lighting a cigarette while transferring petrol between cans. The employer was held vicariously liable for the damage.

Posner (1992) cites vicarious liability (*respondeat superior*) as a clear illustration of his thesis that tort law is efficient. Vicarious liability shows that tort law is not simply designed to find a deep pocket from which to compensate victims, even though many (nonetheless excellent) legal experts seem often to view tort in this way (Rogers, 1994). The employer's vicarious liability is limited to torts inflicted by the employee in the course of the employer's business. Posner rightly argues that this shows that the law is aimed at creating deterrence. Vicarious liability ensures that the employer takes care in the selection and supervision of employees, which is a useful preventative measure that can be interpreted as an aspect of the least-cost avoidance of accidents. However, there is nothing that the employer can do to control negligence outside of working time and away from the job and so the law does not expect this.

Cases involving the personal acts of employees in working time do not confound Posner's argument. In the Australian case *Deatons* v. *Flew* (1949) a barmaid threw a glass of beer at the plaintiff during an altercation (an 'intentional tort' of assault rather than a case of negligence). The employer was not held liable, which seems reasonable as it is not clear that employers could control the mood swings of employees. However, employers can be expected to enforce procedures to be followed in situations like keeping order on business premises. This distinction explains the apparent contradiction between *Deatons* v. *Flew* and *Pettersson* v. *Royal Oak Hotel* (1948), in which vicarious liability followed the act of a barman who threw a piece of glass. In *Pettersson*, a New Zealand case, the barman refused drink to a violent customer and was keeping order when he threw broken glass that hit a bystander.

Further support for Posner's view can be found in vicarious liability cases involving motor cars in England. Following *Ormrod* v. *Crosville Motor Services* (1953), lenders of motor vehicles are vicariously liable for the negligence of a driver acting on the owner's behalf. In these cases, it is not clear whether the driver or the owner would have the deeper pocket. However, it is clear that the owner is put on notice to take care in allowing others to drive the vehicle which is a low-cost control on the suitability of drivers.

6.7 PRODUCT LIABILITY

Product-liability law, which is the area of tort concerned with manufacturers' liability for defective products, has emerged and grown in importance throughout the common-law countries in the late twentieth century. There are two elements to the development of this area of law. First, liability has been extended to the users of products regardless of whether they were the original purchasers. Secondly, the liability standard has moved from negligence to strict liability.

Before the evolution of modern product-liability law, a buyer had to sue the seller of a faulty product under the law of contract. The seller, in turn, was indemnified through his contract with the manufacturer. This meant that a non-purchasing (secondary) user of a product had no redress if injured by it. Liability to secondary users was recognized in England following *Donoghue* v. *Stevenson* (1932), in which the plaintiff recovered damages after she drank ginger beer containing a snail although she had not bought the drink herself, extending the manufacturer's duty of care (i.e. a negligence standard) to all foreseeable users of a product. A similar case extending manufacturers' liability for negligence beyond the immediate buyer in the USA is *MacPherson* v. *Buick Motor Co.* (1916), in which the plaintiff recovered damages from the car manufacturer rather than the dealer.

From an economic point of view, the inclusion into tort law of liability to secondary users avoids the need for the creation of a complex chain of contractual liability. Without liability, people would not be covered against injury from items that they used but had not purchased unless they could claim negligence or had their own insurance. Also, it may be difficult for non-purchasing users to obtain information on the product, so that care by the manufacturer would be the least-cost form of accident avoidance, although this type of argument is not without its critics (Calfee and Rubin, 1992).

In the USA, strict liability for defects in products emerged comparatively early on. In *Escola* v. *Coca Cola* (1944), a waitress was injured by an exploding bottle and Coca Cola was held liable even though no negligence was present. The *Restatement (Second) of Torts*, section 402A (American Law Institute, 1965) clearly adopts the principle of strict liability for defects in products.[7] American law has now begun to move on to a form of absolute product liability in which no defence to liability is permitted. In *Beshada* v. *Johns-Manville Products* (1982), the defendant was held liable for failing to warn of the dangers of asbestos even though these were not known at the time (the 1950s). Many writers see the *Beshada* ruling as indicating a judicial search for a 'deep pocket' to pay damages that amount to social security payments (Priest, 1985).

In England, modern product-liability law operates through Part I of the Consumer Protection Act 1987 which is based on a 1985 EU Directive (EC, 1985) and imposes strict liability upon manufacturers for injuries resulting from defects in their products. A defect arises if the safety of a product is 'not such as persons generally are entitled to expect'. In England, strict liability for products is not absolute since there are defences open to a manufacturer, who may claim, e.g. that the defect was not present when the product was sold. A most important defence is that the state of scientific knowledge at the time the product was made and sold did not allow the producer to discover the defect which rules out the type of ruling that resulted in the *Beshada* case in the USA. In particular, this 'state of the art' defence removes or reduces liability in some cases where drugs are discovered to have adverse effects long after their initial trials.

The law of product liability is a controversial area. In principle, the introduction of strict liability can be efficient, as long as the manufacturer is the least-cost avoider of accidents, which could be because the user of a product has little or no influence over the safe use of a product. Landes and Posner (1987) argue that this became increasingly true as the twentieth century progressed. Increased mechanization and the complexity of products can be regarded as raising the costs of consumers gathering information. If the steps taken by manufacturers at the design and production stage are the dominant influence on product safety, then strict liability does create a full incentive for them to introduce cost-effective safety precautions. Priest (1985) believes that modern product-liability law ignores the incentives required to encourage users to take care and, as mentioned above, has been driven by a wish to see corporations bear the costs of accidents.

For strict liability to be efficient when the user can influence safety outcomes, it is necessary to allow the manufacturer to cite product misuse or voluntary assumption of the risks as defences. The first defence rules out claims by consumers who have undertaken inappropriate acts with products, e.g. allowing electrically powered garden implements to become submerged in water. The manufacturer cannot prevent accidents from inappropriate use at least cost and it is most efficient for the consumer to be fully deterred from such practices. The defence of voluntary assumption of the risk allows consumers to be warned of risks. Then, if the user is the least-cost avoider, consumers will buy the product and assume the risk. If the user is not the least-cost avoider, consumers can avoid the risk-shifting manufacturer's product and pay a premium to buy from a producer prepared to bear the risk. In many US states, these defences are not permitted nor are they permitted in the UK (or, indeed, in the EU). This analysis implies that modern product-liability law is only efficient providing consumer behaviour is of no consequence in influencing the safe use of products.

Absolute liability, as in some US cases, is even more questionable in terms of efficiency. The same questions arise over providing incentives for consumers to take care where the user is the least-cost avoider. Moreover, applying retroactive liability to manufacturers when their contemporary knowledge could not have indicated a danger, as in the *Beshada* case, cannot create incentives to take care.

It is noticeable that most of the post-war growth in litigation in the USA is in the area of product liability (Markesinis, 1990). Rubin and Bailey (1994) explain this growth in terms of the rent-seeking tendencies of lawyers as a special-interest group. Their explanation of the strict-liability character of modern product-liability law is quite distinct from Landes and Posner's (1987) efficiency hypothesis and Priest's (1985) ideological explanation. In particular, Rubin and Bailey note that the US legal system operates to the disadvantage of manufacturers. A decision in one state benefits plaintiffs (and their lawyers) in that state and harms manufacturers in all states, as a manufacturer who sells in a state can be sued there. They also note that the American Association of Trial Lawyers was formed as a powerful interest group right in the heart of the period during which pressure began to mount for reforms of product-liability law. There is also statistical evidence in favour of the rent-seeking thesis: both the number of lawyers per capita (LPC) and the rate of growth of LPC in a state turned out to be statistically significant determinants of revisions to product-liability law. The relevance of this analysis is not confined to the USA because the 1985 EU Directive, which initiated the 1987 Consumer Protection Act in the UK, was influenced by American practices.

6.8 COMPENSATION FOR WRONGFUL DEATH

An old principle in tort law was that death could not be complained of as an injury in a civil court. Although that approach disappeared in common-law countries in the nineteenth century, it remains true that claims are largely based on replacing the income of the deceased for the benefit of descendants. In a general sense, it is impossible to compensate a dead person for their loss, i.e. one cannot value life. However, it is possible to design a compensation scheme that deters unreasonable risk taking with life.

If an average person would accept £10 to accept a 0.00001 increase in the risk of death if some precaution is not taken (e.g. buying a cheaper car without a safety feature), then the court should award £10/0.00001 = £1 million as damages if a fatal accident occurs. This will cause the precaution to be taken whenever the cost is below £10 (e.g. consumers demand and the car maker fits the safety feature if it costs less than £10). The valuation of small risks is less of a problem than might be thought, there are indeed studies of willingness to pay for safety improvements in motor vehicles (Landes and Posner 1987, 189n), although assessment might well prove to be highly costly.

SUMMARY AND CONCLUSIONS

We have concentrated on negligence and product liability in examining the economics of tort law. In negligence cases, the choice is between strict liability, contributory negligence and comparative negligence standards in assessing responsibility for a tort. We showed that, providing the legal standard of care is set at the efficient level and given full information for the court, any form of negligence rule provides a full incentive for efficient precaution by both parties. Strict liability is also efficient as long as the victim is unable to influence the probability of an accident occurring. Relaxing the assumption of full information over levels of care implies that comparative negligence is the superior negligence standard.

Product-liability law has evolved into strict liability over the late twentieth century, with some evidence of absolute liability in the USA. Strict liability for product defects can encourage firms to take care and is efficient if victims cannot influence precaution. However, some writers believe that product liability shows a search for a deep pocket to compensate victims and some argue that the growth of this area of the law has favoured the legal profession.

ENDNOTES

1. The word comes from the Latin root suggesting physical twisting and consequent damage.
2. This is not required for intentional torts like assault or battery, which are actionable *per se*.
3. Arising from the same fire discussed in relation to *The Wagon Mound (No.1)* discussed above.
4. The English rule on damages to property from the operations of railway companies was strict liability, which Landes and Posner (1987) attribute to the greater population density and lower economic value of railways in England compared with the USA.
5. Any dominant strategy equilibrium is Nash. The conclusion that the parties take optimal care depends upon the assumption that courts can discover actual care levels with certainty.
6. Risk aversion arises if an individual would pay to avoid being given an equal chance of winning or losing a set sum of money.
7. The *Restatement* is an effort to codify the law, which, while lacking the formal status of statute, is taken to be a reliable summary of the law in America.

7 | The economics of crime

There is a considerable body of economic analysis examining crime as a special case of rational maximizing behaviour. To some extent, this literature has developed separately from the economic analysis of law as a part of mainstream applied economics. Economists have mostly concerned themselves with the economics of criminal deterrence. There is a recent trend towards integrating this work into the modern economic analysis of law by focusing on the way the system of criminal justice operates compared with areas of private law like tort.

7.1 THE NATURE OF CRIMINAL ACTIVITY

A person commits a crime by violating a statute, e.g. by robbing or killing someone. This may seem an obvious statement but it is not obvious why many injurious acts are regarded as crimes when others are not. Indeed, some non-injurious acts, such as unfinished robberies, can be 'victimless' crimes. Also, in the past, many actions now treated as crimes were treated as torts. We need to examine the key features of criminal law that set it apart from its civil counterpart.

The standard of proof is different in the case of crime. First, the prosecution must prove its case beyond reasonable doubt, which is a tougher criterion than the one used in civil disputes. In a tort case, by contrast, it is enough to show that the defendant was negligent – by the standards of a reasonable person – in causing the injury. The tougher criterion in a criminal case reflects the penalties the court may apply, which are potentially severe. Punishment in a criminal case goes beyond compensating the victim and imposes harm on the criminal.

Secondly, in most cases, the prosecution must show that the criminal intended to commit the crime. There must be *mens rea* or intent to cause harm. This again contrasts with civil cases, e.g. nuisance is defined independently of the state of mind of the tortfeasor. In terms of a spectrum of harm, injurious acts resulting from negligence are the subject of tort actions whereas intentional harm is dealt with by the potentially more severe sanctions of the criminal law. One explanation of this distinction is that criminal law aims to suppress the criminal frame of mind which is identified by the demonstration of *mens rea*.

The exception to the requirement to show intent is the case of the strict-liability crime, such as possession of an offensive weapon or narcotics. In these instances, possession may reasonably be taken to imply intent to use the items. It would anyway be virtually impossible to distinguish accidental from deliberate possession. Therefore, these examples of strict-liability crimes are not really inconsistent with the general requirement for intent to be proved.

The third major distinguishing characteristic of criminal law is that the harm has a public element about it. Crime disrupts social codes of behaviour that are thought to be beneficial to all. Crimes such as murder, assault or robbery are disturbing to many people and not just to their victims. There is a wider public interest in prosecuting the criminal than in suing the typical tortfeasor. As Shavell's (1985, 1993) arguments imply, the victim of a crime (or a relative in a case of murder) has an incentive to sue to reclaim personal losses only. However, this will not obtain compensation for the fear and anxiety experienced by dispersed observers of the crime. Notice that the victim can take an action in tort against a criminal: the criminal law comes in on top of civil remedies. Also, where someone causes an accident through gross negligence such as drunkenness while driving a train, the criminal law steps in to prosecute for criminal negligence. Finally in this regard, the prosecution of public nuisance, e.g. blocking a public highway, by the public authorities also supports the hypothesis that it is mainly the dispersed nature of damage that causes the state to step in.

It may also be that there is generally a low probability of apprehension in the case of many criminal acts, particularly as the criminal intends to hide the crime (Posner, 1985). Therefore, relatively severe penalties will be needed to deter the harm. For example, if there is only a 50% chance of catching the thief of a car valued at £1000, the fine must be set at just over £2000 if the expected value of stealing is to be negative. Action in tort would for the most part succeed only in reclaiming £1000 damages. On a related theme, criminals are often members of impoverished sections of the community who would not be able to pay damages, particularly as they often sell stolen property at below market value. Then, the only real way to create a deterrent is to impose a custodial or other non-monetary sanction. These considerations suggest that the coercive power of the state is useful in deterring criminal behaviour.

Finally, most crime is socially wasteful and represents a classic form of rent-seeking behaviour (Tullock, 1968). Criminals devote resources to pure redistribution of existing goods without creating anything new. Their potential victims also devote resources to security devices, to paying insurance companies and indeed, to funding the cost of the police service. Similarly, a thief may value a stolen item at an amount (e.g. £20) which is below its owner's valuation (e.g. £50). We cannot be sure that resources move to their highest-valued uses when items are stolen. Crime is typically doubly wasteful.[1]

7.2 CRIMINAL DETERRENCE

Gary Becker's (1968) work represents the first serious attempt to apply standard economic analysis to general criminal behaviour. The fundamental point of departure is that people are rational maximizing beings. Therefore, we should find that:

1. crime rates respond to the costs and benefits of committing crimes;
2. people respond to deterring incentives.

It follows that devoting resources to detection, conviction and punishment should influence the level of crime. As Buchanan and Hartley (1992) point out, for this to be true, people need not be rational all the time. It is enough that varying the expected penalty influences criminal behaviour at the margin for deterrence to work. Becker may be credited with articulating the deterrence hypothesis, which has influenced not only economists, but also some sociologists and policy makers.

The main alternatives to the deterrence hypothesis are claims that crime results from biological influences like mental illness or from social factors such as unemployment. The policy implications of these alternative explanations are that we need to tackle problems like unemployment and poverty and/or improve the mental health of the population. To many economists, the alternatives to the deterrence hypothesis are not convincing. In explaining rising crime rates, e.g. for crimes against property in advanced societies in the 1990s, we would have to show that poverty had been rising or that the mental health of the criminal classes had suddenly deteriorated. Strictly biological accounts of crime are also often subject to criticism (Fishbein, 1990). As (the Australians) Buchanan and Hartley (1992) point out, if criminals were genetically predisposed towards a life of crime, it would be hard to explain why the original convict population of Australia did not beget a nation of criminals. Furthermore, the common observation that members of the criminal classes are frequently of below average intelligence (Wilson and Herrnstein, 1985) is not in itself an argument against the deterrence hypothesis: their low intelligence may limit their options, leading them rationally to turn to crime unless deterred. With few exceptions, statistical studies fail to give a major role to non-deterrence factors (Pyle and Deadman, 1994).

7.2.1 Deterrence and the supply and demand for crime

The deterrence hypothesis is illustrated by Figure 7.1. The horizontal axis shows the amount of crime committed by an individual, which could be measured by the number of offences and the vertical axis measures costs and benefits. If the marginal costs (MC_1) of criminal activity rise and the marginal benefits (MB) fall, as shown, there is an optimal level of crime (C^*) where marginal cost intersects marginal benefit. Marginal cost shows the minimum return required before an individual would engage in successive units of crime: it is therefore a supply function for crime. Marginal benefit shows the maximum the individual would pay for the opportunity to undertake successive units of crime, ignoring his costs, and can be regarded as the demand for crime.

For some people, the intersection of supply and demand will give a corner solution to Figure 7.1, e.g. if marginal cost (supply) takes the position MC_2, meaning that they do not engage in crime. As one example, the higher position of marginal cost could be consistent with worrying about the effect on one's reputation if criminal associations were apparent. The costs of criminal activity are not necessarily just monetary ones associated with preparing to commit crimes. Similarly, marginal benefits are not limited to monetary gains, e.g. some sadistic thugs obtain direct pleasure from engaging in acts of violence. We would nonetheless need to measure the individual's willingness to pay for the benefits or for avoiding costs.

Economics suggests we can influence individuals to reduce their criminal activity by undertaking policies to shift the marginal cost function upwards and the marginal benefit function downwards. Becker (1968) argues that comparing the costs and benefits of clearing up a particular crime allows us to find an optimum level of crime prevention. It is important to remember that no policies are costless, and it is unlikely to be sensible to try and stop all crime, which would almost certainly be too costly to achieve. We pick up on the idea of optimal crime and punishment further below (section 7.3.1).

The deterrence approach is not necessarily incompatible with alternative approaches emphasizing wider social factors or apparently non-economic individual characteristics. For example, in Figure 7.1, a

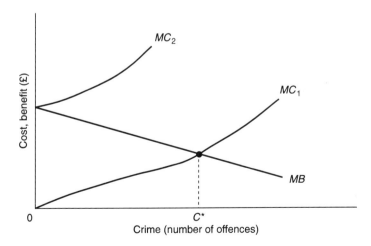

Figure 7.1 Rational crime. MB = marginal benefit of crime; MC_1 = marginal cost of crime; MC_2 = alternative marginal cost of crime.

psychological predisposition towards crime might shift the marginal cost function to the right, reflecting lower psychic (conscience-based) costs from engaging in crime. We can fit various shift factors like this into a model of rational crime. The real question is empirical: which factors influence criminal behaviour in a major way?

The deterrence hypothesis can be formulated, following Becker (1968), using a little calculus. Taking any crime as an example, we can write:

$$EU = pU(Y - f) + (1 - p) U (Y)$$

where p = probability of capture and punishment; U = utility (assumed measurable); EU = expected utility; f = value of punishment; Y = income if undetected. Increasing p by a small amount (dp) implies EU changes by $dp[U(Y - f) - U(Y)]$, which must be negative. The cost-benefit calculation of the rational criminal implies that increasing the probability of detection, perhaps by expanding the police force,[2] deters criminal behaviour. Similarly, increasing the severity of the punishment (f) by a small amount (df) implies EU changes by $df(p)(\partial U/\partial f)$, which is again negative since $\partial U/\partial f$ (the rate of change of utility with respect to punishment) should be negative. Increasing the probability of capture and punishment and increasing the severity of the punishment both reduce the criminal's expected utility and should deter crime.

Cameron (1988) points out that there are several possible economic reasons why deterrence might not be found. First, private deterrence effort might fall as public deterrence increases. Individuals might be less vigilant about crime if they felt the authorities had it under control. Secondly, some crime could be displaced to another offence type, time or location. Also, if criminals have target incomes, deterrence could imply that more crime would occur, e.g. there could be more attempted break-ins that the police managed to halt. Finally in this respect, the deterrence of established criminals could encourage the entry of replacements into the crime 'industry': deterring organized drug traffickers might let in amateur drug 'mules'.

However, statistical work tends to support the deterrence hypothesis in terms of the effect of arrest and conviction rates and sentence length. We look more closely (section 7.2.3) at some of the statistical results after a brief examination of the impact of deterrence variables on the behaviour of a risk-taking individual.

7.2.2 Risk taking and deterrence

Becker (1968) argues that increasing the probability of capture and punishment should deter more strongly than increasing the severity of sentencing, if criminals are risk takers. This suggestion can be examined with the aid of Figure 7.2 which shows a utility function for a risk taker. Utility is shown on the vertical axis and is assumed to be measurable for purposes of illustration. The money value of pay-offs is

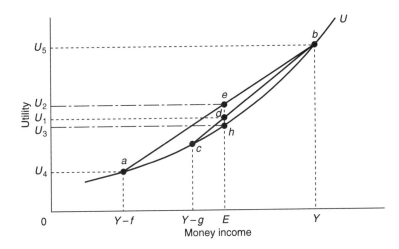

Figure 7.2 Risk taking and deterrence. U = utility.

shown on the horizontal axis. The utility function is convex when viewed from below which is consistent with risk taking. To keep things simple, we also assume that the crime involves the theft of money and may be punished by imposing a monetary fine.

Figure 7.2 shows four possible levels of money income for a criminal. The highest level, Y, results if a crime is successfully completed without detection. The two lower levels, $(Y - f)$ and $(Y - g)$, give the post-crime income after the imposition with certainty of either a high fine, f, or a low fine, g. However, detection is not certain. Point e, which is halfway along a line joining points a and b on the utility function, shows the expected outcome if the probability of punishment is 0.5. Reading down from e, the expected money income is given by E (i.e. $(0.5(Y - f)$ $+ 0.5Y))$. The expected utility associated with e is shown as U_2 on the vertical axis $(0.5U_4 + 0.5U_5)$. If point e were closer to a, the probability of punishment would be higher.

It follows that point d, directly below e on a line joining c to b and reflecting the lower fine valued at g, results in the same expected income of E. Point d is more than half the distance from b to c. Therefore, d represents a lower fine but higher probability of punishment compared with point e. Since U_1 is less than U_2, the criminal prefers e to d. A low fine coupled with a high probability of punishment is a greater deterrent than a high fine with a low probability when both packages give the same expected income.

This result depends upon the convex shape of the utility function which reflects risk taking by the criminal. To show that convexity implies risk taking, consider an individual at point h with an income of E. The utility from E is U_3. Since e is above h, the individual prefers a gamble in which there is a 0.5 probability of income being either higher or lower by the same amount and where the expected value of income is unchanged. The convexity of the utility function implies the individual is risk loving.

7.2.3 Tests of the deterrence hypothesis

Statistical tests tend to support the deterrence hypothesis in terms of the effect of arrest and conviction rates and sentence length on the amount of crime. The studies examine the effects of a range of criminal-justice and more general variables in determining a variety of types of crime, covering both property and violent crime. Property crime mainly comprises burglary and theft whereas violent crime consists of robberies like muggings as well as the more obvious categories of murder and assault. One common but surprising result of the empirical work is that expenditure on the police does not appear to deter crime (Carr-Hill and Stern, 1979). Cameron (1988) interprets the failure of expenditure on police forces to have negative effects on crime variables as indicative of a failure for statistical studies to support the deterrence hypothesis. This is an unreasonable conclusion: expenditure on the police is not necessarily correlated with arrests if the extra members of the force are desk bound. We now look more closely at some of the statistical results.

Cameron (1988) suggests the typical statistical model of crime has the following three ingredients:

$$C/N = f(A/C, S, Z)$$
$$A/C = f(C/N, P, Z)$$
$$P = f(C/N, Z)$$

where C = crime rate; A = arrest rate; N = population; S = sentence length; P = expenditure on or number of police and Z = vector (list) of other exogenous variables. The studies have a number of commonly occurring results. First, they support the deterrence hypothesis but give different detailed results for different crimes. Secondly, they give different weights to the effect of detection and conviction relative to the severity of sentencing in deterring crime. Finally, studies can be plagued by data problems, e.g. it can be difficult to obtain consistent long-run data in studies for the USA owing to the separate state jurisdictions. We look first at a series of studies testing the deterrence hypothesis primarily in relation to property crime.

Ehrlich's (1973) pioneering statistical work was based on US robbery data for 1940, 1950 and 1960 and used regression techniques. He found that a higher probability of conviction implied a lower robbery rate. In addition, a higher average sentence implied a lower robbery rate for 1940 and 1960. This study is usually interpreted as giving early support to the deterrence hypothesis. One criticism of it is that data on the criminal justice system and crime variables may not be fully comparable across different states. A study following on from Ehrlich (1973) is Blumstein and Nagin (1977) who examined evasion of the US military draft in the 1960s and 1970s. Data on the US draft are consistent across different states. A greater probability of conviction implied lower evasion of the draft, supporting the deterrence hypothesis.

Wolpin (1978a) used data from England and Wales for the period 1894–67 to test the deterrence hypothesis using statistical time-series analysis. The advantage of these data was that they had been compiled on a consistent basis for a long period. Wolpin's study thereby avoids the problems attached to using US data. He found evidence of a deterrence effect from both the probability of punishment and from the severity of sentencing, particularly for property crime. Wolpin's results show that the deterrent from increasing the probability of punishment exceeds that from increasing the severity of sentencing. This last result is consistent with Becker's (1968) suggestion that there should be a greater deterrence effect from increasing the probability of capture and punishment compared with increasing the severity of sentencing, if criminals are risk takers.

Willis (1983) also used data from England and Wales, and used the clear-up rate for particular crimes as a measure of the probability of capturing and punishing criminals. Although Willis's focus was partly on regional variations in crime, the study usefully produced general results supporting Wolpin (1978a). Again, the strongest deterrence came from increasing the probability of punishment, although there was also deterrence from increasing the severity of sentences. Willis's study highlights differences between categories of crime. A 1% increase in the clear-up rate:

1. reduces thefts by 0.8%
2. reduces sex crimes by 1%
3. has no effect on violent crime.

These figures describe the elasticity of crime with respect to the clear-up rate. This elasticity can be defined as the proportional change in the crime variable in response to a 1% increase in the clear-up rate. In everyday terms, elasticity is a standardized measure of the responsiveness of a variable to changes in another, with a higher figure indicating greater responsiveness. Note the complete inelasticity of violent crime (excluding sex crime) in this study which raises the question whether some forms of violence may be less firmly based in rational behaviour than property crime.

Work carried out by Pyle (1983) using several UK data sets for the period 1950–80 also found deterrence from both the probability of conviction and from increases in the severity of sentences. He also found that increasing the probability of conviction had the stronger deterrence effect. The elasticity of offences with respect to the conviction rate was 0.9 but was only 0.3 with respect to sentence length. Pyle also derived results showing how deterrence differs among property crimes. A 1% increase in the clear-up rate reduces:

1. burglaries by 1.6%
2. robbery by 0.7%
3. thefts by 0.2%.

In a study based on data from Australian states and territories, Withers (1984) concluded that the major reliable determinants of crime rates were committal and imprisonment rates. Committal rates reflect the probability of trial whereas the imprisonment rate is a severity measure. Despite Wither's (1984, p.182) 'prior expectation', more attitudinal variables, such as television-viewing habits, were not statistically significant determinants of crime.[3]

Summing up, statistical studies support the existence of deterrence effects from variables reflecting the probability of punishment and the severity of sentencing. Increasing the probability of punishment has a greater effect than increasing the severity of sentences. Property crime, in particular, would seem to be highly influenced by deterrence factors. The support found for the deterrence hypothesis is of great academic interest. It shows that criminal behaviour is like most forms of behaviour and is influenced by costs and benefits.

7.2.4 Cost of deterrence

Before the results of deterrence studies become useful for formulating public policy towards crime, we need information on the cost of particular deterrence instruments. Just because an instrument is technically highly deterring does not mean that it is good value for money: a less deterring but cheaper one might be better. Pyle (1983, 1989, 1993) has developed his work in terms of assessing the cost effectiveness of alternative instruments of deterrence.

Pyle (1989, 1993) has calculated the cost of achieving a 1% reduction in property crime by alternative means, as shown in Table 7.1. The obvious conclusion is that although the elasticity of deterrence is technically higher for increases in the probability of conviction, increasing the severity of sentences is more cost effective as a means of beating property crime. Increasing police numbers to increase the probability of conviction looks like particularly poor value. Interestingly, between 1979 and 1991 when recorded total crime increased by 112%, the UK authorities increased the number of police by 12% and increased the number of people imprisoned by 8%. The policy response runs somewhat counter to the findings in Table 7.1. According to figures published by the British Crime Survey, crime rose by a further 18% between 1991 and 1993, although Home Office figures

Table 7.1 Cost of reducing property crime by 1%

Option	Cost (£m)
Increased police numbers	51.2
Increased number of offenders imprisoned	4.9
Increased average length of sentence	3.6

Source: Pyle (1989).

show a fall of 5.5% for the year to June 1994.[4] Governments may wish to increase police numbers for political reasons as this is a highly visible response to rising crime.

7.2.5 Unemployment and crime

The effect on crime rates of changes in unemployment levels has been subjected to much statistical testing and is currently topical. The unemployment hypothesis suggests people are driven to crime by deprivation and is often interpreted as an alternative to the deterrence hypothesis. However, the unemployment hypothesis need not be inconsistent with Becker's (1968) view of crime: the unemployed have a lower opportunity cost attached to using their time in criminal pursuits. In fact, there turns out to be little support in empirical work for an effect from unemployment.

Cook and Zarkin (1985) use regression techniques on US data to show that there are small increases in burglaries and robberies during times of recession. However, their results show there is no effect on homicide rates – and thefts of motor vehicles actually fall in a recession and rise in the up-swing. The studies by Wolpin (1978a) and Willis (1983), discussed in connection with the deterrence hypothesis, used data for England and Wales and showed a weak effect on crime from unemployment. The same conclusion is reached by Pyle (1989), also using data on England and Wales and by Withers (1984) using Australian data. The survey by Box (1987) also concludes that the effect of unemployment is weak.

Field (1990) uses changes in consumption levels rather than unemployment to assess the effects of deprivation on crime. The reasoning behind this is that consumption changes have a more immediate motivational impact than becoming unemployed. Field undertakes a time-series analysis using UK data and finds evidence of a 'bounce-back' effect. Decreases in consumption are initially followed by an increase in property crime but the crime level returns to its normal trend value in the longer term. Field concludes that there is no real long-run relationship between changes in consumption levels and crime rates.

Using data for Scotland, Reilly and Witt (1992) estimated several models which all appeared to support a robust link between crime and unemployment. Their data comprised 15 annual observations from 1974–88 for each of the six regions of Scotland, taking the general crime rate as the dependent variable. Pyle and Deadman (1994) are highly critical of this study as they could not replicate its results using a data set updated to include 1988–91. The earlier study ignores a period of falling unemployment from 1987–90 which occurred while crime continued on a rising trend. Adding just three observations to the data set renders the unemployment variable statistically insignificant in Reilly and Witt's models. Pyle and Deadman also carried out a separate time-series analysis, using quarterly data to increase the available number of observations, which also failed to find a statistically significant role for unemployment.

Pyle and Deadman (1994) point out that testing theories of crime using cross-sectional data (e.g. looking across different regions) is particularly problematic. A correlation between, e.g. crime and unemployment may not show a causal relationship but, rather, may reflect the influence of a third variable such as poor educational standards. Pyle and Deadman are particularly concerned about crime spillovers: an area with high unemployment may be less able to raise local taxes to spend on policing and may therefore attract criminals from other areas. The unemployed would not be committing the crimes but researchers would find a high correlation between unemployment and crime. A similar effect would follow if reduced policing in a poorer area simply encouraged the existing criminals to greater activity. Again, a meaningless correlation would be observed between crime and unemployment. These criticisms, if valid, could undermine Reilly and Witt's (1992) findings for the unextended data set over the period 1974–88.

7.2.6 Violent crime

Most countries have experienced increases in violent crime levels in recent years. In the UK violence against the person, which includes murder, wounding and assault, grew from under 10 000 to over 200 000 annual incidents between 1946 and 1991 with most of this growth occurring in the less serious area of assault (Pyle, 1993). The figure for 1991 is equivalent to a rate of 363 per 100 000 of population. More recent Home Office figures show violent crime still to be rising: by 5% in the year to June 1994.[5] In the USA, according to broadly comparable figures from the Department of Justice, the violent-crime rate stood at 675 per 100 000 of population in 1991, having exhibited similar growth.

Violent crime may be subject to a wider range of influences than property crime. For example, Withers (1984) found that deterrence variables were at best weakly significant determinants of violent crimes. Secondly, studies of capital punishment, which we look at below (section 7.3.3), sometimes support the deterrence hypothesis in relation to murder (Ehrlich, 1975, 1977) and sometimes do not (Passell and Taylor, 1977). A number of studies reveal a role for wider influences on violent crime compared with crime against property.

Field (1990) found a positive correlation between increases in violent crime and upturns in economic activity. The explanation offered is that boom times lead to increased use of leisure facilities and greater interpersonal contact. These are associated with an increase in violent crime. Field also found a positive correlation between the consumption of alcohol and the incidence of violent offences. Walmsley (1986) reaches similar conclusions and cites detailed work showing that over 25% of violent incidents in some British cities occur immediately after the public houses close. Policy responses to these findings could include such measures as staggering closure times and increasing policing in sensitive areas at closure times or perhaps increasing the cost of alcoholic beverages (Pyle, 1993).

However, we should not forget that some empirical work shows that criminal-justice variables also deter violent crime. In the USA, Murray and Cox (1979) tracked 317 youths after they were released following their first custodial sentences. The youths had an average record of 13 arrests each prior to their imprisonment for an average of ten months. Their offences included homicide, rape, assault, car theft, armed robbery and burglary. After imprisonment, their arrest records fell by two-thirds on average. A comparison group of non-imprisoned juvenile offenders did not show the same reduction in the rate of rearrest. It is unlikely that the imprisoned youths were learning from other crooks how to avoid arrest to an extent that would account for such a large drop. As Murray and Cox comment, no school is as good as that!

Witte (1980) also looked at rearrest rates, and examined the characteristics of 641 men released over a three-year period in North Carolina. The higher the probability of conviction for a crime, the lower was the number of subsequent arrests per month released. Increases in the severity of prior punishment had a stronger deterrent effect compared with increases in the probability of conviction for violent crime. Increasing the probability of conviction had a stronger deterrent effect on reoffending in the case of crimes against property.

It is true that non-deterrence variables like alcohol consumption and wealth effects have a greater influence on the rate of violent crime than on the rate of property crime. Nonetheless, many applied studies indicate that deterrence variables are still relevant to the decision to commit violent crime.

7.3 PUNISHMENTS

In this section we examine various economic issues concerning the use of punishment as a means of influencing criminal behaviour. Mainly this involves comparing the use of fines with imprisonment. However, there are other sanctions that deserve some attention. Capital punishment, in particular, has generated a considerable literature and is considered separately in its own subsection (section 7.3.3).

7.3.1 Optimal punishment

Pyle's (1983) work suggests it is cost effective to increase the severity of sentencing compared with, e.g. increasing policing levels. His conclusions came from comparing the costs of using different methods to achieve a 10% reduction in levels of property crime. This was very much a cost-effectiveness study and still does not give optimal levels for particular policies. The distinction between cost effective and optimal levels of deterrence is illustrated by Figure 7.3.

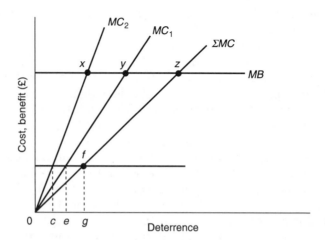

Figure 7.3 Cost-effectiveness of deterrents. MC = marginal cost of deterrence; MB = marginal benefit of deterrence.

In Figure 7.3, we assume there are two alternative forms of deterrence, which is measured as a projected reduction in a crime rate. Marginal cost for the high-cost deterrent (e.g. policing) is shown by MC_2, whereas MC_1 refers to a low-cost alternative (e.g. increasing sentence length). In the case of policing, MC_2 measures the costs of increasing policing hours to achieve an additional unit of deterrence. Similarly, MC_1 shows the marginal cost of increasing average sentence length to achieve the additional unit of deterrence. The marginal benefit of deterrence is assumed to be constant and equal for the two forms of deterrence, as shown by the line labelled MB.

If there are spending constraints, then we maximize deterrence using the available alternatives keeping within the budget constraint. Maximum deterrence for any budget is found by using the cheapest solution (prison) initially and then by switching between policing and prison, depending on which is cheapest to use to obtain an increment of deterrence. For example, $0e$ prison and $0c$ policing together give the lowest possible cost for achieving $0g$ deterrence (at a marginal cost of a for either method). We can show the marginal cost of deterrence from combining the two methods by horizontally summing MC_1 and MC_2, giving the line labelled ΣMC in Figure 7.3. The area under ΣMC gives the total cost of particular levels of deterrence, e.g. $0fg$ is the cost of $0g$ deterrence. It follows that a given budget of $0fg$ should be spent on $0c$ policing and $0e$ prison for cost effective deterrence.

If we had no spending constraints, we would expand deterrence to a level associated with point z, where marginal benefit equals marginal cost. This would place us at point x for expenditure on police and at point y for prison. Notice that in the optimum for both the constrained and unconstrained case both forms of deterrence have the same marginal cost.

7.3.2 Imprisonment versus fines

Imprisoning an offender has one major advantage for the population at large: it incapacitates him and prevents further offences being committed against the general public.[6] At the same time, rehabilitation of the criminal is made possible. Also, we know from earlier sections of this chapter that there is a deterrent effect on the incarcerated and on others. A final advantage of imprisonment is that it may gratify a sense of retribution for law-abiding members of society. All of these effects may be regarded as economic benefits.

The costs of imprisonment are generally high, however, which explains why alternatives such as fines are often used. First there are direct costs of imprisonment: the costs of buildings, meals, and prison officers. In the UK in 1994 these were an average of approximately £27 000 per year for each prisoner, although the costs of special units such as the one at Barlinnie in Scotland can be much higher at around £70 000.[7] There are also less obvious costs in the shape of the opportunity costs of prisoners' skills and time which they cannot use while incarcerated.

Fines raise money for the state and are virtually costless to operate. They are thus a very attractive option where there are no special reasons to use imprisonment. If offenders were always solvent, the authorities would prefer fines to prison (unless there were non-economic grounds for jail) as fines are less costly to administer. This is illustrated in Figure 7.4, which is based on deterrence indifference curves – for the criminal – between the severity of a fine and of imprisonment. Any deterrence indifference curve (like DI or DI_1) shows the combinations of fine and imprisonment that will produce the same reduction in a particular form of criminal behaviour. Higher indifference curves show greater deterrence.

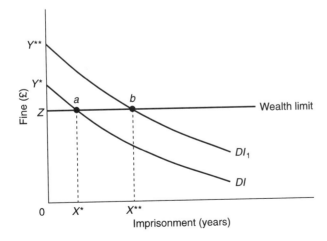

Figure 7.4 Fines versus imprisonment.

With no constraint on the criminal's wealth, the fine is the least-cost solution. We can reach any level of deterrence, such as Y^* or Y^{**}, simply by imposing a heavy enough fine and there is no problem about the criminal paying this. With the limit on wealth shown in Figure 7.4 there is a problem. The criminal cannot be made to pay more than Z as a fine. The authorities can only achieve increases in criminal deterrence by moving to points on the indifference curves like a and b, which require X^* and X^{**} years of imprisonment along with a fine of Z, which will be costly. The existence of a wealth constraint for the criminal may imply that budgetary limits for the authorities restrict deterrence to DI, if, e.g. X^* is the maximum level of affordable imprisonment. Without the constraint, the authorities could just set a high fine and achieve deterrence on DI_1 at point Y^{**}.

Apart from fines and imprisonment, other sanctions comprise such things as orders for probation or for compulsory community service. Probation involves the close supervision of a convicted offender and occurs outside of prison. Costs are saved but there is still the possibility of encouraging rehabilitation. Compulsory community service imposes costs on convicted criminals but again avoids the costs of imprisonment. In the US case, unusually among advanced societies, there is also the possibility of capital punishment which we discuss in a more specialized subsection below.

7.3.3 Capital punishment

Capital punishment is mostly abolished in developed countries. Nonetheless, there are periodic debates in the UK and overseas about whether it should be reintroduced. Also, the death penalty is still used by 36 states in the USA. The use of capital punishment is a continuing issue of public-policy debate in many countries. One question concerns whether there is a deterrent effect on murder from having a death penalty.

An early empirical study by Ehrlich (1975) used a Becker-type model in which the murderer maximizes utility by comparing the costs and benefits of the crime. Time-series data were used for the USA for the period 1933–69. Ehrlich represented the benefits of murder by property-crime variables because murder was correlated with property crime. The benefits of murder were determined by data on unemployment, levels of wealth and the age structure and racial composition of the population. The costs of murder (to the murderer) were measured by alternative measures of the hazard of punishment: the probability of arrest for murder; the probability of conviction given arrest and the probability of execution given conviction. Ehrlich predicted the relative strength of these deterrents to be in the order just given.

Ehrlich's results showed that the murder rate was negatively and significantly correlated with the arrest, conviction and execution probabilities, with the relative strength of deterrence in this order as predicted. One striking conclusion was that one extra execution in a year would deter eight murders, which was famously quoted in the US Supreme Court, in the case of *Gregg* v. *Georgia* in 1976. A less quoted result was that the deterrent effect of improved labour-market conditions was greater than for the justice variables. Ehrlich (1977) also supports these results.

There are a number of possible criticisms of Ehrlich's work. First, does deterrence logically follow from conviction? Capital punishment might make juries less willing to convict, in which case it might not act as a deterrent. There was in fact a fall in the number of murderers found insane by courts in the UK after the abolition of capital punishment in 1965, which suggested the courts were previously looking for excuses not to convict. In this connection, Lempert (1981) re-estimated Ehrlich's model and found that an increase in the use of the death penalty decreased the probability of conviction by 17%.

Secondly, some subsequent researchers found it difficult to replicate Ehrlich's results.One statistical criticism of the work is that its conclusions seem to be sensitive to the functional (e.g. log-linear) form used. Changing the formulation can change the results. Also, Ehrlich's results appear to be sensitive to the time period chosen. Passell and Taylor (1977) re-estimated Ehrlich's model but excluded data for the period 1962–69, in which executions dropped from 47 to zero and crime rose sharply. They found no significant relationship between executions and murder for 1933–61, with the unlikely implication that capital punishment was a deterrent in the USA only for the period after 1962. Leamer (1983) uses a model of capital punishment in his demonstrations of how statistics may be misused to support prior beliefs. Also on a statistical basis, Hoenack and Weiler (1980) argue that the link between capital punishment and deterrence may not exist if studies have been picking up the response of the criminal-justice system to murder.

However, there are several studies that strongly support Ehrlich's broad conclusions. Wolpin (1978b) replicates Ehrlich (1975) on data for England and Wales for 1929–68 and concludes that one extra execution in a year would have deterred four murders. In more recent work, Deadman and Pyle (1993) use the modern technique of intervention analysis on time-series data for England and Wales over the period 1880–1989 and for Scotland for 1884–1989. Their hypothesis is that if socio-economic, demographic and law enforcement variables change slowly over time then murder data should show some inertia. The data in fact show evidence of a significant shift in the trend for murder after abolition of the death penalty in 1965. The effect of abolition is equivalent to about 52 extra murders a year for the UK.

There is some evidence that clearly supports a deterrent effect for capital punishment. However, it does not follow from this that there is a strong economic argument in favour of using a death penalty for murder. The costs of capital punishment are high, so even if it is a deterrent it is not necessarily cost-effective. For example, in the USA there are high costs attached to running an exhaustive appeal system and operating 'death row'. It may also be argued that the costs of mistakes are very high when an irreversible penalty of this sort is used. At the same time, it has been argued by Mishan (1989) that not using a death penalty for murder in the UK imposes high costs on the victims of murder and their families if Wolpin (1978b) and Deadman and Pyle (1993) are indeed correct.

There is some concern in the USA that the death penalty may be racially discriminatory. From 1977–90, 143 executions were carried out by 16 states, mostly in the South. Of these, 87 (61%) were of white convicts and 56 (39%) were of blacks. Most executions occur in California, Florida, Texas and Illinois. In fact, some of this perceived racial effect may be explained by other factors. Dnes and Nuxoll (1995) use cross-sectional data for all US states to show that the average level of income in a state is a determinant of its use of the death penalty. Poorer states have significantly higher execution rates. Interestingly, there is a 'Southern' effect in the data after controlling for race and income levels. The result is consistent with Becker's (1968) conjecture that increased severity is used by poorer societies in earlier times to compensate for a shortage of policing resources.

The economic analysis of capital punishment can help policy makers in deciding whether to use or eschew the use of a death penalty for murder. Empirical studies have helped to clarify the deterrent effect of capital punishment and have given an idea of the impact of abolition in the UK.

7.4 DRUG ENFORCEMENT

Serious drug use has grown in most parts of the world since the 1960s. Most addiction is associated with heroin, although there have been recent trends towards cocaine use, including 'crack' cocaine. Public concern arises because of perceptions of the debilitating effect of addiction and the association of crime with drug addiction. Addicts seem unable to hold down regular jobs and therefore support their habits with crime (Kaplan, 1983).

Much public policy, particularly in the USA where it is really the only policy, is concerned with restricting supplies. However, economic analysis questions this. If addicts have an inelastic demand for a drug (i.e. one that does not change much in response to price changes) supply restrictions merely increase the price and should increase any associated crime. This unintended consequence of government intervention is illustrated by Figure 7.5. where addicts' demand is given by D_a and that for non-addicts by D_{na}.

Shifting the supply function to the left in Figure 7.5 causes addicts to pay more but hardly reduces their use of heroin, owing to the

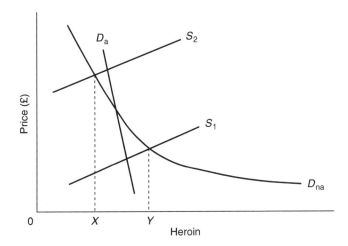

Figure 7.5 Supply restrictions for heroin. D = demand of addicts; S = supply of heroin.

inelasticity of D_a. However, casual users who are not addicted (D_{na}) are more sensitive to changes in price and can be deterred this way, as shown by the larger fall in equilibrium sales from Y to X. The supply curve is shifted left by policies that crack down on supplies entering a country, e.g. increasing customs inspections.

Figure 7.5 suggests a dual policy: make an addictive drug freely available to registered addicts but restrict the supplies to casual users. Addicts will be less attracted to crime and may be supervised. Clinical supervision of addicts is also useful in controlling needle use and the associated transmission of diseases. Policy in the UK has broadly followed this approach. Until 1967, UK physicians were allowed to prescribe morphine or heroin to addicts. This was really a legacy of the days when most addicts had accidentally become addicted as a result of medical treatment. The system came under pressure as a result of social changes in the 1960s when there was a fivefold increase in the number of addicts. From 1967, the prescription of opiates was limited to specially licensed clinics with attached rehabilitation facilities. Since 1967, the UK has moved to a policy of prescribing methadone as a substitute for opiates. The new policy is also broadly consistent with the analysis of Figure 7.5.

The policy towards drug addiction in the USA emphasizes restrictions on supply and does not follow the logic of distinguishing between addicts and social users. A number of European countries have moved towards supplying addicts and restricting social use in recent years. In 1993, the Swiss city of Zürich, which has a serious drug problem, began to supply heroin to addicts at very low prices. Such a development makes great economic sense.

7.5 THE ECONOMICS OF SOME NEW DEVELOPMENTS IN CRIMINAL JUSTICE

We now examine a number of contemporary issues connected with the system of criminal justice that are linked by their novelty rather than anything else. All are amenable to economic analysis.

7.5.1 Plea bargaining

In the USA, plea bargaining is an integral part of the system of criminal justice. Under this arrangement, the accused agrees to plead guilty in exchange for some reduction in the sentence sought by the prosecution. A typical pattern might be for the accused to plead guilty to a lesser set of charges than those being brought in exchange for an agreed sentence that the prosecution will recommend. Similar, but not identical, arrangements have been proposed for the UK. We first examine a straightforward case of US-style plea bargaining.

Figure 7.6 shows the pay-offs to a defendant from going to trial. These depend upon whether conviction or acquittal is the result and whether or not the judge is easygoing or tough. Figure 7.6 describes a courtroom game in 'extensive form', i.e. we follow all the possible directions a trial could take, beginning at the origin at the left of the diagram. The probability attached to each branch (relative to the preceding node) is printed alongside it. For simplicity, each branch is regarded as equally likely. The defendant is released if acquitted (with probability = 0.5) and incurs no penalty. However, if found guilty, the defendant is equally likely to face a 'tough' or 'soft' judge. A tough judge will impose a sentence of three years whereas a soft one will impose only one year.

If the prosecutor and defendant agree on the probabilities and assuming for simplicity that both are risk neutral, the defendant would plead guilty in exchange for a promised sentence of up to one year.[8] Both sides then save the cost of going to trial. The attraction of plea bargaining is easy to see: everyone knows where they stand relative to a prediction for the trial and can save the costs of prosecution or defence.

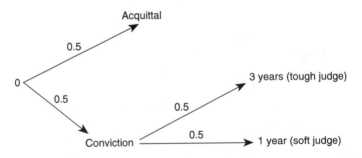

Figure 7.6 Trial game.

In June 1993, a system of sentence discounts was proposed for the UK by the Royal Commission on Criminal Justice headed by Lord Runciman. The discount would be greater the earlier the guilty plea were made but would be given relative to the maximum sentence for the offence. The possible discount would be announced by the judge at the beginning of a trial, whereas at present, a judge can apply a discount retrospectively after a criminal co-operates by pleading guilty. The new system is a little different from the US situation where the prosecution recommends the sentence. However the logic of UK plea bargaining is much the same.

At present in the UK, there are many 'cracked' trials. Approximately 83% of defendants who elect to receive a Crown Court trial change their plea at the last minute. Presumably they want to see if they have a soft or a tough judge and jury, and what sort of evidence seems likely. This is entirely consistent with an economic model like the one in Figure 7.6. Plea bargaining should reduce the number of cracked trials.

7.5.2 Neighbourhood watch

The system of neighbourhood watch spread from the USA to several countries in the 1980s. A group of neighbours agree to be vigilant on crime prevention, e.g. taking care over locking premises and making efforts to report suspicious behaviour. The idea is generally to increase awareness about crime. These schemes do not have a good track record in the UK. This is not surprising as economic analysis suggests that neighbourhood watch suffers from a free-rider problem. Table 7.2 illustrates this free-rider problem for a simple two-household neighbourhood, and is a development of a model used by Pyle (1993).

The pay-offs in Table 7.2 are measured as the value of property lost through theft over a period of time. If both households join, both are vigilant in the neighbourhood as a whole and each loses £5000, which is a total of £10 000 worth of theft. If one stays out but the other joins, total theft increases. However, the free rider can apply more time to protecting his own property and suffers only £4000 loss. The household that agrees to watch loses £7000. If neither joins the scheme, a total loss of £12 000 occurs through theft and is shared equally.

The rational neighbour would free ride in Table 7.2 and stay out. This is because joining carries the risk that your neighbour will free ride and that you will lose £7000. By free riding yourself, the worst that could happen is that you lose £6000 if your neighbour does the same.

Table 7.2 Neighbourhood watch

		Household B	
		Join	Stay out
Household A	Join	5, 5	7, 4
	Stay out	4, 7	6, 6

(pay-offs to A, B: £000)

Free riding is a dominant strategy (better in every comparison with joining) in Table 7.2 for both parties. Therefore, they both stay out and are driven to the worst possible corner of the table, with joint losses of £12 000.

Empirical work supports the prediction that neighbourhood watch schemes will perform weakly. Bennett (1989) evaluates schemes in Acton and Wimbledon in a study that included a displacement area on the boundary of Wimbledon and a control area (Redbridge). Neither the displacement or control area had neighbourhood watch. In theory, crime should go to a displacement area if neighbourhood watch works. Also, crime trends should be better with neighbourhood watch than in the control area.

Over a two-year period, crime rose by 40% in Acton, fell 17% in Wimbledon, fell by 9% in the displacement area and fell 39% in the control area. These results cast doubt on the benefits of neighbourhood watch in the UK.

7.5.3 Privatization of prisons

There has been a move towards the privatization of prisons in a number of countries. Private prisons are not new, e.g. they existed in the UK from medieval times up to the late eighteenth century and in some southern states of the USA until the early nineteenth century. The contemporary move towards the privatization of custodial care is part of a general move towards the contracting out of many services that were traditionally seen as a part of government activity. Governments have been led to consider these options as demands on their budgets from areas such as welfare payments have grown. The privatization of prisons raises a number of issues, including those of accountability and propriety (Logan, 1990), but we concentrate on the cost side here.

The Wolds Remand Centre in Humberside, which opened in April 1992, was Britain's first contemporary privatized jail. It is run by the Group 4 security firm on a fixed-price contract paying approximately £5 million per year, although this excludes the costs of utilities such as electricity. Under the contract, Group 4 caters for around 320 remand prisoners. Group 4 also operates privatized escort services between other prisons and the courts.[9] In May 1993, a second privatized prison opened at Blakenhurst catering for a mixture of remand and convicted prisoners. Blakenhurst is run by United Kingdom Detention Services, which is a conglomerate including Mowlem and MacAlpine (two construction companies) and the Corrections Corporation of America. It must be emphasized that, in the case of prisons, privatization does not significantly involve selling assets previously owned by the state. Rather, in the typical case, contracts are awarded to the firm offering to build and run a new prison at the lowest cost subject to certain requirements covering the quality of the service.

The intention behind privatization is to cut costs while at least maintaining the existing quality of service. In 1994, major expansion

Table 7.3 Costs of state and privately-run jails (per prisoner place per week)

Prison	Cost per week (£)
Frankland	752
Brixton	535
Norwich	434
Winchester	401
Strangeways	350
Wolds	350
Blakenhurst	310

Source: Moran (1994).

was announced for the private correctional sector as a result of early encouraging results. The Home Office has identified 21 prisons, including all nine open prisons for men and Feltham Young Offenders' Institution in West London, as candidates for privatization.[10] The intention is to choose some cases with bad escape and cost records to assess whether private management can improve things. In 1994, another private prison which is run by Premier Prison Services opened in Doncaster.

The costs of the Wolds and Blakenhurst and a number of state-run prisons are shown in Table 7.3. The privately-managed prisons are at the bottom of Table 7.3 indicating that their costs compare favourably with the state prisons. Care must be taken in this comparison, however, as the Wolds and Blakenhurst are relatively low-security prisons and do not face the elaborate and costly requirements of a maximum-security unit: a point made by Borna (1986) in relation to US data on the cost savings from privatizing prisons. However, while it still is very early to be confident that private prisons have lower costs, Table 7.3 suggests that contracting out stimulates competitive cost saving: the lowest-cost state-run prison in the table (Strangeways) is one where (in July 1993) the Prison Service successfully outbid private-sector rivals for a contract to run the prison.

The USA has rather more recent experience of privatizing prisons and had 12 such institutions in 1988. Again the prisoners tend to be low-risk groups such as those on remand or awaiting deportation. However, US evidence on reductions in costs and improvements in the quality of service is not always encouraging (Borna, 1986; Weiss, 1989). On the other hand, some privatization exercises do show cost reductions. Cooter and Ulen (1988) quote the example of Behavioral Systems Southwest which was incarcerating approximately 650 low-risk prisoners per day in leased hotels and large houses in the 1980s. Behavioral Systems' costs were $25 per prisoner per day, compared with $75–$100 in the state sector.

Pyle (1993) argues that contracting out may not reduce the resource cost of prisons. If rent seeking occurs among would-be contractors then there may be a great waste of resources. Rent seeking may arise if contractors devote resources to influencing the authorities towards granting them contracts. Comparing operating costs per prisoner will not show rent-seeking costs. Pyle may well be correct in this argument although it should be remembered that some promotional expenditure is clearly required to communicate information to the authorities. Another worry may be that private-prison companies might lobby for strong law enforcement and stiff sentences to improve their business prospects (Cooter and Ulen, 1988), which is also a form of rent seeking.

A further concern could be that companies might underbid for prison contracts. They could place a very low bid to obtain the contract and attempt to renegotiate later, claiming that costs were higher than anticipated and threatening to close down unless the terms were revised in their favour. Underbidding is a form of hold-up strategy similar to the cases discussed in Chapter 4. The threat of serious disruption might cause the authorities to permit renegotiation. There have been no cases of renegotiation in the privatized prisons but it is still early days. Concern raised in the House of Commons in 1995 about the Wolds, where costs were estimated as likely to be £8 million higher than Group 4's bid, referred to the costs of utilities which were excluded from the terms of the original competition.[11]

7.5.4 Electronic tagging

A further modern development in correctional techniques is electronic tagging. Again, this was first developed in the USA but is now spreading around the world. An electronic device is incorporated into an ankle bracelet. If a person leaves a specified building the device informs the authority. Individuals can be subjected to house arrest, possibly as part of a parole arrangement, which saves a great deal of the costs of a normal custodial sentence.

In 1989, three pilot schemes were operated in the UK in Nottingham, Tower Hamlets and Newcastle-upon-Tyne. These ran for six months and covered 50 offenders (Mair and Nee, 1990; Pyle, 1993). The results were not particularly encouraging: 18 offenders absconded and 11 committed crimes while tagged. The costs worked out at £20 000 per offender per year which was about the same as prison costs at that time. According to Pyle (1993, p.14), plans to extend the experiment in 1990 were quietly dropped at one stage although a provision remained in the Criminal Justice Act 1991 to allow tagging. In July 1995, the Home Office announced a further experiment with tagging based in Norwich.

SUMMARY AND CONCLUSIONS

This chapter has shown how economic analysis may be used to aid our understanding of crime and punishment. There is statistical evidence to suggest that individuals engage in crime as a rational activity and are deterred by changes in criminal-justice variables. This appears to be particularly true in the case of property crime. Increases in the probability of eventual punishment appear to have the strongest deterrent effect. Nonetheless, in cost-effectiveness comparisons, increasing the severity of sentences appears to be the cheapest way to obtain a given reduction in criminal activity. It would appear that if society is serious about tackling modern crime, a toughening of sentencing is likely to be the most successful approach.

Economic analysis is also useful in examining a host of management issues from the criminal-justice system. These issues arise mainly as a response to rising costs. The modern trend is towards drawing in investment from the private sector to help in the running of prisons. However, experiments with neighbourhood watch and with electronic tagging have not been cost-effective.

ENDNOTES

1. Although some crime is not obviously wasteful, e.g. marijuana production and distribution is illegal but is not obviously different from the activities of firms in the tobacco industry.
2. There is empirical evidence to suggest that expanding police numbers is a poor method of creating deterrence. We discuss this issue further later in this chapter (section 7.2.4).
3. However, the proportion of British-born and the proportion of European-born members of the population were statistically significant.
4. See 'Crime Figures Show Overall Fall but Violence Increases', *The Times*, Wednesday September 28, 1994.
5. *The Times, op.cit.*
6. Qualification is necessary as offences are committed within prisons.
7. See 'Staff Turn Blind Eye to Prisoners', *The Times*, Friday August 26, 1994 for some further details.
8. Risk neutrality requires that an individual does not dislike (risk aversion) or desire (risk loving) a pay-off because it is an expected value rather than a certain pay-off of the same amount.
9. Which was the brunt of many jokes in the UK in its early days as Group 4 lost a number of prisoners.
10. See 'Prisons Shortlisted for Privatisation', *The Times*, Tuesday August 16, 1994.
11. See 'Cost of running private jail £8m more than Group 4 bid', *The Times*, Friday February 10, 1995.

8 Contingency fees, cost rules and litigation

In this chapter, we examine several, largely procedural, issues connected with litigation. First, we consider the implications of permitting lawyers to work for contingency fees (i.e. on a no-win, no-fee basis). We also examine the impact on the incentive to litigate of following English cost rules, under which the loser pays the winner's costs, compared with American rules under which each party meets his own lawyers' fees. Finally in this chapter, we look at differences in rates of litigation across countries.

8.1 CONTINGENCY FEES

A traditional difference between US jurisdictions and England (and other Commonwealth countries like Australia and New Zealand) is that in the USA lawyers may work for contingency fees whereas in England this has been prohibited. England is in the process of moving towards a form of contingency fee following the Courts and Legal Services Act 1990. A contingency-fee system allows the lawyer's fee to be contingent on the results gained for a client. In the USA, the contingency fee is an agreed proportion of the client's gain: if there is no gain then there is no fee. In the UK, a hybrid system is to be introduced allowing a lawyer to charge normal hourly rates plus an agreed percentage mark-up on these rates (the 'speculative mark-up') in the event of success, with no fee being paid if the case is lost. It is important to note a key difference between England and the USA in considering the impact of contingency fees: in the USA each party pays his own lawyers' fees whereas in England the loser pays the litigation costs of both parties. In England, lawyers will need to use insurance schemes to meet the costs of unsuccessful litigants operating on a contingency-fee basis.

There are several interesting economic questions concerning contingency fees. First, there is great interest in the incentive properties of the system. In particular, it is held that contingency fees influence the incentive lawyers have to represent their clients' interests faithfully, rather than to pursue sub-goals (Dana and Spier, 1993; Rubinfeld and Scotchmer, 1993; Gravelle and Waterson, 1994; Rickman, 1994). A second and related major area of interest focuses on the impact of contingency fees on the amount of litigation, measured in terms of the volume of litigation and settlement rates for cases (Cooter and Rubinfeld, 1989). We examine these issues in this section, taking the example of US proportional contingency fees for simplicity.

8.1.1 Contingency fees and principal–agent problems

Economic analysis suggests that there can be a major problem of incentive compatibility between a client and a lawyer working for an hourly fee. The relationship between client and lawyer exhibits classic aspects of the principal–agent problem: the client, as principal in the case, must motivate the lawyer, who is the agent, to pursue the client's interests. Hourly fees may not do this, as it is difficult for the client to know how diligently the lawyer is working. The lawyer may, e.g. prolong the case to maximize the hourly fees, which is a case of moral hazard (Rees 1985) stemming from the hidden nature of the lawyer's actions.[1] A classic solution to the principal's problem in cases where the agent's actions are hidden but output may be observed is to make the agent's rewards contingent on the level of output. By this reasoning, contingency fees for lawyers may be seen as a useful device for ensuring that they deliver services efficiently.

What then determines the level of the contingency fee? The usual assumption made in investigating the determination of the contingency fee is that the lawyer is better able than the client to bear the risks of litigation, owing to the lawyer's involvement in a wide range of cases over which risks may be diversified (Rickman, 1994). The lawyer is therefore treated as risk neutral in not discounting pay-offs to reflect risk. The client is regarded as risk averse which means that a smaller but certain pay-off is preferred to a larger but risky one. The client's utility function over the returns to litigation is therefore convex when viewed from above, as illustrated by the function U in Figure 8.1.

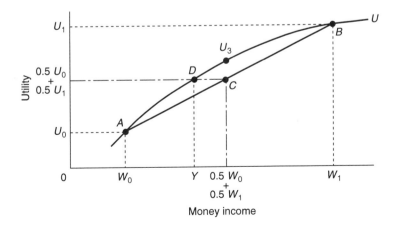

Figure 8.1 Risk sharing between lawyer and client.

In Figure 8.1, the client is assumed to face an equal chance of winning or losing a case. If he wins, his income level is W_1 (with utility level U_1) whereas if he loses, income is only W_0 (with utility U_0). Point C, which is halfway along the straight line connecting points A and B on the utility function shows the expected income from litigation if read in conjunction with the horizontal axis and, reading from the vertical axis, shows the client's expected utility. Note that the point on the utility function directly above C shows a higher level of utility (U_3) because it assumes the same level of income is paid with certainty. Reading across from C to point D, we can deduce that the same utility is obtained from the lower level of income Y, provided that this is available with certainty. Thus, there is scope for risk sharing: as long as the lawyer is risk neutral, he could offer a sum just larger than $Y - W_0$ to buy the case. The client would be better off from shifting the risk in this way and the lawyer would expect to make a profit of $[0.5(W_1 + W_0) - Y]$.

We now show what happens to risk sharing following the introduction of a contingency-fee system. Figure 8.2 shows one effect as a reduction in the difference between income in the win and lose states following the change. The spread is between points a and b with hourly fees but is only from a to d with contingency fees: the client no longer pays lawyer's fees in the event of losing the case. Still assuming an equal chance of success or failure in litigating, the point of 'certainty equivalence' gives a higher monetary amount and income level for the client in the case of a contingency fee (c_2 compared with c_1).

There are no welfare consequences from introducing contingency fees in an example like the one in Figure 8.2. This is because we implicitly assume that the litigation goes ahead under either method of paying the lawyer, as the expected increase in the client's income is positive. Contingency fees merely redistribute income from the lawyer to the client under these circumstances. However, if there are impecu-

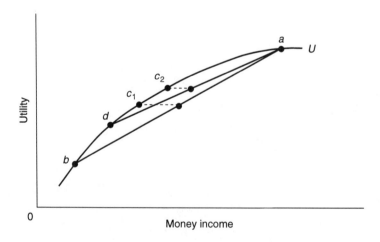

Figure 8.2 Contingency fees and the returns to litigation.

nious clients who cannot raise the funds to litigate under hourly fees, then, other things being equal, contingency fees encourage worthwhile litigation. This in turn will deter accidents as more tortfeasors are pursued for damages.

Figures 8.1 and 8.2 imply that lawyers would often wish to buy valuable cases from risk-averse clients in return for contingency fees of 100%. In such cases, risk-neutral lawyers would provide full insurance for clients. We do not in fact see this as a general phenomenon in the USA where contingency-fee representation has been normal for some time. Also, we should not expect to see this in the case of England, where a watered-down version of the contingency fee is being introduced following the Courts and Legal Services Act 1990. This is quite simply because the respective legal systems do not permit full trade in legal claims and would not necessarily enforce contracts that bought and sold cases. Figure 8.2 is really a model, based on risk sharing, of the pricing of cases under either hourly or contingency fees in an unregulated environment. The US position is that contract claims are saleable whereas tort claims generally are not (Posner, 1992, p.569).

When clients are restricted to bargaining in terms of the percentage contingency fee, or – in the English case – the speculative mark-up, a number of factors will influence the size of the percentage fee. Rubinfeld and Scotchmer (1993) argue that private information held by clients and lawyers will be the chief influence on fees. Private information cannot be communicated convincingly to another party. A lawyer's confidence (based on skill) in winning the case would encourage lower cost-based and higher percentage contingency fees. Conversely, confidence by the client, who may have private information about a defendant, would tend to encourage a lower contingency fee. Also, there is less of a tendency to use contingency fees in cases where the client can easily monitor the efforts of the lawyer. Kritzer (1990) shows that business organizations used hourly fees in 81% of cases in hiring lawyers, compared with a figure of 10% for individuals. The monitoring experience of business clients, together with their ability to diversify risk over cases, would also imply a smaller percentage for the contingency fee whenever one was used.

8.1.2   Contingency fees and litigation levels

It is often argued that a contingency-fee system can increase the volume of litigation and/or alter settlement rates for cases. The anxiety over increasing the volume of litigation stems from the observation that the cost of losing a case is reduced by contingency fees. Impecunious clients are able to pursue cases that would otherwise not be litigated. The anxiety over settlement rates reflects a possible agency problem attached to contingency fees: the lawyer may have an incentive to settle early, obtain the fee and move on to other cases. However, the literature generally shows mixed results for the impact of contingency fees on the number of cases and on settlement rates.

Taking settlement rates first, Schwartz and Mitchell (1970) showed early on that diminishing returns to a lawyer's effort implies that the effective hourly rate under contingency fees falls over time. There is, therefore, a tendency to wish to settle early on, even though further effort would improve the client's expected pay-off. However, Johnson (1981) uses a similar model to Schwartz and Mitchell (1970) to show that hourly fees also have the predictable effect of encouraging the lawyer to extend the case. Clearly both fee systems can have agency problems. Gravelle and Waterson (1994) show that the contingency-fee lawyer's tendency to settle early can also arise in a setting characterized by English cost rules, where the losing party pays the winner's costs. Swanson (1991) argues that risk-averse clients will benefit from the reduction in the risks associated with trials when lawyer's incentives to settle are sharpened. Rickman (1994) argues that two possibly off-setting tendencies are set up by contingency fees. The lawyer is led to press the client's interests harder but may also wish to settle earlier, both owing to the lawyer's financial interest. Empirical work also appears to be mixed in its results. Kritzer (1990) found that contingency-fee lawyers put less effort into small cases compared with hourly paid lawyers but that the difference was reversed for larger cases, which does not support the existence of a conflict of interest. Thomason (1991) found that contingency-fee lawyers settled sooner and for smaller amounts compared with litigants in person in industrial-injury cases which supports a conflict of interest. However, it may be that worries over settlement rates miss the point. Client's use contingency fees to shift risk, which makes them better off, and earlier settlement makes lawyers (and defendants) better off. The implied welfare levels may be as high as possible given the need that impecunious clients have for using contingency fees.

Looking now at the volume of litigation, there is a commonly held view that contingency fees encourage litigation and might be partly responsible for the perceived litigious nature of American society. In England, concern over the effect of contingency fees on the volume of litigation was expressed in the consultative Green Paper (Lord Chancellor's Department, 1989) that preceded the Courts and Legal Services Act 1990. In fact there are a number of influences that might explain the difference between high rates of litigation in the USA and the lower rates in countries like England and we examine some of these later in this chapter. However, the use of contingency fees could, in principle, either increase or decrease litigation rates (Cooter and Rubinfeld, 1989; Miceli and Segerson, 1991; Rickman, 1994; Gravelle and Waterson, 1994). This is because there are at least two offsetting influences to the increased incentive to litigate for the impecunious litigant that follows from reducing the spread of the pay-offs in Figure 8.2. The first is the increased deterrence of tortfeasors that follows from less costly litigation for victims of accidents. If potential tortfeasors know they will face legal action over accidents they may be led to act more carefully. Also, lawyers may more carefully screen cases before

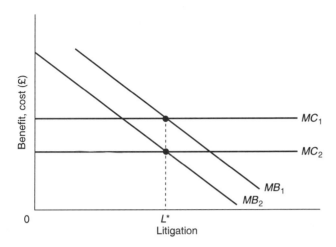

Figure 8.3 Offsetting effects from contingency fees. MC = marginal cost of litigation; MB = marginal benefit of litigation.

taking them on under a contingency-fee arrangement. Both of these factors could result in fewer cases reaching the courts, rather as in the 'raid-or-trade' model (section 2.6) of property rights formation (Anderson and McChesney, 1994), which is based on Cooter and Rubinfeld's (1989) analysis of the incentive to litigate and in which the discovery of more effective weapons could lead to less fighting.

In Figure 8.3, contingency fees reduce the marginal costs of litigation for a client but more careful screening by lawyers reduces the client's perception of the marginal benefits of litigation. As drawn, the two effects are completely offsetting so that no change results from introducing contingency fees. In practice, the introduction of contingency fees in England will give an excellent opportunity to study empirically which factors dominate and whether litigation rates increase or decrease following the change. The possible offsetting effects of contingency fees can arise both under US cost rules, where parties bear their own costs and under English rules, where the loser pays the costs of both parties. Therefore, differences in litigation rates across jurisdictions require a more broadly-based explanation.

8.2 ENGLISH AND AMERICAN COST RULES

In England and other Commonwealth countries, the loser in a civil case pays the legal costs of the winner, including lawyers' fees. There is 'indemnity' of lawyers' fees, sometimes called 'fee shifting'. In the USA, each party is responsible for his own lawyers' fees, which are the major costs in a case, although the winner may claim the administrative costs of the case from the loser. At least, this is the broad position: under rule 68 of the Federal Rules of Civil Procedure in the USA, if the defendant offers a compromise and the plaintiff proceeds to a court action but fails to win more, the plaintiff must pay all of his costs. Rule 68 provides a limited amount of one-way indemnity in favour of the defendant. Similarly, in England, the defendant can protect himself by registering an early offer of settlement: if the plaintiff proceeds to court and wins, the defendant only pays costs proportional to any positive difference between his offer and the damages awarded by the court. Both of these procedural devices recognize offers of compromise and give the plaintiff an incentive to be careful in considering whether additional court action is worthwhile. Broadly, however, the comparison is between litigants meeting most of their own costs (American) and 'loser pays all' (England).

We can use the model constructed in section 8.1 to examine the impact of English and American cost rules on the incentive to litigate. Figure 8.4 shows that the spread of utility from winning or losing a case is reduced for a plaintiff under American rules (U_1 to U_2) compared with English cost rules (U_3 to U_0). We assume that, under English rules, the costs paid by the plaintiff to the defendant on losing (VW) equal the costs received if the plaintiff wins (XY). Because the plaintiff is assumed to be risk averse, the loss of utility from paying costs on losing (U_2 to U_0) exceeds the gain in utility from receiving costs after winning (U_1 to U_3) and the certainty equivalent, or value of the case, falls under English rules (C) compared with American rules (C'). On this reasoning, based on a utility function that is convex viewed from above, English rules would tend to deter litigation.

The view that English cost rules deter litigation is frequently encountered among lawyers (Markesinis, 1990) and legislators. For example, in the 'Contract with America' launched by the Republican Party following its winning a majority of seats in the US Congress in 1995, a proposal was made to introduce English cost rules in American

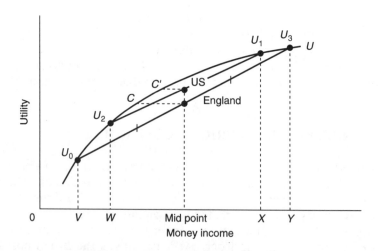

Figure 8.4 American and English cost rules.

courts. Similarly in the Green Paper on contingency fees in England (Lord Chancellor's Department, 1989), it is suggested that different cost rules, rather than contingency fees, are responsible for greater litigation rates in the USA compared with England.

In fact, greater litigation rates in the USA (see section 8.3 for details) need not result from American cost rules. Just as English rules deter risk-averse plaintiffs from taking action, so too would consequential increases in the spread of outcomes deter defendants from defending cases. The literature on the impact of cost rules (Shavell, 1982; Bowles, 1987; Cooter and Rubinfeld, 1989; Snyder and Hughes, 1990; Hughes and Snyder, 1995) therefore makes no clear theoretical prediction over the impact of English rules. The net result of deterring both plaintiff and defendant depends upon their relative levels of risk aversion and the amount of costs expected by each party from winning or losing a case. Indeed it is possible to apply the Coase theorem to argue that the cost-shifting rule cannot affect the final outcome of a case (Donohue, 1991). It is therefore an empirical matter whether English rules deter litigation on balance.

There is a shortage of empirical work in this area but exceptions are Snyder and Hughes (1990) and Hughes and Snyder (1995) which use US data from Florida where English rules were applied in cases of medical malpractice from 1980–85. Hughes and Snyder conclude that plaintiffs and defendants are encouraged to be careful by English rules and spend more on legal fees and that plaintiffs going to trial are more likely to win. Their results are consistent with the clear perception among lawyers and legislators that English rules deter 'claim mining', which refers to the practice of suing in the hope that someone will settle rather than incur the costs of defending themselves. Under English rules spurious suits result in a costs bill for the claim miner whose bluff is called.

8.3 CLASS ACTIONS

An interesting difference between the USA and England is that the USA allows class actions. In US jurisdictions, individuals may sue on behalf of a class of plaintiffs, providing the court is prepared to certify the claim as a class action. The class action may make it worthwhile for an individual to sue when the individual stakes are small but when aggregate damages may be high, which is potentially efficient as it confronts a tortfeasor with the costs of his actions. If successful in a class action, a plaintiff's lawyers must make attempts to pay damages to the class of victims concerned. However, this is often prohibitively expensive and the plaintiff and his lawyers typically receive a disproportionately large share of the award. It is the prospect of the large share that motivates plaintiffs in class actions.

If the defendant in a class action settles before trial, there may be a problem. The lawyer in a class action may lack the motivation to press a class action to its conclusion in court. Rather, the lawyer may settle for a large fee and small award to the plaintiff. The US courts regulate lawyers' fees in settlements of class actions but lawyers may be able to persuade judges that they have spent a lot of time on a case. Some empirical work supports the existence of this settlement effect (Rosenfield, 1976). However, in practice, the settlement effect may be controlled by the way courts control lawyers' fees and by the existence of contingency-fee litigation in class actions (Lynk, 1990).

In the USA, devices like class actions and contingency fees operate to reduce the plaintiff's costs of pursuing legal claims. In England, a well developed system of legal aid operates under which the state subsidizes the legal costs of plaintiffs and defendants who are assessed as having significant cases and whose access to justice might otherwise be barred owing to lack of finances.[2] However, it is clear from the operation of the legal aid assessment board that it would not subsidize apparently trivial claims. This resistance could rule out cases where individual stakes are small but add up to a large amount. Therefore, the class action could be useful within a system characterized by legal aid.

In the UK in 1995, the Lord Chancellor announced plans to limit the availability of funds for legal aid for both criminal and civil cases, as the system increasingly ran into financial difficulty (Gray, 1994). The most likely way forward is for lawyers to be awarded legal aid contracts based partly upon their bidding the lowest fees to obtain the work. In this increasingly financially stringent environment, the class action could have a useful role in ensuring that tortfeasors face the costs of their actions.

8.4 LITIGATION MANIA?

There is a growing perception in many jurisdictions that individuals are becoming increasingly litigious. There is a further belief that the USA is the most litigious of the advanced societies.[3] As Markesinis (1990) shows, this belief is not well-founded as far as general litigation is concerned as the USA is not wildly out of line with England. However, the USA does have an unusually high level of litigation in tort law compared with England, particularly for medical malpractice and product liability cases, although the rate of litigation in tort in America is comparable to that in Germany (a civil-law jurisdiction). The comparisons may be best described as showing England as having unusually low rates of tort litigation.

One measure of the amount of private legal action is the total number of civil actions undertaken in a jurisdiction in a given year. Comparisons between countries must be adjusted to allow for different sized populations. Markesinis (1990, pp.240–44) shows that in the late 1980s, both the UK and USA had approximately 60 000 civil actions per million members of the population a year. The picture changes in examining tort cases, where the figure for the USA is 3750 per million

(1987) compared with 1200 per million in the UK. Interestingly, Germany has rates of tort litigation that are comparable to the US figures. The similarity between Germany and the USA seems to rule out an explanation of American litigiousness based on the need to compensate losses in the absence of a developed system of social security: Germany has a well-developed social security system and has similar levels of tort litigation.

Markesinis (1990, p.242) examines several suggested explanations of the difference in litigation rates between England and the USA. He notes that many US judges are elected officials who become politicized. US judges therefore have a more open commitment to changing the law and adopt a more innovative approach whereas English judges (who are appointed with tenure) tend to be traditionalist in outlook and are more inclined to follow existing holdings (*stare decisis*). Markesinis implies that this may make American litigants more optimistic about a judge's treatment of their cases.

Much US private law is rather pro plaintiff in nature. The development of strict liability, and then absolute liability, in product-liability torts is a well-known example of this, as is the development of no-fault compensation for motoring injuries. Markesinis (1990, p.242) notes that the Association of Trial Lawyers of America (ATLA) has developed as a pressure group that opposes attempts to diminish the effects of pro-plaintiff legislation and judicial decisions. The ATLA also mobilizes to support the election of pro-plaintiff judges. Rubin and Bailey (1994) also cite the role of the ATLA in shaping product-liability law as an example of rent seeking and as showing how the law may develop to favour special-interest groups. Rubin and Bailey's argument runs counter to Posner's (1992, p.523) conclusions that the common law tends to develop in a wealth-maximizing fashion.

Markesinis (1990, p.245) notes that contingency fees may make access to law cheaper and encourage more litigation in the USA. However, he also notes that contingency-fee lawyers would be highly selective in the cases they chose. The overall effect is unclear as we concluded earlier in this chapter (section 8.1.2). Apparently, in-house doctors are often used by law firms to advise over whether to take on a medical-malpractice case which leads to 85% of potential plaintiffs being turned down.

One of the crucial legal differences between England and the USA is the persistence in the USA of jury trials for a wide range of civil cases. In England, juries have been progressively abolished for civil trials (but not for criminal trials) from 1833 onwards: today, juries may be used for cases involving fraud, defamation, malicious prosecution and false imprisonment (Supreme Court Act 1981, section 69). In the USA no such reforms have occurred and it is often noted (as it also is in defamation trials in England) that juries tend to take a pro-plaintiff, deep-pocket view of defendants in cases involving medical malpractice or product liability. Markesinis quotes American data which shows that government defendants pay three times more than private defendants and corporate defendants pay four-and-a-half times more. This denial of equal justice will also have the effect of encouraging potential plaintiffs to sue government agent departments and business corporations.

Curiously, Markesinis has little to say about the relative impact of English and American cost rules. We have already concluded (section 8.2) that empirical evidence suggests that English rules deter claim mining and act as a brake on spurious cases.

Finally, Markesinis (1990, p. 255) quotes the comments of Berger CJ to the American Bar Association in 1982: 'One reason our courts have become over-burdened is that Americans are increasingly turning to the courts for relief from personal wrongs. . . . [and to] fill the void created by the decline of church, family and neighborhood unity'. According to this view, the courts are used by members of a developed but impersonal society as an early resort to resolve adversity.

There is no simple explanation of the differentially high tort litigation rates in the USA, compared with its common-law cousin England. In the USA, a combination of lower costs attached to the early use of litigation and an absence of institutional alternatives partly explains the greater recourse to the law.

SUMMARY AND CONCLUSIONS

In this chapter we have applied economic analysis to several, largely procedural, issues connected with litigation. First, we showed that permitting lawyers to work for contingency fees does not necessarily encourage litigation. Similarly, there is an ambiguous effect on the incentive to litigate of following English compared with American cost rules although empirical work supports a disincentive for claim mining under English rules. Thirdly, we suggested that introducing the class action may be worth considering in England as the system of legal aid increasingly encounters financial constraints. Finally in this chapter, while differences between English and American rates of litigation are often overemphasized, we examined several broadly economic factors that partially explain the higher US rate of tort litigation.

ENDNOTES

1. In general, principal–agent relationships may suffer from problems of hidden actions or of hidden information. Hidden information leads to problems of adverse selection, e.g. a litigant who is ignorant of the true capacity of individual lawyers will be willing to pay fees based on average ability, which may mean that above-average lawyers leave the profession.
2. These are not necessarily poor people, e.g. in 1995, the sons of Robert Maxwell received millions of pounds in legal aid to defend themselves against criminal charges.
3. Markesinis (1990, p.245) cites the case of a 15-year-old girl filing a claim for $50 against her boyfriend for the cost of wasted make-up, etc., after the boy stood her up on a date.

Postscript

It is interesting to speculate why the economic analysis of law is so well established in North America but remains relatively underdeveloped in England and in most Commonwealth countries. Part of the explanation may lie in the nature of legal training in North America, where law degrees tend to be taken by postgraduates who have already had exposure to other subjects in their first degrees, whereas law is often taken as a first degree in England. The legal academic in North America is probably therefore more open to the insights of other subjects. US judges have a reputation for legal innovation, compared with their more conservative English cousins, that may stem from this different educational background. One certainly cannot point to major differences in the systems of law: the English and North American legal systems (especially in the Canadian case) are very close cousins indeed. The outlook of the English and Americans is also similar in placing a high value on personal freedom under the rule of law.

One factor that might also partly explain the reluctance of some English academic lawyers to embrace the economic analysis of law is a feeling that somehow the subject reflects a hard-nosed American affection for the market economy. An obvious comment would be that England has become a pretty hard-nosed place of late too. Leaving that aside, it appears to be true that highly mobile American society relies heavily on impersonal, often market-based approaches to allocating resources and to avoiding interpersonal conflict. English society has often relied on non-market social mechanisms (e.g. the disapprobation shown to generators of nuisance in settled village society). However, English society is heading in much the same direction as its American counterpart these days. There are signs already that there has been considerable recent growth in interest in the economic structure of the law in England.

I hope that this book serves as a useful introduction to the economic analysis of law which draws in English and Commonwealth cases and applies to them the same economic analysis routinely applied to American cases. There is much to be gained from carrying out comparative studies in the economic analysis of law. If the principles are sound there should be no difficulty applying them outside of their original jurisdiction. A comparative theme has been maintained throughout this book and should be of interest on both sides of the Atlantic.

Cases, statutes and references

CASES

Adams *v.* Bullock, 227 N.Y. 208 (1919)
Alaska Packers' Association *v.* Domenico, 117 F 99 (9th Circuit 1902)
Alcock *v.* Chief Constable of South Yorkshire Police [1992] 1 AC 310 (HL)
Allied Marine Transport Ltd *v.* Vale do Rio Doce Navegaçao SA, The Leonidas D [1985] 1 WLR 925 (CA)
Anglia Television *v.* Reed [1972] 1 QB 60 (CA)
Anns *v.* Merton London Borough Council [1978] AC 728 (HL)
Attorney General *v.* City of Birmingham Corporation [1858] 4 K&J 528
Bach *v.* Longman (1777) [1993] Jacob & Alexander 128
Barnett *v.* Chelsea and Kensington Hospital Management Committee [1969] 1 QB 428
Beshada *v.* Johns-Manville Products, 90 N.J. 191 (1982)
Blyth *v.* Birmingham Waterworks Co. (1856) 11 Ex 781
Boomer *v.* Atlantic Cement Co. 26 NY 2d 219 (Court of Appeals NY, 1970)
Bourhill *v.* Young [1943] AC 92
British Crane Hire Corporation *v.* Ipswich Plant Hire [1975] QB 303 (CA)
British Westinghouse Electric & Manufacturing Co. Ltd *v.* Underground Electric Railways Co. of London Ltd [1912] AC 673
Buckley *v.* Smith Transport (1946) OR 798 (Ontario Court of Appeal)
Canadian National Railway *v.* Norsk Pacific Steamship Co. [1992] 1 SCR 1021 (Supreme Court of Canada)
Carlill *v.* Carbolic Smoke Ball Co. [1893] 1 QB 256
Chappell & Co. Ltd *v.* Nestlé Co. Ltd [1960] AC 87 (HL)
Cullinane *v.* British 'Rema' Manufacturing Co. Ltd [1954] 1 QB 292 (CA)
Davies *v.* Mann (1842) 152 ER 588
Davis Contractors Ltd *v.* Fareham UDC [1956] AC 696 (HL)
Deatons *v.* Flew (1949) 79 CLR 370
Dimskal Shipping Co. SA *v.* International Transport Workers' Federation; The Eria Luck [1992] 2 AC 152 (HL)

Donoghue *v.* Stevenson [1932] AC 562

Entores *v.* Miles Far East Corp. [1955] 2 QB 327 (CA)

Escola *v.* Coca Cola, 24 Cal. 2d 453 (1944)

Fry *v.* Lane (1888) 40 Ch 312

Gordon *v.* Selico Co. (1986) 278 EG 53 (CA)

Graham *v.* Scissor-Tail Inc. 28 Cal 3d 807 (1981)

Gregg *v.* Georgia, 428 US 153 (1976) (Supreme Court)

Hadley *v.* Baxendale (1854) 9 Exch 341

Haley *v.* London Electricity Board [1965] AC 778 (HL)

Hamer *v.* Sidway, 27 NE 256 (Court of Appeals NY, 1891)

Harris *v.* Watson (1791) Peake 102

Hartog *v.* Colin and Shields [1939] 3 All ER 566

Hill *v.* Chief Constable of West Yorkshire [1989] AC 53 (HL)

Hydraulic Engineering Co. Ltd *v.* McHaffie, Goslett & Co. (1878) 4
  QBD 670

Jacob & Youngs *v.* Kent 230 NY 239 (1921)

Jefferson *v.* Derbyshire Farmers Ltd [1921] 2 KB 281 (CA)

Jobson *v.* Johnson [1989] 1 WLR 1026 (CA)

Kemper (M.F.) Construction Co. *v.* City of Los Angeles *et al.*, 235 P 2d
  7 (1951)

Kennaway *v.* Thompson [1981] QB 88 (CA)

Khorasandjian *v.* Bush [1993] QB 727 (CA)

Koufos *v.* C. Czarnikow Ltd [1969] 1 AC 350 (HL)

Laidlaw *v.* Organ, 15 US (2 Wheat) 178 (1817)

Leroy Fibre Co. *v.* Chicago, Milwaukee and St Paul Railway, 232 US
  240 (1914)

Levy *v.* McDonald's Hamburgers, *The Times*, Saturday February 11,
  1995

Livingstone *v.* Rawyards Coal (1880) 5 App Cas 25

Lloyds Bank *v.* Bundy [1975] QB 326 (CA)

Lobb (Alec) (Garages) Ltd *v.* Total Oil Great Britain Ltd [1985] 1
  WLR 173 (CA)

Mabo and Others *v.* The State of Queensland (1992) 175 CLR 1

McHale *v.* Watson (1965–66) 115 CLR 119 (High Court of Australia)

MacPherson *v.* Buick Motor Co. 217 NY 382 (1916)

McRae *v.* Commonwealth Disposals Commission (1951) 84 CLR 377
  (High Court of Australia)

Miller *v.* Jackson [1977] QB 966 (CA)

Motherwell *v.* Motherwell (1976) 73 DLR (3d) 62

Nash *v.* Inman [1908] 2 KB 1 (CA)

National Westminster Bank *v.* Morgan [1985] AC 686 (HL)

Obde *v.* Schlemeyer, 56 Wash 2d 449 (1960)

Ormrod *v.* Crosville Motor Services, Murphy, Third Party [1953] 1
  WLR 1120 (CA)

Page One Records Ltd *v.* Britton [1968] 1 WLR 157

Palsgraf *v.* Long Island Railway Co., 162 NE 99 (1928)

Panayiotou (Georgios) v. Sony Music Entertainment (UK) [1994] Ch 142

Pennington v. Brinsop Hall Coal Co. (1877) 5 Ch 769

Pettersson v. Royal Oak Hotel [1948] NZLR 136

Photo Production v. Securicor Transport [1980] AC 827 (HL)

Posner v. Scott-Lewis [1987] Ch 25

Pride of Derby and Derbyshire Angling Association v. British Celanese [1953] Ch 149 (CA)

R. v. Clarke (1927) 40 CLR 227 (High Court of Australia)

R. v. Sparrow [1990] 1 SCR 404

Radford v. De Froberville [1978] 1 All ER 33

Raffles v. Wichelhaus (1864) 2 Hurl & C 906 (Ex)

Re Selectmove (1994) BCC 349 (CA)

Rickards v. Sun Oil Co., 23 NJ Misc 89 (1945)

Robbins Dry Dock & Repair Co. v. Flint, 275 US 303 (1927)

Robinson v. Harman (1848) 1 Ex 850, 154 ER 363

Robinson v. Post Office [1974] 1 WLR 1176 (CA)

Routledge v. Grant (1828) 4 Bing 653

Rylands v. Fletcher (1868) LR 3 HL 330

Schroeder (A.) Music Publishing Co. Ltd v. Macaulay (Formerly Instone) [1974] 1 WLR 1308 (HL)

Shadwell v. Shadwell (1860) 9 CB NS 159 (Court of Common Bench)

Shelfer v. City of London Electric Lighting Co. [1895] 1 Ch 287

Sherwood v. Walker, 66 Mich 568 (1877)

Sky Petroleum Ltd v. VIP Petroleum Ltd [1974] 1 WLR 576

Spartan Steel & Alloys v. Martin and Co. (Contractors) [1973] QB 27 (CA)

Spur Industries, Inc. v. Del E. Webb Development Co., 49 P 2d 701 (Court of Appeals AZ, 1972)

Stephenson v. Waite Tileman Ltd [1973] 1 NZLR 152 (New Zealand Court of Appeal)

Stilk v. Myrick (1809) 2 Camp. 317

Stringfellow v. McCain Foods [1984] RPC 501

Sturges v. Bridgman (1879) 11 Ch 852

Taylor v. Caldwell (1863) 3 B & S 826 (QB)

Thompson (W.L.) Ltd v. Robinson (Gunmakers) Ltd [1955] Ch 177

Tsakiroglou & Co. v. Noblee Thorl GmbH [1962] AC 93 (HL)

Union Oil Co. v. Oppen, 501 F 2d 558 (9th Circuit, 1974)

US v. Carroll Towing Co. 159 F 2d 169 (1947)

Vernon v. General Accident, *The Times*, Tuesday February 7, 1995 (CA)

Victoria Park Racing Ground Co. Ltd v. Taylor [1937] ALR 597

Vosburg v. Putney, 80 Wis 623 (1891)

Wagon Mound (No.1) [1961] AC 388 (PC)

Wagon Mound (No.2) [1967] 1 AC 617 (PC)

Warner Brothers Pictures Inc. v. Nelson [1937] 1 KB 209

Warren v. Mendy [1989] 1 WLR 853 (CA)

Williams *v.* Roffey Brothers & Nicholls (Contractors) Ltd [1991] 1 QB
   1 (CA)
Williams *v.* Walker-Thomas Furniture Co., 350 F 2d 445 (DC Circuit,
   1965)
Yuen Kun Yeu *v.* Attorney General of Hong Kong [1988] AC 175 (PC)

STATUTES

Acquisition of Land (Assessment of Compensation) Act 1919
Clean Water Act (USA) 1972
Consumer Credit Act 1974
Consumer Protection Act 1987, Pt 1
Copyright, Designs and Patents Act 1988
Courts and Legal Services Act 1990
Criminal Justice Act 1991
Employment Protection (Consolidation) Act 1978
Environmental Protection Act 1990
Fair Trading Act 1973
Homesteading Act (USA) 1862
Land Clauses Consolidation Act (1845)
Law Reform (Contributory Negligence) Act 1945
Misrepresentation Act 1967
Patents Act 1977
Sale of Goods Act 1979, s 52
Standard State Zoning Act (USA) 1926
Statute of Anne 1709
Statute of Monopolies 1623
Supreme Court Act 1981, s 69
Town and Country Planning Act 1990
Trade Marks Act 1994
Unfair Contract Terms Act 1977
United States Uniform Commercial Code 1958, ss 2–205, 2–302, 2–615

REFERENCES

Agnello, R.J. and Donnelley, L.P. (1975) Property rights and
   efficiency in the oyster industry, *Journal of Law and Economics*, 18,
   521–33.
Aivazan, V.A., Trebilcock, M.J. and Penny, M. (1984) The law of
   contract modification: the uncertain quest for a benchmark of
   enforceability. *Osgoode Hall Law Journal*, 22, 173–212.
American Law Institute (1965) *Restatement (Second) of Torts*.
American Law Institute (1981) *Restatement (Second) of Contracts*.
Anderson, T.L. (ed.) (1993) *Property Rights and Indian Economies*,
   Rowman and Littlefield, Lanham MD.

Anderson, T.L. and Hill, P.J. (1975) The evolution of property rights: a study of the American West. *Journal of Law and Economics*, 18, 163–79.

Anderson, T.L. and McChesney, F.S. (1994) Raid or trade? An economic model of Indian–white relations. *Journal of Law and Economics*, 37, 39–74.

Anderson, T.L. and Simmons, R.T. (1993) *The Political Economy of Customs and Culture: Informal Solutions to the Commons Problem*, Rowan and Littlefield, Lanham MD.

Axelrod, R. (1984) *The Evolution of Cooperation*, Basic Books, New York.

Baker, C.E. (1975) The ideology of the economic analysis of law. *Philosophy and Public Affairs*, 5, 3–38.

Becker, G. (1968) Crime and punishment: an economic approach. *Journal of Political Economy*, 69, 169–217.

Bennett, T. (1989) *Evaluating Neighbourhood Watch*, Gower, Aldershot.

Benson, B.L. (1994) Are public goods really common pools? Consideration of the evolution of policing and highways in England. *Economic Enquiry*, 32, 249–71.

Bernstein, L. (1992) Opting out of the legal system: extra-legal contractual relations in the diamond industry. *Journal of Legal Studies*, 21, 115–58.

Besen, S.M. and Raskind, L.J. (1991) An introduction to the law and economics of intellectual property. *Journal of Economic Perspectives*, 5, 3–27.

Bishop, W. and Sutton, J. (1986) Efficiency and justice in tort damages: the shortcomings of the pecuniary loss rule. *Journal of Legal Studies*, 15, 347–70.

Blackstone, W. (1766) *Commentaries on the Laws of England*, Professional Books Ltd, Abingdon.

Blumstein, A. and Nagin, D. (1977) A stronger test of the deterrence hypothesis. *Stanford Law Review*, 29, 241–76.

Borna, S. (1986) Free enterprise goes to prison. *British Journal of Criminology*, 26, 321–43.

Bowles, R. (1987) Settlement range and cost allocation rules. *Journal of Law, Economics and Organization*, 3, 177–84.

Box, S. (1987) *Recession, Crime and Punishment*, Macmillan, London.

Breyer, S. (1970) The uneasy case for copyright: a study of copyright in books, photocopies and computer programs. *Harvard Law Review*, 84, 281–351.

Buchanan, C. and Hartley, P.R. (1992) *Criminal Choice: The Economic Theory of Crime and its Implications for Crime Control*, Policy Monograph 24, Centre for Independent Studies, St Leonards, New South Wales.

Buchanan, J.M. (1965) An economic theory of clubs. *Economica*, 32, 1–14.

Buchanan, J.M. and Stubblebine, W.M. (1962) Externality. *Economica*, 29, 371–84.

Buchanan, J.M., Tollison, R.D. and Tullock, G. (eds) (1980) *Towards a Theory of the Rent Seeking Society*, A & M Press, College Station, Texas.

Calabresi, G. (1970) *The Costs of Accidents: A Legal and Economic Analysis*, Yale University Press, New Haven.

Calabresi, G. and Melamed, A.D. (1972) Property rules, liability rules and inalienability: one view of the cathedral. *Harvard Law Review*, 85, 1089–128.

Calfee, J and Rubin, P. (1992) Some implications of damage payments for non-pecuniary losses. *Journal of Legal Studies*, 21, 371–411.

Cameron, S. (1988) Economics of crime deterrence, *Kyklos*, 41, 301–23.

Carr-Hill, R. and Stern, N.H. (1979) *Crime, the Police and Criminal Statistics*, Academic Press, New York.

Carter, R.A.L, and Palmer, J.P. (1991) Real rates, expected rates, and damage awards. *Journal of Legal Studies*, 20, 439–62.

Carter, R.A.L, and Palmer, J.P. (1994) Simple calculations to reduce litigation costs in personal injury cases: additional empirical support for the offset rule. *Osgoode Hall Law Journal*, 32, 197–223.

Chung, T. (1993) Efficiency of comparative negligence: a game-theoretic analysis. *Journal of Legal Studies*, 22, 395–404.

Clark, C. (1976) *Mathematical Bioeconomics*, John Wiley, New York.

Coase, R.H. (1937) The nature of the firm. *Economica*, NS 4, 386–405.

Coase, R.H. (1960) The problem of social cost. *Journal of Law and Economics*, 3, 1–44.

Coase, R.H. (1974) The lighthouse in economics. *Journal of Law and Economics*, 17, 357–76.

Coase, R.H. (1988) Notes on the problem of social cost, in *The Firm, the Market and the Law*, University of Chicago Press, Chicago, pp.157–85.

Connell, E.S. (1984) *Son of the Morning Star: Custer and the Little Bighorn*, Harper Collins, New York.

Cook, P.J. and Graham, D.A. (1977) The demand for insurance and protection: the case of irreplaceable commodities. *Quarterly Journal of Economics*, 91, 143–56.

Cook, P.J. and Zarkin, G.A. (1985) Crime and the business cycle. *Journal of Legal Studies*, 14, 115–28.

Cooter, R.D. and Rubinfeld, D.L. (1989) Economic analysis of legal disputes and their resolution. *Journal of Economic Literature*, 27, 1067–97.

Cooter, R.D. and Ulen, T.S. (1986) The economic case for comparative negligence. *New York University Law Review*, 61, 1067–110.

Cooter, R.D and Ulen, T.S. (1988) *Law and Economics*, Harper Collins, New York.

Cowling, K. and Meuller, D. (1978) The social costs of monopoly. *Economic Journal*, 88, 727–48.

Crutchfield, J. and Pontecorvo, G. (1969) *The Pacific Salmon Fisheries: A Study in Irrational Conservation*, Johns Hopkins University Press, Baltimore.

Dam, K.W. (1994) The economic underpinnings of patent law. *Journal of Legal Studies*, 23, 247–72.

Dana, J.D. and Spier, K.E. (1993) Expertise and contingent fees: the role of asymmetric information in attorney compensation. *Journal of Law, Economics and Organization*, 9, 349–67.

Deadman, D.F. and Pyle, D.J. (1993) The effect of the abolition of capital punishment in Gt Britain: an application of intervention analysis. *Journal of Applied Statistics*, 20, 191–206.

De Jasay, A. (1989) *Social Contract, Free Ride*, Clarendon Press, Oxford.

Demsetz, H. (1967) Towards a theory of property rights. *American Economic Review*, 57, 347–59.

Demsetz H. (1969) Information and efficiency: another viewpoint. *Journal of Law and Economics*, 12, 1–22.

Demsetz, H. (1970) The private production of public goods. *Journal of Law and Economics*, 13, 292–306.

Demsetz, H. (1982) Barriers to entry. *American Economic Review*, 72, 47–57.

Diamond, P.A. (1974) Accident law and resource allocation. *Bell Journal of Economics and Management Science*, 366–405.

Dnes, A. (1985) Rent seeking behaviour and open-access fishing. *Scottish Journal of Political Economy*, 32, 159–70.

Dnes, A. (1989) Rent seeking, conflict and property rights. *Scottish Journal of Political Economy*, 36, 366–74.

Dnes, A. (1993) A case-study analysis of franchise contracts. *Journal of Legal Studies*, 22, 367–94.

Dnes, A. (1995) The law and economics of contract modifications: the case of *Williams* v. *Roffey*. *International Review of Law and Economics*, 15, 225–40.

Dnes, A. and Nuxoll, D. (1995) The Rich Society Effect and Capital Punishment. *Discussion Paper*. Virginia Polytechnic Institute and State University.

Domberger, S., Meadowcroft, S. and Thompson, D. (1986) Competitive tendering and efficiency. *Fiscal Studies*, 7, 69–87.

Donohue, J.J. (1991) Opting for the British rule, or if Posner and Shavell can't remember the Coase theorem, who will? *Harvard Law Review*, 104, 1094–119.

Dworkin, R.M. (1980) Is wealth a value? *Journal of Legal Studies*, 9, 191–226.

Dworkin, R.M (1986) *Law's Empire*, Belknap, Cambridge MA.

EC (1985) Directive 85/374, Liability for Defective Products. *Official Journal*, L 210/29 (25.7.1985).

Ehrlich, I. (1973) Participation in illegitimate activities: a theoretical and empirical investigation. *Journal of Political Economy*, 81, 521–64.

Ehrlich, I. (1975) The deterrent effect of capital punishment: a question of life and death. *American Economic Review*, 65, 397–417.

Ehrlich, I. (1977) Capital punishment and deterrence: some further thoughts. *Journal of Political Economy*, 85, 741–88.

Eisenberg, J. (1982) The bargain principle and its limits. *Harvard Law Review*, 95, 741–52.

Epstein, R.A. (1975) Unconscionability: a critical appraisal. *Journal of Law and Economics*, 18, 293–315.

Epstein, R.A. (1993) Holdouts, externalities and the single owner: one more salute to Ronald Coase. *Journal of Law and Economics*, 36, 553–87.

Farrell, J. (1987) Information and the Coase theorem. *Journal of Economic Perspectives*, 1, 113–29.

Feldthusen, B.P. (1989) *Economic Negligence: The Recovery of Pure Economic Loss*, Carswell, Toronto.

Field, S. (1990) Trends in Crime and Their Interpretation. *Home Office Research Paper 119*.

Fischel, W.A. (1985) *The Economics of Zoning Laws*, Johns Hopkins University Press, Baltimore.

Fischel, W.A. (1995a) *Regulatory Takings: Law, Economics, and Politics*, Harvard University Press, Cambridge MA.

Fischel, W.A (1995b) The offer/ask disparity and just compensation for takings. *International Review of Law and Economics*, 15, 187–203.

Fishbein D. (1990) Biological perspectives in criminology. *Criminology*, 28, 27–72.

Friedman, D (1989) An economic analysis of alternative damage rules for breach of contract. *Journal of Law and Economics*, 32, 281–310.

Furubotn, E. (1987) Privatizing the commons. *Southern Economic Journal*, 54, 219–24.

Furubotn, E. (1989) Distributional issues in contracting for property rights. *Journal of Institutional and Theoretical Economics*, 145, 25–31.

Furubotn, E. (1994) *Future Development of the New Institutional Economics: Extension of the Neoclassical Model or New Construct?* Jena Lecture, Max Planck Institute for Research into Economic Systems, Jena, Germany.

Furubotn, E. and Pejovich, S. (1972) Property rights and economic theory: a survey of recent literature. *Journal of Economic Literature*, 10, 1137–63.

Furubotn, E. and Pejovich, S. (eds) (1974) *The Economics of Property Rights*, Ballinger, Cambridge MA.

Galal, A., Jones, L., Tandon, P. and Vogelsant, I. (1992) *Welfare Consequences of Selling Public Enterprise*, World Bank, Washington.

Gambetta, D. (1993) *The Sicilian Mafia: The Business of Private Protection*, Harvard University Press, Cambridge, MA.

Gilmore, G (1986) *The Death of Contract*, Ohio State University Press, Ohio.

Goetz, C. and Scott, R. (1977) Liquidated damages, penalties and the just compensation principle: some notes on an enforcement model of efficient breach. *Columbia Law Review*, 77, 554–94.

Goldberg, V. (1988) Impossibility and related excuses. *Journal of Institutional and Theoretical Economics*, 144, 100–16.

Goldberg, V. (1994) Recovery for economic loss following the *Exxon Valdez* oil spill. *Journal of Legal Studies*, 23, 1–41.

Gordon, H.S. (1954) The economic theory of a common-property resource: the fishery. *Journal of Political Economy*, 62, 124–42.

Gravelle, H. and Waterson, M. (1994) No win, no fee: some economics of contingent legal fees. *Economic Journal*, 104, 1205–20.

Gray, A. (1994) The reform of legal aid. *Oxford Review of Economic Policy*, 10, 51–67.

Grossman, G.M. and Schapiro, C. (1987) Dynamic R&D competition. *Economic Journal*, 97, 372–87.

Haddock, D. and Curran, C. (1985] An economic theory of comparative negligence. *Journal of Legal Studies*, 14, 49–72.

Halson, R. (1991a) Opportunism, economic duress and contractual modifications. *Law Quarterly Review*, 107, 649–78.

Halson, R. (1991b) The modification of contractual obligations. *Current Legal Problems*, 44, 111–33.

Harrison, G.W. and McKee, M. (1985) Experimental evaluation of the Coase theorem. *Journal of Law and Economics*, 28, 653–70.

Harrison, G.W., Hoffman, E., Rutström, E.E. and Spitzer, M.L. (1987) Coasian solutions to the externality problem in experimental economics. *Economic Journal*, 97, 388–402.

Hicks, J.R. (1943) The four consumer surpluses. *Review of Economic Studies*, 11, 31–41.

Hobbes, T. [1651) *Leviathan*, Penguin, Harmondsworth.

Hoenack, S.A. and Weiler, W.C. (1980) A structural model of murder behavior and the criminal justice system. *American Economic Review*, 70, 327–41.

Hoffman, E. and Spitzer, M.L. (1982) The Coase theorem: some empirical tests. *Journal of Law and Economics*, 25, 73–98.

Hoffman, E. and Spitzer, M.L. (1986) Experimental tests of the Coase theorem with large bargaining groups. *Journal of Legal Studies*, 15, 149–71.

Hughes, J.W. and Snyder, E.A. (1995) Litigation under the English and American rules: theory and evidence. *Journal of Law and Economics*, 38, 225–50.

Hulme, S.E.K. (1993) Aspects of the High Court's handling of Mabo, in *The High Court of Australia in Mabo*, papers delivered to the Samuel Griffith Society, Association of Mining and Exploration Companies, Leederville, Western Australia, pp. 23–65.

Hviid, M. (1995) Relational contracts and repeated games, in *Contracts and Economic Organization: Socio-Legal Initiatives* (eds I.D. Campbell and P. Vincent-Jones), Dartmouth, Aldershot.

Jacob, R. and Alexander, D. (1993) *A Guide to Intellectual Property*, Sweet & Maxwell, London.

Johnson, E. (1981) Lawyer's choice: a theoretical appraisal of litigation investment decisions. *Law and Society Review*, 15, 567–610.

Joskow, P. (1977) Commercial impossibility: the uranium market and the Westinghouse case. *Journal of Legal Studies*, 6, 119–76.

Kahneman, D., Knetsch, J.L. and Thaler, R.H. (1990) Experimental tests of the endowment effect and the Coase theorem. *Journal of Political Economy*, 98, 1325–48.

Kaplan, J. (1983) *The Hardest Drug: Heroin and Public Policy*, University of Chicago Press, Chicago.

Kennedy, D. (1981) Cost–benefit analysis of entitlement problems: a critique. *Stanford Law Review*, 33, 387–445.

Klein, B. and Leffler, K.B. (1981) The role of market forces in assuring contractual performance. *Journal of Political Economy*, 89, 615–41.

Klein, B., Crawford, R.A. and Alchian, A. (1978) Vertical integration, appropriable rents and the competitive contracting process. *Journal of Law and Economics*, 21, 297–326.

Klein, D.B. (1990) The voluntary provision of public goods? The turnpike companies of early America. *Economic Enquiry*, 28, 788–812.

Knetsch, J.L. (1983) *Property Rights and Compensation – Compulsory Acquisition and Other Losses*, Butterworths, Toronto.

Knetsch, J.L. (1989) The endowment effect and evidence of non-reversible indifference curves. *American Economic Review*, 79, 1277–84.

Knetsch, J.L. and Sinden, J.A. (1984) Willingness to pay and compensation demanded: experimental evidence of an unexpected disparity in measures of value. *Quarterly Journal of Economics*, 99, 507–21.

Kritzer, H. (1990) *The Justice Brokers: Lawyers and Ordinary Litigation*, Oxford University Press, Oxford.

Kronman, A.T. (1978) Mistake, disclosure, information and the law of contracts. *Journal of Legal Studies*, 7, 1–34.

Kull, A. (1992) Reconsidering gratuitous promises. *Journal of Legal Studies*, 21, 39–67.

Landes, W.M. and Posner, R.A. (1978) Salvors, finders, good samaritans and other rescuers: an economic study of law and altruism. *Journal of Legal Studies*, 7, 83–128.

Landes, W.M. and Posner, R.A. (1987) *The Economic Structure of Tort Law*, Harvard University Press, Cambridge MA.

Leamer, E.F. (1983) Let's take the con out of econometrics. *American Economic Review*, 23, 31–43.

Lempert, R. (1981) Desert and deterrence: an assessment of the moral bases of the case for capital punishment. *Michigan Law Review*, 79, 1177–231.

Libecap, G. (1978) Economic variables and the development of the law: the case of Western mineral right. *Journal of Economic History*, 38, 338–62.

Libecap, G. (1989) Distributional issues in contracting for property rights. *Journal of Institutional and Theoretical Economics*, 145, 6–24.

Lindahl, E. (1919) Just taxation – a positive solution, in *Classics in the Theory of Public Finance*, R.A. Musgrave and A.T. Peacock, St Martin's Press, New York.

Littlechild, S.C. (1981) Misleading calculations of the social costs of monopoly power. *Economic Journal*, 91, 348–63.

Logan, C.H. (1990) *Private Prisons*, Oxford University Press, Oxford.

Lord Chancellor's Department (1989) *Contingency Fees*, Cm. 571, HMSO, London.

Lueck, D. (1989) The economic nature of wildlife law. *Journal of Legal Studies*, 18, 291–324.

Lynk, W. (1990) The courts and the market: an economic analysis of contingent fees in class-action litigation. *Journal of Legal Studies*, 19, 247–60.

Macneil, I.R. (1974) The many futures of contracts. *Southern California Law Review*, 48, 691–816.

Macneil, I.R. (1978) Contracts: adjustment of long-term economic relations under classical, neoclassical and relational contract law. *Northwestern Law Review*, 72, 854–905.

Mair, G. and Nee, C. (1990) Electronic monitoring: the trials and their results. *Home Office Research Study 120*.

Manne, H.G (1966) *Insider Trading and the Stock Market*, Free Press, New York.

Markesinis, B. (1990) Litigation mania in England, Germany and the USA: are we so very different? *Cambridge Law Journal*, 49, 233–76.

Marshall, J.D., Knetsch, J.L. and Sinden, J.A. (1986) Agents' evaluation and the disparity in measures of economic loss. *Journal of Economic Behavior and Organization*, 7, 115–27.

Meiners, R.E. and Yandle, B. (1993) *Taking the Environment Seriously*, Rowman and Littlefield, Lanham MD.

Merrill, T. (1986) Property rules, liability rules and adverse possession. *Northwestern University Law Review*, 79, 1122–54.

Miceli, T.J. and Segerson, K. (1991) Contingent fees for lawyers: the impact on litigation and accident prevention. *Journal of Legal Studies*, 20, 381–99.

Miceli, T.J. and Sirmans, C.F. (1995) An economic theory of adverse possession. *International Review of Law and Economics*, 15, 161–73.

Mishan, E.J. (1981) *Introduction to Normative Economics*, Oxford University Press, Oxford.

Mishan, E.J. (1989) The economics of capital punishment. *Economic Affairs*, 9, 9–12.

Moran, P. (1994) The hard cell? The private management of prisons. *Review of Policy Issues*, 1, 57–68.

Mortensen, D.T. (1982) Property rights and efficiency in mating, racing and related games. *American Economic Review*, 72, 968–79.

Mumey, G.A. (1971) The Coase theorem: a re-examination. *Quarterly Journal of Economics*, 85, 718–23.

Murray, C.A. and Cox, L.A. (1979) *Beyond Probation: Juvenile Corrections and the Chronic Offender*, Sage, Beverley Hills and London.

North, D.C. (1990) *Institutions, Institutional Change and Economic Performance*, Cambridge University Press, Cambridge.

Nutter, W. (1968) The Coase theorem on social cost: a footnote. *Journal of Law and Economics*, 11, 503–7.

Ogus, A. (1990) Property rights and freedom of economic activity, in *Constitutionalism and Rights: The Influence of the United States Constitution Abroad* (eds L. Henkin and A. Rosenthal), Columbia University Press, New York.

Ogus, A. and Richardson, G. (1977) Economics and the environment: a study of private nuisance. *Cambridge Law Journal*, 36, 285–325.

Ogus, A and Veljanovski, C.J (1984) *Readings in the Economics of Law and Regulation*, Oxford University Press, Oxford.

Ordover, J.A. (1991) A patent system for both diffusion and exclusion. *Journal of Economic Perspectives*, 5, 43–60.

Passell, P. and Taylor, J.B. (1977) The deterrence effect of capital punishment. *American Economic Review*, 67, 445–51.

Peacock, A.T. and Rowley, C.K. (1972) Welfare economics and the public regulation of natural monopoly. *Journal of Public Economics*, 1, 227–44.

Pearson Commission (1978) *Royal Commission on Civil Liability and Compensation for Personal Injury*, Cmnd 70054, HMSO, London.

Pigou, A.C. (1938) *The Economics of Welfare*, Macmillan, London.

Posner, E.A. (1995) Contract law in the welfare state: a defense of the unconscionability doctrine, usury laws and related limitations on freedom of contract. *Journal of Legal Studies*, 24, 283–319.

Posner, R.A. (1972) A theory of negligence. *Journal of Legal Studies*, 1, 29–96.

Posner, R.A. (1973) Strict liability: a comment. *Journal of Legal Studies*, 2, 205–22.

Posner, R.A. (1975) The social costs of monopoly and regulation. *Journal of Political Economy*, 83, 807–27.

Posner, R.A. (1977) Gratuitous promises in economics and law. *Journal of Legal Studies*, 6, 411–26.

Posner, R.A. (1980) A theory of primitive society, with special reference to law. *Journal of Law and Economics*, 23, 1–53.

Posner, R.A. (1981) *The Economics of Justice*, Harvard University Press, Cambridge MA.

Posner, R.A. (1985) An economic theory of criminal law. *Columbia Law Review*, 85, 1193–231.

Posner, R.A (1992) *Economic Analysis of Law*, Little Brown & Co., Boston.

Posner, R.A. (1993) Ronald Coase and methodology. *Journal of Economic Perspectives*, 7, 195–210.

Posner, R.A. and Rosenfeld, A.M. (1977) Impossibility and related doctrines in contract law: an economic analysis. *Journal of Legal Studies*, 6, 83–118.

Priest, G.L. (1985) The invention of enterprise liability: a critical history of the intellectual history of modern tort law. *Journal of Legal Studies*, 14, 461–527.

Priest, G.L. (1993) The origins of utility regulation and the 'theories of regulation' debate. *Journal of Law and Economics*, 36, 289–323.

Pryke, R. (1982) The comparative performance of public and private enterprise. *Fiscal Studies*, 3, 68–81.

Pyle, D.J. (1983) *The Economics of Crime and Law Enforcement*, Macmillan, London.

Pyle, D.J. (1989) Economics of crime in Britain. *Economic Affairs*, 9, 6–9.

Pyle, D.J. (1993) *An Economist Looks at Crime in Britain*, paper given to the European Policy Forum/Social Market Fund.

Pyle, D.J. and Deadman, D.F. (1994) Crime and unemployment in Scotland: some further results. *Scottish Journal of Political Economy*, 41, 314–24.

Rasmusen, E. and Ayres, I. (1993) Mutual and unilateral mistake in contract law. *Journal of Legal Studies*, 22, 309–44.

Raub, W. and Keren, G. (1993) Hostages as a commitment device. *Journal of Economic Behavior and Organization*, 21, 43–63.

Rees, R. (1985) The theory of principle and agent: parts 1 and 2. *Bulletin of Economic Research*, 37, 3–26 and 77–95.

Regan, D. (1972) The problem of social cost revisited. *Journal of Law and Economics*, 15, 427–37.

Reilly, B. and Witt, R. (1992) Crime and unemployment in Scotland: an econometric analysis using regional data. *Scottish Journal of Political Economy*, 39, 13–28.

Ricketts, M.J. (1987) Rent seeking, entrepreneurship, subjectivism and property rights. *Journal of Institutional and Theoretical Economics*, 143, 457–66.

Rickman, N. (1994) The economics of contingency fees in personal injury litigation. *Oxford Review of Economic Policy*, 10, 34–50.

Rogers, W. (1994) *The Law of Tort*, Sweet and Maxwell, London.

Rosenfield, A.M. (1976) An empirical test of class-action settlement. *Journal of Legal Studies*, 5, 113–20.

Roth, A.E. (1988) Laboratory experimentation in economics: a methodological overview. *Economic Journal*, 98, 974–1031.

Roth, A.E. and Murnighan, J. (1982) The role of information in bargaining: an experimental study. *Econometrica*, 50, 1123–42.

Rubin, P. (1977) Why is the common law efficient? *Journal of Legal Studies*, 6, 51–64.

Rubin, P. and Bailey, M. (1994) The role of lawyers in changing the law. *Journal of Legal Studies*, 23, 807–32.

Rubinfeld, D.L. and Scotchmer, S. (1993) Contingent fees for attorneys: an economic analysis. *RAND Journal of Economics*, 24, 343–56.

Samuelson, P.A. (1955) Diagrammatic exposition of a theory of public expenditure. *Review of Economics and Statistics*, 36, 386–9.

Schelling, T.C. (1960) *The Strategy of Conflict*, Harvard University Press, Cambridge MA.

Schwartz, A. (1977) A reexamination of non-substantive unconscionability. *Virginia Law Review*, 63, 1053–83.

Schwartz, A. (1988) Proposals for products liability reform: a theoretical synthesis. *Yale Law Journal*, 97, 353–419.

Schwartz, A. (1992) Relational contracts in the courts: an analysis of incomplete agreements and judicial strategies. *Journal of Legal Studies*, 21, 271–318.

Schwartz, M. and Mitchell, D. (1970) An economic analysis of contingency fee and personal injury litigation. *Stanford Law Review*, 22, 1125–62.

Selten, R (1978) The chainstore paradox. *Theory and Decision*, 9, 127–59.

Shavell, S. (1980a) Damage measures for breach of contract. *Bell Journal of Economics*, 11, 466–90.

Shavell, S. (1980b) Strict liability v. negligence. *Journal of Legal Studies*, 9, 1–26.

Shavell, S. (1982) Suit, settlement and trial: a theoretical analysis of alternative methods for allocating legal costs. *Journal of Legal Studies*, 11, 55–81.

Shavell, S. (1985) Criminal law and the optimal use of non-monetary sanctions as a deterrent. *Columbia Law Review*, 85, 1232–62.

Shavell, S. (1993) The optimal structure of law enforcement. *Journal of Law and Economics*, 36, 255–87.

Shogren, J.F. (1993) Experimental markets and environmental policy. *Agricultural and Resource Economics Review*, 22, 117–29.

Shogren, J.F., Shin, S.Y., Hayes, D.J. and Kliebenstein, J.B. (1994) Resolving differences in willingness to pay and willingness to accept. *American Economic Review*, 84, 255–70.

Simon, H. (1957) *Models of Man*, John Wiley, New York.

Smith, A. (1776) *An Enquiry into the Nature and Causes of the Wealth of Nations* (eds R.H. Campbell, A.S. Skinner and W.B. Todd, 1976), Clarendon, Oxford.

Smith, V.L. (1989) Theory, experiment and economics. *Journal of Economic Perspectives*, 3, 151–69.

Snyder, E.A. and Hughes, J.W. (1990) The English rule for allocating legal costs: evidence confronts theory. *Journal of Law, Economics and Organization*, 6, 345–80.

Stephen, F. (1987) Property rules and liability rules in the regulation of land development: an analysis of development control in Great Britain and Ontario. *International Review of Law and Economics*, 7, 33–50.

Stephen, F. (1988) *The Economics of the Law*, Harvester Wheatsheaf, Brighton.

Stigler, G.J. (1966) *The Theory of Price*, 3rd edn, Macmillan, New York.

Stigler, G.J. (1971) The theory of economic regulation. *Bell Journal of Economics*, 2, 3–21.

Sturgess, G.L. and Wright, M. (1993) *Water Rights in NSW: the Evolution of a Property Rights System*, CIS Policy Monograph 26.

Swanson, T.M. (1991) The importance of contingency fee arrangements. *Oxford Review of Legal Studies*, 11, 193–226.

Sykes, A.O. (1990) The doctrine of commercial impracticability in a second-best world. *Journal of Legal Studies*, 19, 43–94.

Thaler, R. (1980) Toward a positive theory of consumer choice. *Journal of Economic Behavior and Organization*, 1, 39–60.

Thomason, T. (1991) Are attorneys paid what they are worth? Contingent fees and the settlement process. *Journal of Legal Studies*, 20, 187–223.

Tideman, T.N. and Tullock, G. (1976) A new and superior process for making social choices. *Journal of Political Economy*, 84, 1145–59.

Trebilcock, M.J. (1993) *The Limits of Freedom of Contract*, Harvard University Press, Cambridge MA.

Trebilcock, M.J. and Dewees, D.N (1981) Judicial control of standard form contracts, in *The Economic Approach to Law* (eds P. Burrows and C.J. Veljanovski), Butterworths, London.

Tromans, S. (1982) Nuisance – prevention or payment. *Cambridge Law Journal*, 41, 87–109.

Tullock G. (1968) The welfare costs of tariffs, monopoly and theft. *Western Economic Journal*, 5, 224–32.

Turvey, R. (1963) On divergences between social cost and private cost. *Economica*, 30, 309–13.

Tversky, A. and Kahneman, D. (1991) Loss aversion in riskless choice: a reference-dependent model. *Quarterly Journal of Economics*, 106, 1039–61.

Ulen, T.S. (1984) The efficiency of specific performance: toward a unified theory of contract remedies. *Michigan Law Review*, 83, 358–403.

Umbeck, J. (1981) Might makes rights: a theory of the formation and initial distribution of property rights. *Economic Enquiry*, 19, 38–51.

Veljanovski, C.J. (1982) The Coase theorems and the economic theory of markets and law. *Kyklos*, 35, 66–81.

Walmsely, J. (1986) Personal violence. *Home Office Research Paper 89*, HMSO, London.

Waterson, M. (1990) The economics of product patents. *American Economic Review*, 80, 860–9.

Weiss, R. (1989) Private prisons and the state, in *Privatising Criminal Justice*, (ed. R. Mathews), Sage, London.

Wellisz, S. (1964) On external economies and the government-assisted invisible hand. *Economica*, NS 31, 345–62.

White, M.J. (1988) Contract breach and contract discharge due to impossibility: a unified theory. *Journal of Legal Studies*, 17, 353–76.

White, M.J. (1989) An empirical test of the comparative and contributory negligence rules in accident law. *RAND Journal of Economics*, 20, 308–30.

Williamson, O.E. (1975) *Markets and Hierarchies: Analysis and Antitrust Implications*, Macmillan/The Free Press, New York.

Williamson, O.E. (1976) Franchise bidding for natural monopoly: in general and with respect to CATV. *Bell Journal of Economics*, 7, 73–104.

Williamson, O.E. (1985) *The Economic Institutions of Capitalism*, Macmillan/The Free Press, New York.

Williamson, O.E (1993) The evolving science of organization. *Journal of Institutional and Theoretical Economics*, 149, 36–63.

Willis, K. (1983) Spatial variations in crime in England and Wales. *Regional Studies*, 17, 261–72.

Wilson, J. and Herrnstein, R. (1985) *Crime and Human Nature*, Simon and Schuster, New York.

Withers, G. (1984) Crime, punishment and deterrence in Australia: an empirical investigation. *Economic Record*, 60, 176–85.

Witte, A. (1980) Estimating the economic model of crime with individual data. *Quarterly Journal of Economics*, 94, 57–84.

Wolpin, K. (1978a) An economic analysis of crime and punishment in England and Wales 1894–1967. *Journal of Political Economy*, 86, 815–40.

Wolpin, K. (1978b) Capital punishment and homicide: the English experience. *American Economic Review*, 68, 422–7.

Van Zandt, D.E. (1993) The lessons of the lighthouse. *Journal of Legal Studies*, 22, 47–72.

Cases index

Statutes index

Author index

Subject index